IMAGES
of America

RIVER OAKS

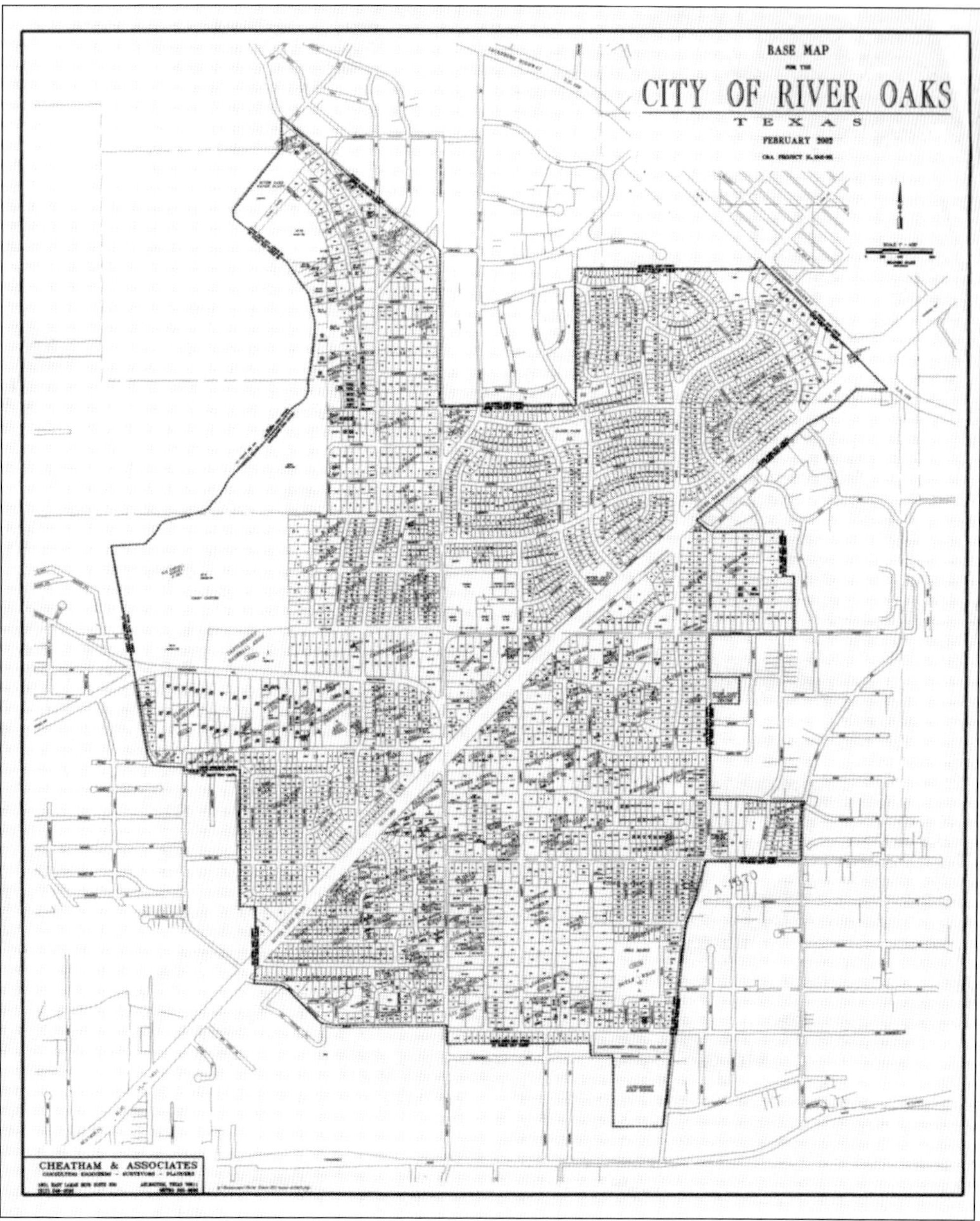

The map of the city of River Oaks shows the locked boundaries of the city surrounded by Fort Worth and other cities. River Oaks has no room for expansion, and most lots are already developed, giving the city limited room for economic expansion. (Courtesy of the River Oaks Historical Society.)

On the Cover: River Oaks started as a rural farming community near the West Fork of the Trinity River that grew into a small blue-collar city. Its citizens took care of their families, their neighbors, and their community. The River Oaks Theater, seen here in 1961, was owned by the Interstate Theater Circuit and provided much-appreciated entertainment to the citizens of the city. (Courtesy of David Bloomfield.)

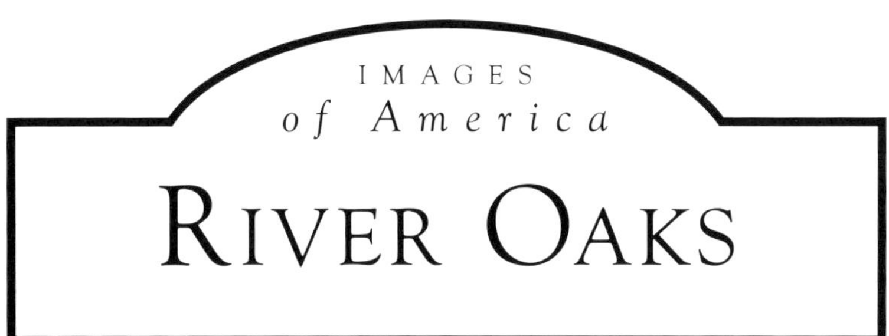

Darren Houk and Mark A. Nobles

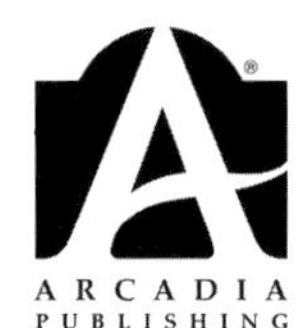

ISBN 978-1-4671-6214-2

Published by Arcadia Publishing
Charleston, South Carolina

Printed in the United States of America

Library of Congress Control Number: 2024939525

For all general information, please contact Arcadia Publishing:
Telephone 843-853-2070
Fax 843-853-0044
E-mail sales@arcadiapublishing.com

Visit us on the Internet at www.arcadiapublishing.com

This book is gratefully dedicated to the past, present, and future citizens of the city of River Oaks.

Contents

Acknowledgments

The authors would like to acknowledge the considerable help and cooperation of the city council and city manager of River Oaks in the writing of this book. Council members John Claridge, Brent Forester, Steve Holland, Yolie Rodrigues, and Leigh Ann Turner, along with city manager Marvin Gregory, have provided tireless work and leadership in all the 75th-anniversary celebration activities.

River Oaks Event Center directors Shirley Wheat and Shirley Bloomfield, lovingly referred to as the "Two Shirleys," graciously provided time, information, and photographs from the event center archives and their own private collections. The River Oaks Lions Club serves as the repository for the River Oaks Historical Society's archival collection. We would like to specifically thank Lions Jim Byrom and Randy Hooper for making this extensive collection available.

We made extensive use of old newspaper archives in researching this book. Newspaper editorial practices in the 1940s, 1950s, and 1960s often called for identifying married women by their husband's first name. We endeavored to find the women's first names but often were unable to do so. Our apologies to these wonderful women and their families for being unable to properly identify them.

Our editor at Arcadia Publishing, Caroline Vickerson, was unbelievably patient, encouraging, and knowledgeable. We are grateful to her for guiding us to completion. There are many people who encouraged, guided, and illuminated our journey, specifically Shirley Bunker, Jack Atkinson, Johnny Rutherford, Linda Claridge, Paulina Espinosa, Karl Waigand, Eric Perkins, and Barry Machos. We would also like to thank the River Oaks Economic Development Corporation directors Dan Chisholm, Buck Bybee, Steve Holland, Charles Richardson, Heather Knight, and Raul Espinosa. The Castleberry Independent School District is always supportive of the community, and we would like to thank Supt. Renee Smith-Faulkner for her assistance. This has truly been a community project reflecting the close-knit, get-it-done spirit that has always been the hallmark of the city of River Oaks. This hidden gem of a city in the swirling metropolis of North Texas has always been more than content in its own skin. The city of River Oaks is content to be the city of River Oaks, and that is what makes it special and unique.

Introduction

The first settlers to the area that would become the city of River Oaks were drawn by the rich, fertile soil, large, abundant oak trees, and the proximity to the West Fork of the Trinity River. Settlement in the area began slightly later than in other parts of Tarrant County. James Ventioner, a native of France, settled in the River Oaks area around 1859. Between 1854 and 1856, Paul Isbell arrived from Kentucky and established a plantation on the site now mostly occupied by the Naval Air Station (NAS) Joint Reserve Base (JRB) Fort Worth. These early settlers prospered, and soon others joined. Life was quiet, peaceful, and good. Soon enough, they built schools, started businesses, laid roads, and raised houses. The four commercial buildings that made up Willett's Corner were developed by Hugh and Helen Willett beginning in 1936. It was the first commercial area in River Oaks. The buildings were built by the Shankel Brothers Contractors. River Oaks had no sewage system when Willett's Corner was developed. It is believed that the dual outhouse built on the property was the area's first, with one dedicated stall for men and another only for women.

The initial construction of Castleberry School was carried out in 1935–1937 by the Works Progress Administration (WPA). The WPA built what is now the west portion of the main building, which replaced an 1898 one-room schoolhouse. The school was enlarged repeatedly in the 1940s as the local population grew. The postwar population explosion required almost constant expansion of additional facilities. The long, low, white-stuccoed form of the original building, set on landscaped grounds, makes Castleberry School the most prominent historic civic landmark in River Oaks.

In 1941, the voters unanimously approved incorporating as a village. Since the area incorporated was not located entirely in the Castleberry area, the village was named for the oak trees in the area and became River Oaks Village. On May 7, 1946, the board of aldermen changed the name to the city of River Oaks. The city charter was officially enacted on January 11, 1949. The city has grown from the 1800s to a population of 6,985 people. Originally, River Oaks was developed as a bedroom community, since the location was so close to the bomber plant and Carswell Air Force Base, which was designated as a joint reserve base in 1994 to be shared by the Navy, Marines, Air Force, and Texas National Guard. The base is now known as the Naval Air Station Joint Reserve Base Fort Worth. Over the years, the city has been a prime location for base personnel to locate. The population of River Oaks has varied only slightly over the decades since. In an effort to make the city better for citizens, Thurston Park was opened on September 6, 1947. The park was expanded in 1962. With the creation of the first park board, the park was expanded, and the name was changed to McGee Park in honor of James David McGee, who was killed in World War II. The park serves as the host for many youth baseball leagues. There are two existing ball fields with lighting and bleachers, a concession stand, restrooms, playground equipment, picnic tables and shelter, a basketball court, and parking. Most of the housing in the city was built in the late 1940s. The construction of the air base, which was activated by the Army in 1942, became the catalyst for community development. River Oaks had a population of 2,000 by the end of the 1940s. During the 1950s, water and sewer systems were completed, streets were paved, and a library was built. The River Oaks Public Works Department has replaced 65 percent of the existing water lines in the city and has relined over 10,000 feet of old existing sewer mains. Due to persistent flooding issues, the city recently completed an extensive drainage study to reevaluate and plan for future improvements to the current city drainage system.

Every city is best defined by its inhabitants, and River Oaks has a long line of distinguished citizens who exemplify a blue-collar, industrious, and rebellious spirit that rebukes the more humdrum "bedroom community" label hung upon it. Many of the original families still have descendants living in the city whose streets bear their names. River Oaks boasts an Olympian, several Pro Rodeo Hall of Fame members, an International Hot Rod Association Hall of Fame member, and an International Motor Sports Hall of Fame member. With two racing hall of fame members, it is not a stretch to guess the city also has a long and storied car culture stretching back to the 1950s.

The most remarkable aspect of the city of River Oaks is how unremarkable it is. No one has ever moved to River Oaks seeking fame or riches. People came to live solid, middle-class lives and raise a family in a safe, friendly, middle-class town. The city of River Oaks is the stereotype of the American Dream. River Oaks is rows and rows of well-kept lawns. It is waving at your neighbor and having a chat over the fence. It is knowing the name of the person who takes your order at the café. Living in River Oaks is picking up the phone and calling your councilperson, or even the mayor, when you have a question and having them pick up the phone and listen to your concerns. When speaking to people about the city of River Oaks, they sometimes confuse it with the glitzy, uber-rich, flashy neighborhood of the same name in Houston. River Oaks is anything but flashy. River Oaks is friendly, dependable, and hard-working. If most Texans think of the richest neighborhood in Texas way down in Houston when they hear River Oaks, that is fine. It isn't money or anything tangible that makes the city of River Oaks special—it is the people and the quality of life.

One

Before There Was a City

White Settlement, Westworth Village, and River Oaks occupy part of an area of western Tarrant County extending from Fort Worth to the Parker County line. From the 1850s until the early 1900s, the entire area was collectively known as White Settlement. The three cities have been locked together ever since.

In 1849, the first settler, James Ventioner, a native of France, built a log cabin in the River Oaks area. Ventioner donated land for a school where the present-day Castleberry Elementary is located. When Zack Castleberry moved his family to the area, he donated his water well when the first school was built. Both families were attracted to the area because of the rich farmland and beautiful oak trees. The men and their families prospered, and soon other families moved to the area. The community soon became known as Castleberry.

In 1854 and 1856, two caravans arrived in the area from Kentucky. One of the Kentuckians, Paul Isbell, acquired around 1,000 acres in the area and became a leader in the volunteer guard that cleared the section of hostile Indians. His son, Reuben Isbell, built one of the earliest houses in the River Oaks area after his marriage to Elizabeth Ventioner, daughter of James Ventioner.

The area remained primarily rural until World War II. In 1942, the establishment of the Consolidated Aircraft Corporation's bomber plant and the Tarrant Field Airdrome, later Carswell Air Force Base, on the south shore of Lake Worth facilitated the need for local housing and turned the area into a booming bedroom community.

This explosive growth, and Fort Worth eyeing the communities for annexation, led White Settlement, Westworth Village, and River Oaks to incorporate. In 1941, the voters unanimously approved incorporating River Oaks as a village. Since the area incorporated was not located entirely in the Castleberry area, the village was renamed for the surrounding oak trees and became River Oaks Village until May 7, 1946, when the board of aldermen changed the name to the city of River Oaks; the city charter was officially enacted on January 11, 1949.

River Oaks is located in a naturally wooded area defined by the meandering course of the West Fork of the Trinity River. The city of River Oaks is approximately 1.9 square miles in area, and city limits are set, since there is no extraterritorial jurisdiction or unincorporated territory for expansion.

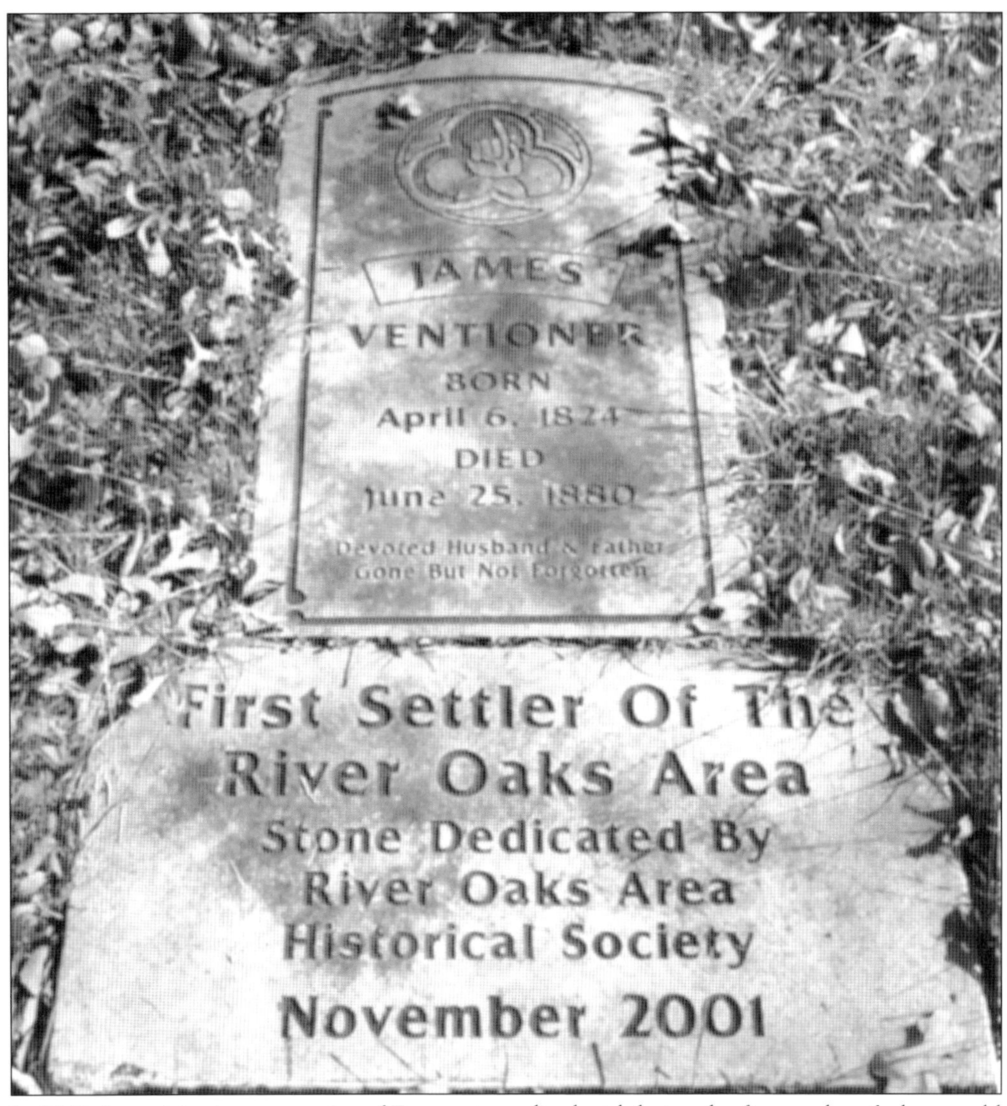

In 1849, James Ventioner, a native of France, is credited with being the first settler of what would grow into being the city of River Oaks. His farm spread from what is now Northside High School, west beyond Ohio Garden Road and northward to present-day Roberts Cut Off Road. His log cabin was built on what is now Roaring Springs Road near Shady Oaks Country Club. He was drawn to the rich farmland and plentiful oak trees in the area. The first recorded marriage in the area was between James Ventioner Jr., who came to Texas with his father, and Mildred Farmer on July 13, 1851. (Courtesy of the River Oaks Historical Society.)

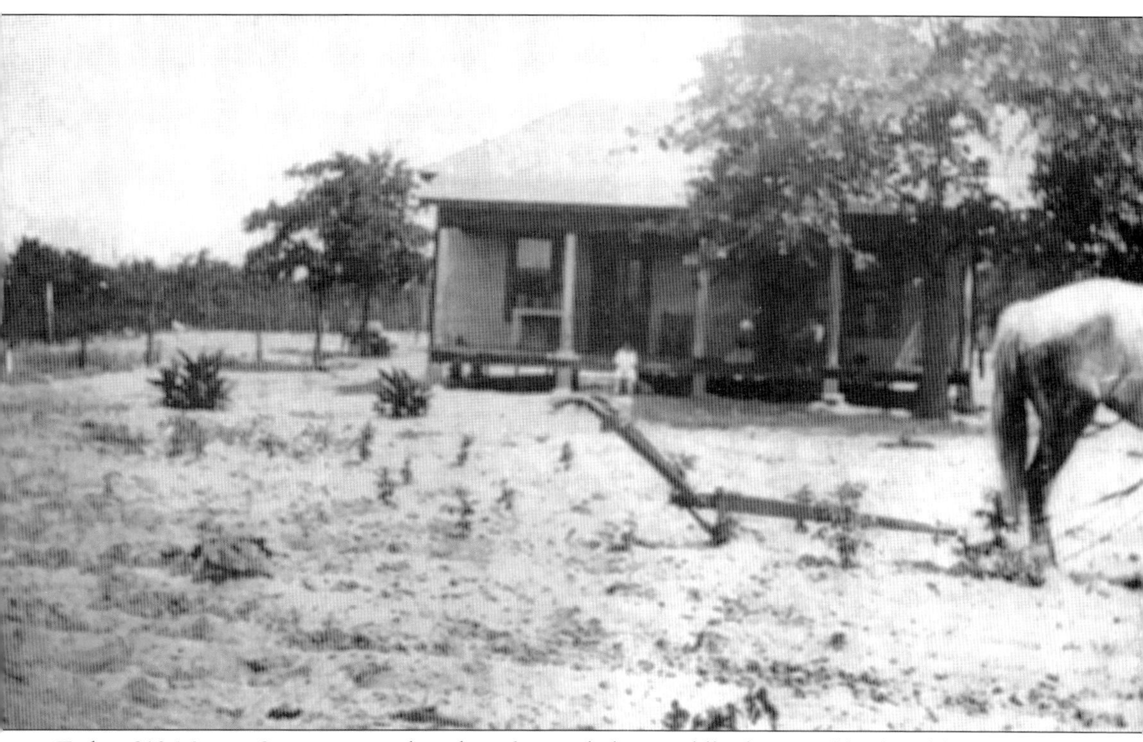

Today, 312 Merritt Street sits on the edge of a tree-laden, middle-class neighborhood less than a mile from Fort Worth's bustling River District. In this undated photograph, the property is rural, and the family evidently does a fair amount of farming on the property. The person on the steps is identified only as Mario. (Courtesy of the River Oaks Historical Society.)

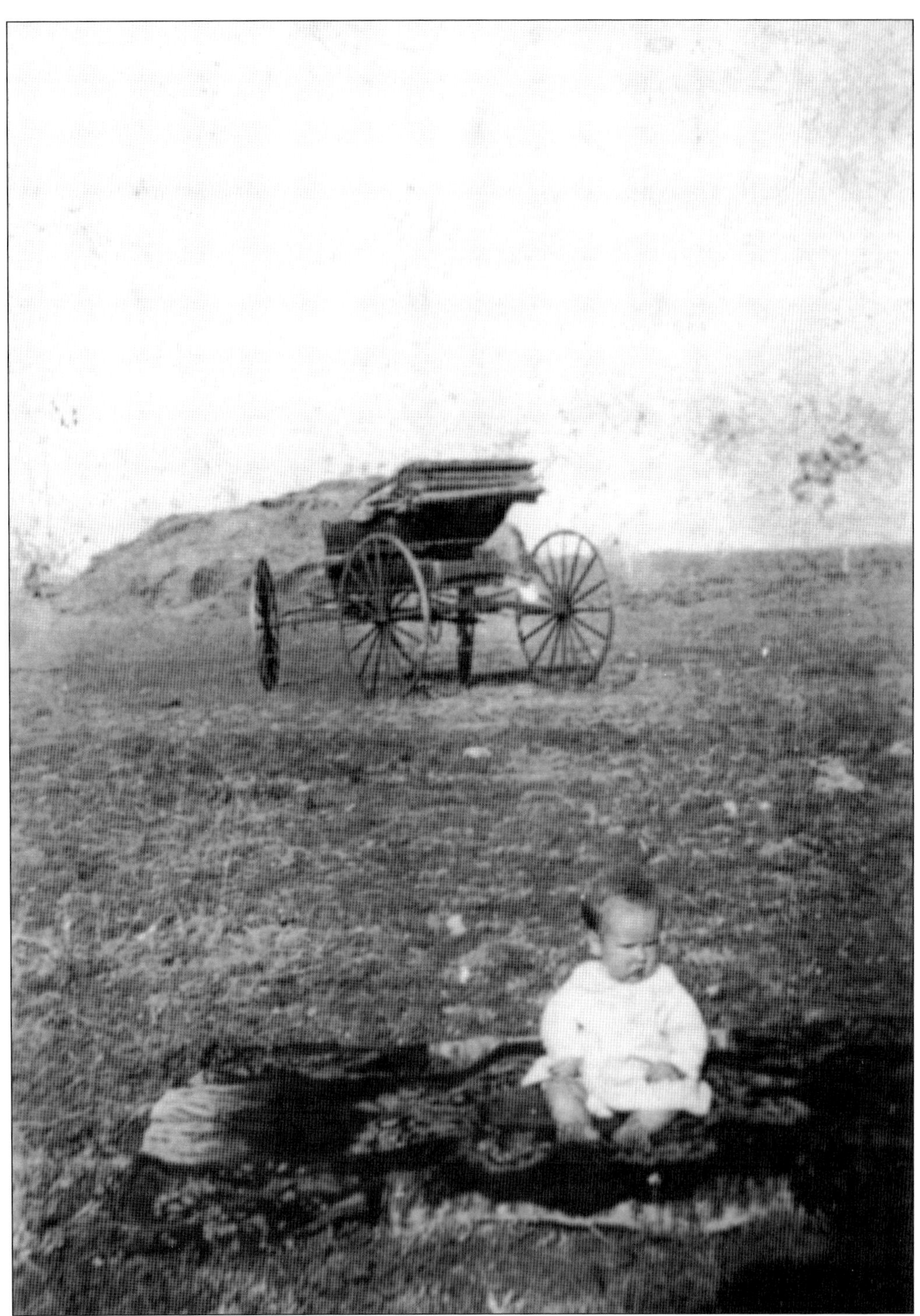

Aubry Hallum's family owned a portion of the land on which the Tarrant Field Airdrome was built in 1932. Aubry was only a baby when this undated picture was taken. While the location of this picture is unknown, it quite possibly could be a runway for the present-day NAS JRB Fort Worth. (Courtesy of the River Oaks Historical Society.)

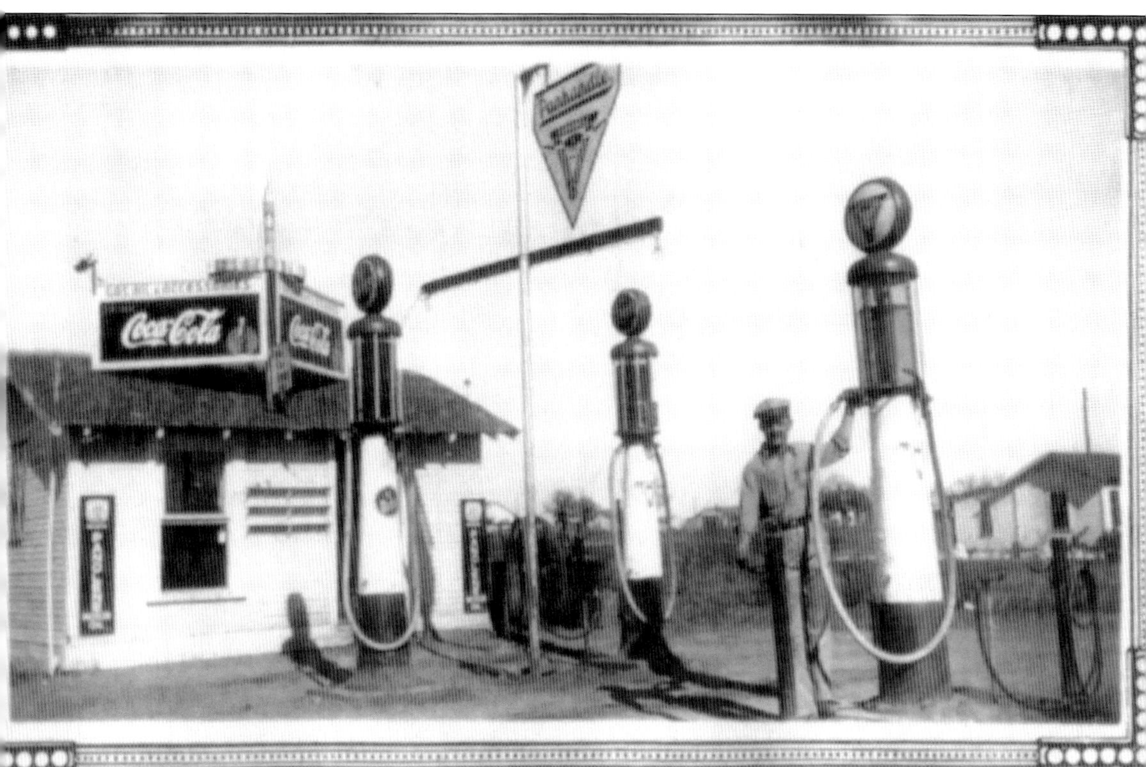

Built in 1938, Willett's Gas Station was later moved from the northeast corner of Yale Street and Meandering Road to the northwest corner to make room for the barbershop and other structures Hugh Willett intended to build. (Courtesy of Shirley Bunker.)

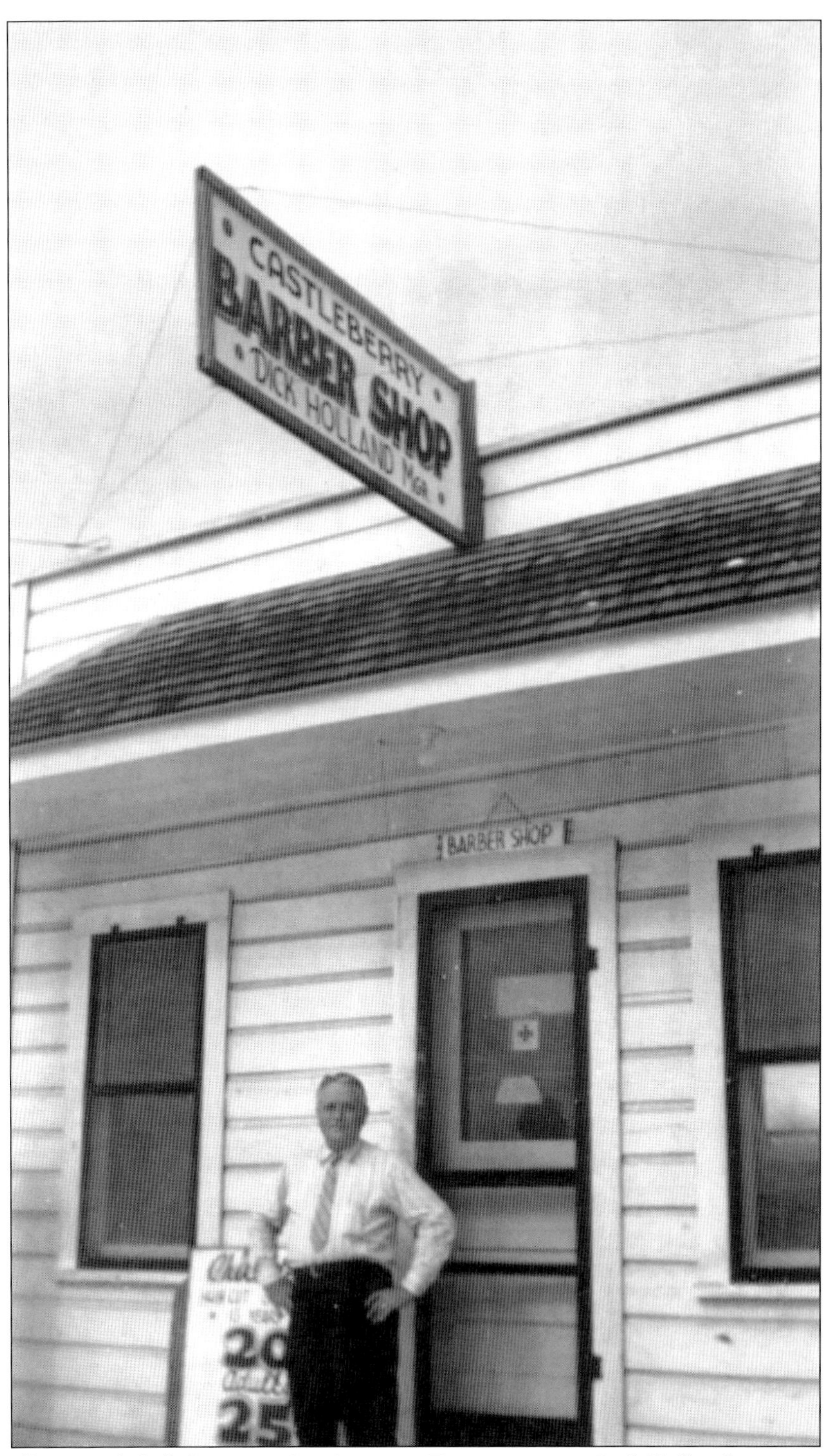

Hugh Willett traveled all the way to San Antonio, Texas, to recruit Dick Holland to move to River Oaks and run his barbershop. Willett's Corner was an early hub of commerce in the River Oaks area with several businesses and nearby homes. (Courtesy of the River Oaks Historical Society.)

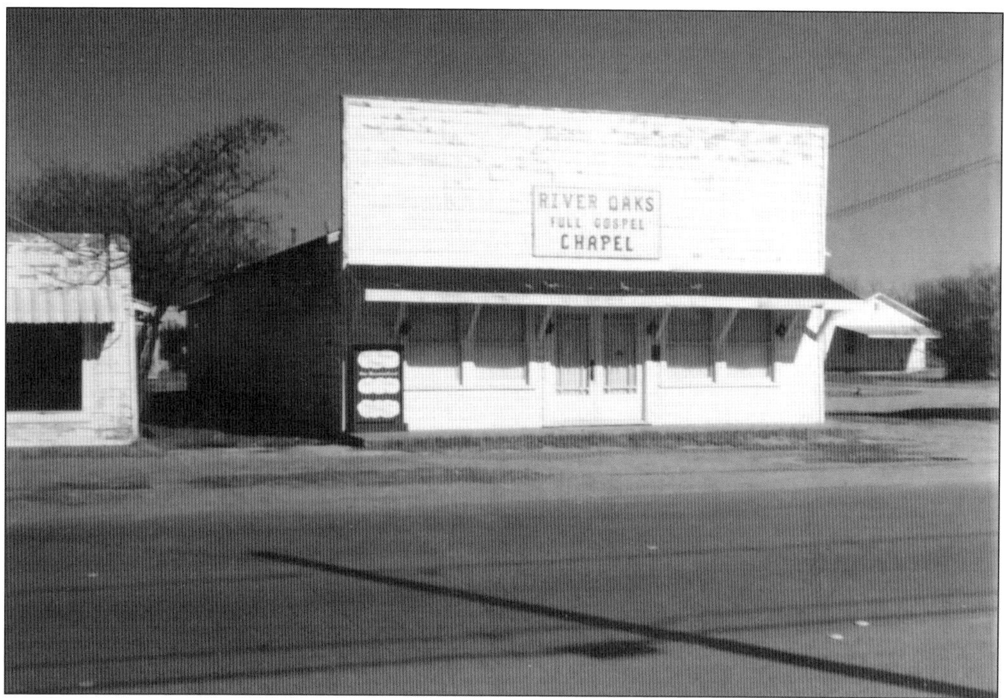

Over several decades, the buildings comprising the commercial property went through several iterations, including a church, a snow cone stand, and other small businesses, and they gradually fell into disrepair before being bought by a roofing company in 2010 and extensively remodeled and brought back to life. A residential and commercial roofing company now occupies the corner. Shirley Bunker, daughter of Hugh Willett, the original builder of Willett's Corner, still lives in a house behind one of the original buildings on Yale Street. The surviving buildings are eligible for the National Register; however, no steps have been taken as yet to place the commercial district on the register. (Both, courtesy of Shirley Bunker.)

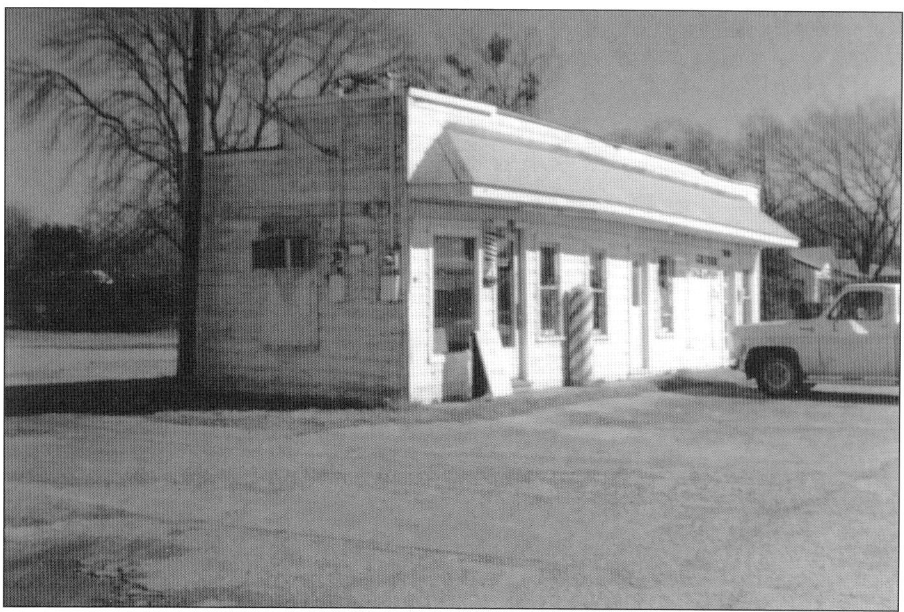

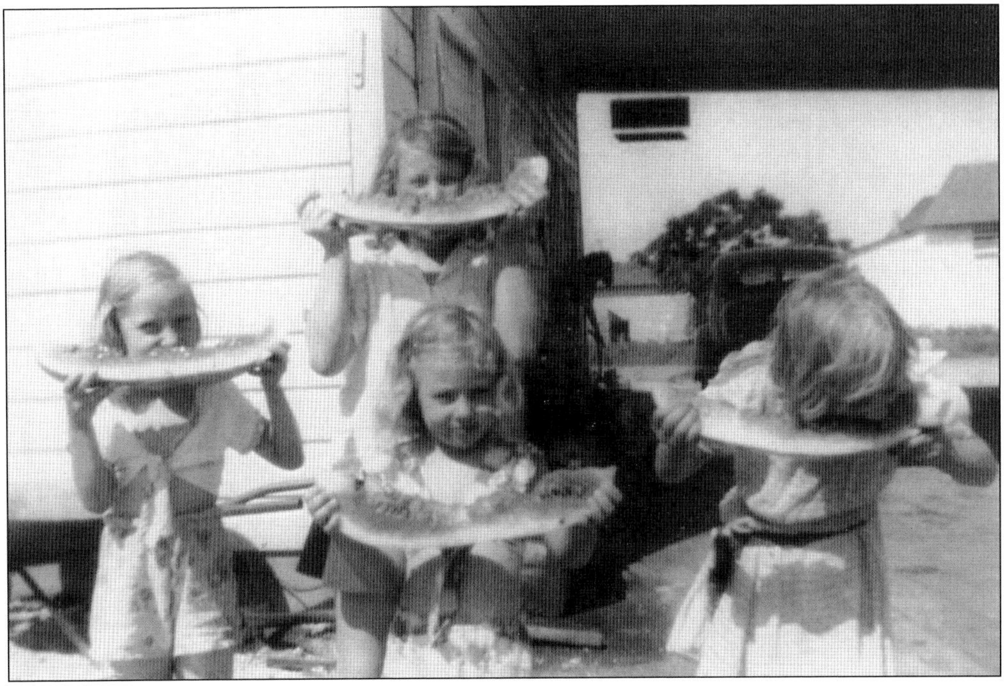

The Willett family was enterprising and hardworking; even the children pitched in, working in the various stores. That did not mean, however, that there was no time on a hot summer day to enjoy an ice-cold watermelon from the grocery. Pictured here are four children enjoying a summer watermelon at Willet's Corner. (Courtesy of Shirley Bunker.)

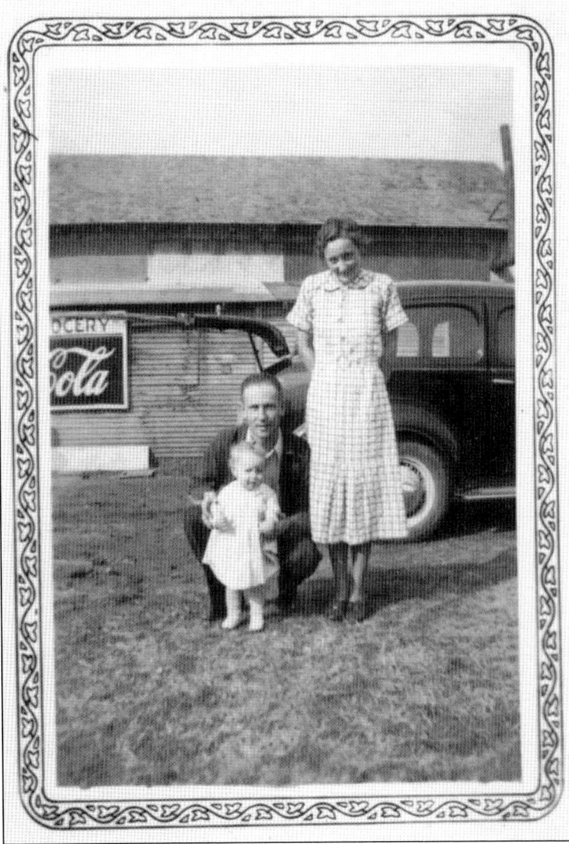

Hugh Willett, holding baby Lavone Willett, and Helen Willett pose for a picture beside the store on what looks to be a crisp spring day. (Courtesy of Shirley Bunker.)

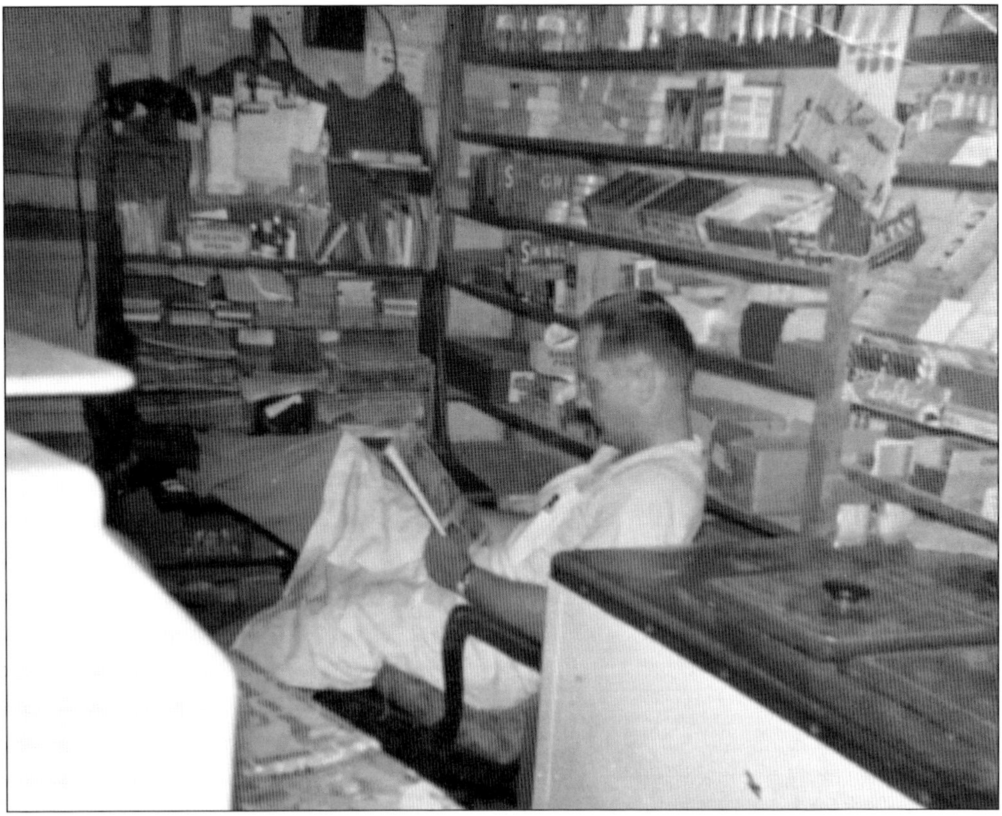

Hugh Willett is pictured here some time in the 1950s keeping up with the local news during a slow time at the grocery store. Willett's Corner, at the intersection of Yale Street and Meandering Road, was an oasis for the still-rural River Oaks area. Families could get gas for their autos, food for themselves, and feed for their animals and livestock, as well as a haircut and sundries. Willett's Corner was the sole commercial concentration in the River Oaks area. It consisted of five wood-frame structures, all built by Shankel Brothers Contractors. Construction on Willett's Corner began in 1936. (Both, courtesy of Shirley Bunker.)

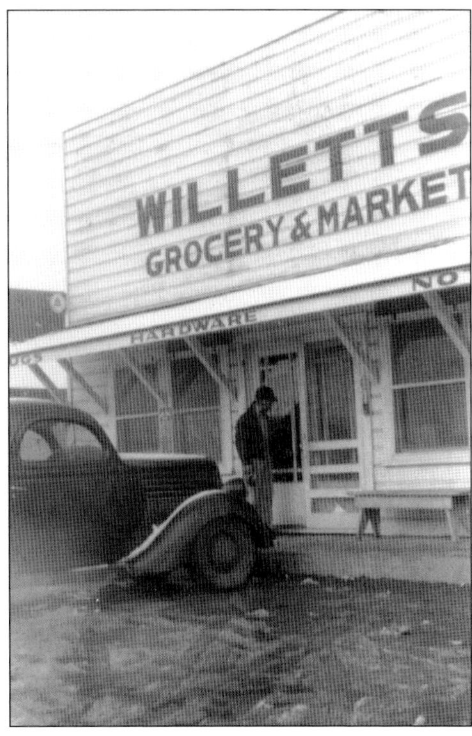

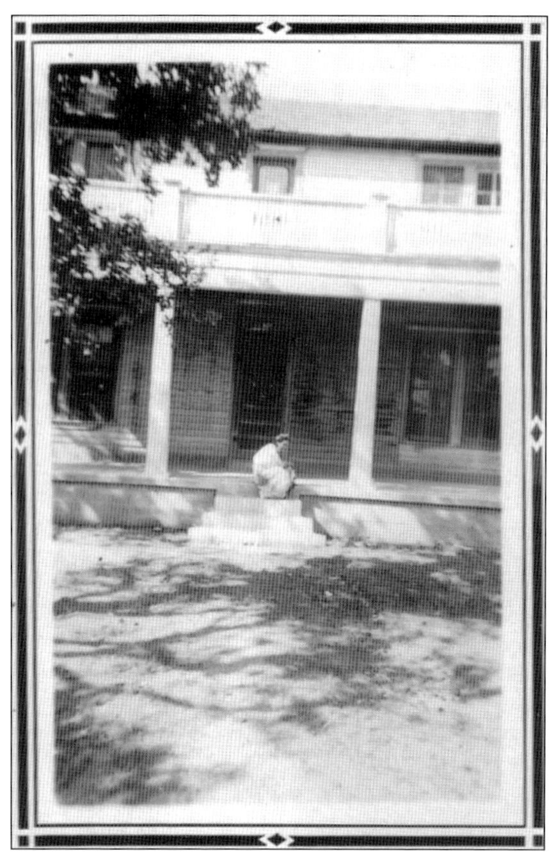

Reuben Isbell, son of early River Oaks area settler Paul Isbell, built the two-story gabled house at 725 Springer Road in 1890. At the time, the lot was on a wooded rise on their 320-acre tract. Reuben built the house for his wife, Martha Elizabeth Ventioner, daughter of James Ventioner, another early settler in the area. The unusual two-story gabled portico may not be original, but if it was added, it was added early. Over the years, the house was sheathed in asbestos siding and enlarged on the east side and rear in order to be converted to two apartments. The woman in the photographs is reportedly Ima Bloomfield. Paul Isbell migrated to River Oaks from Todd County, Kentucky, in 1854. Isbell Street in River Oaks was named in the pioneer family's honor. (Both, courtesy of the River Oaks Historical Society.)

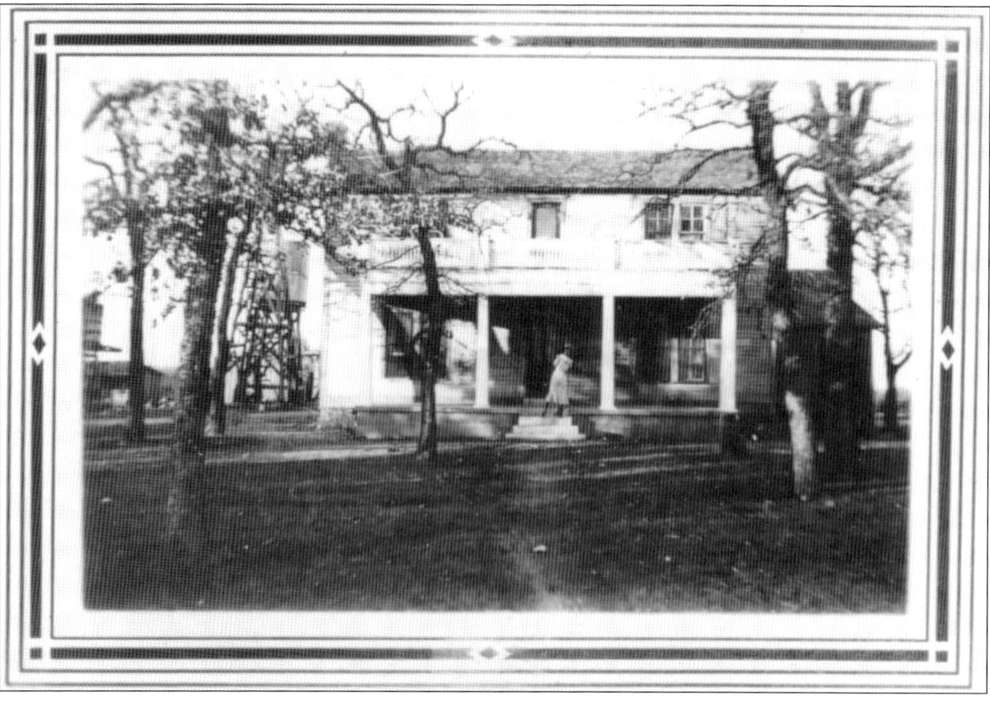

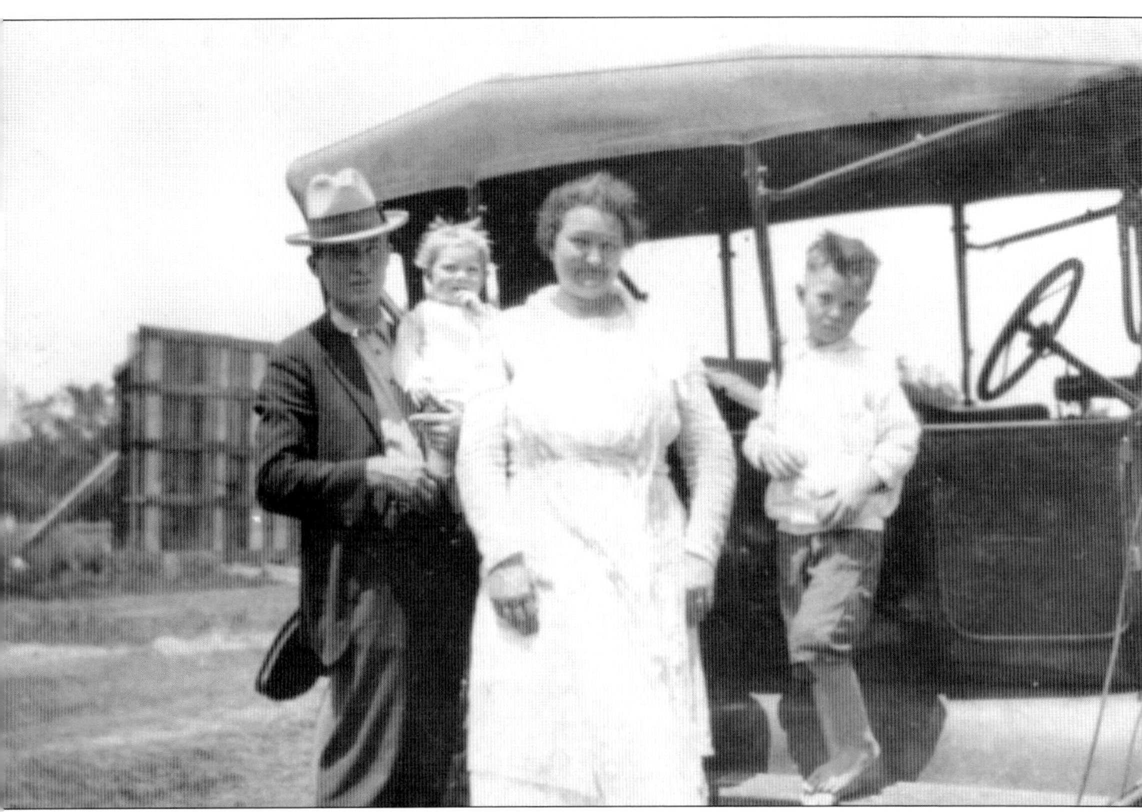

From left to right are Mert Bloomfield Sr., holding his son Mert Jr.; his wife, Maggie Bloomfield; and their oldest son, Ed Bloomfield (standing on the running board of the family automobile). Mert Sr. moved his family to River Oaks in 1926 from Dallas. Mert Sr. was a carpenter, and Mert Jr. soon followed in his father's footsteps in the same trade. As time passed and necessity prevailed, Mert became a person who could do just about anything and was said to be good at whatever he set out to do. Besides carpentry, he could do plumbing, electrical, brickwork, mechanical work on vehicles, and welding. Mert was involved with many of the buildings in the area by overseeing, helping, or advising in some way. Mert became the lead building contractor for many buildings and various projects in the North Texas area from about 1945 until his retirement in the late 1980s. He especially enjoyed fishing, and he and Marguerite and friends spent many years fishing from their little red and white fiberglass boat he affectionately named "Babe" in honor of his wife. (Courtesy of the River Oaks Historical Society.)

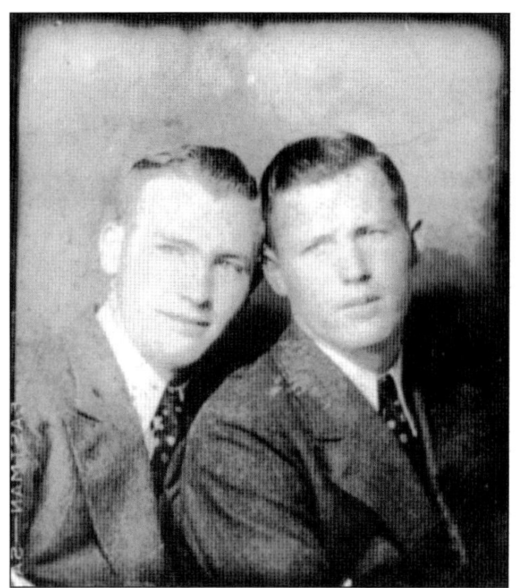

Twins Rick and Bob Gray were lifelong River Oaks residents and are shown in their Sunday best in this undated photograph. Their family owned a trailer park on Robert's Cut Off Road, and Bob Gray served as a volunteer fireman for a time with the city. (Courtesy of the River Oaks Historical Society.)

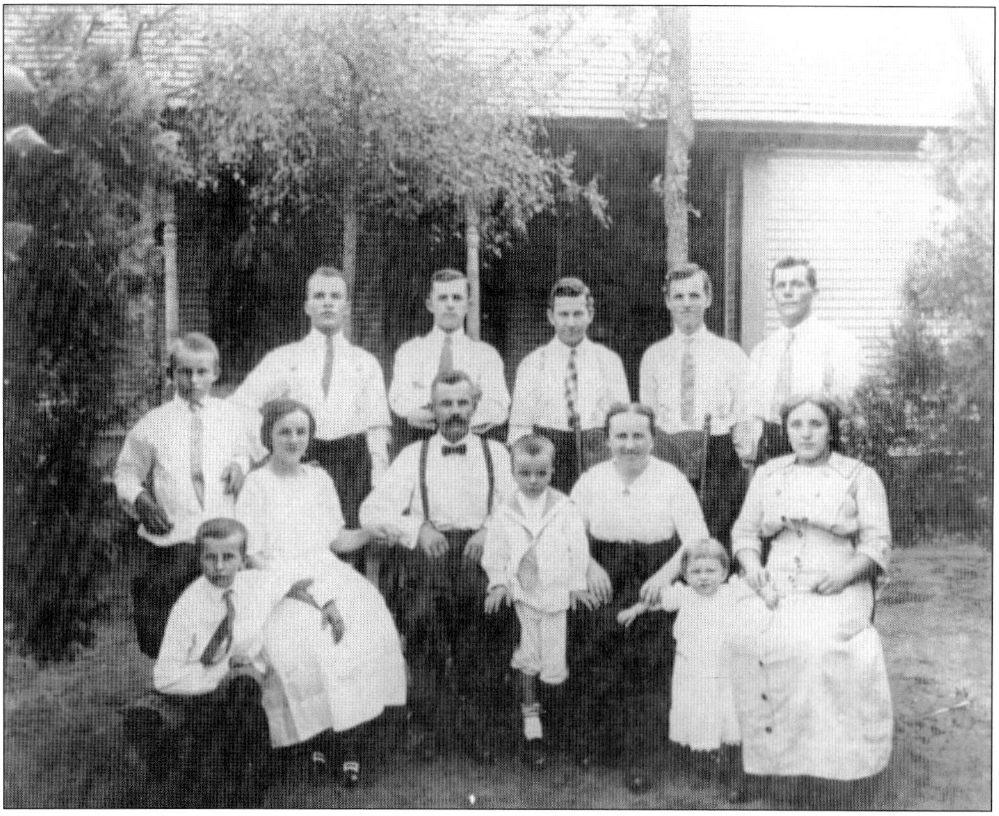

The Piper family were early landowners in what would become the city of River Oaks. Present-day Black Oak Street was originally named Piper Street in their honor. Family members shown in this undated photograph are, from left to right, (first row) Carl Piper (kneeling), Theresa Piper Schilder, Laurenze Piper, Ferdinand Piper (standing), Theresa Piper, Walter Schieme (standing), and Marie Piper Schieme; (second row) John Piper, Rudolph Piper, Frank Schieme, Frank Piper, unidentified, and Lorenz Piper Jr. (Courtesy of the River Oaks Historical Society.)

Two

City Government, Police, and Fire

River Oaks is an incorporated mostly residential community on State Highway 183 within the western boundary of Fort Worth in west central Tarrant County. The driving force that led to incorporation came in 1941, when the Fort Worth Chamber of Commerce deeded 1,450 acres to the federal government to construct a plant to build B-24 bombers and a landing field, which would later become Carswell Air Force Base. Construction began in April 1941. Local citizens felt the residential and commercial boom that would follow would lead Fort Worth to attempt annexation of surrounding land. This led local residents to vote to incorporate their community, and the community voted to change its name to River Oaks Village. The construction of the air base, which was activated by the Army in 1942, became the catalyst for community development. On September 6, 1947, the city opened Thurston Park, its first playground. In 1962, the city created its first park board.

River Oaks organized its volunteer fire department in October 1946. In 2013, River Oaks Fire Department (ROFD) became a part-time, stipend-paid fire department. On April 1, 1947, Ordinance No. 58 created the River Oaks Police Department and the office of police chief. The city of River Oaks has its own school system, Castleberry Independent School District, that provides educational facilities for elementary, middle, and high school students.

River Oaks had a population of 2,000 by the end of the 1940s. During the 1950s, water and sewer systems were completed, streets were paved, and a library was built. In 1960, the population of River Oaks surpassed 8,000. The dramatic population increase was due to the increased activity at Carswell and to the arrival of the General Dynamics Corporation near River Oaks. For the next few decades, the population level remained above 8,000. During the 1980s, the number of residents dropped as a result of decreased activity at the air base and the decline in defense contracts received by General Dynamics. At the time of the last census in 2020, the population was 7,629.

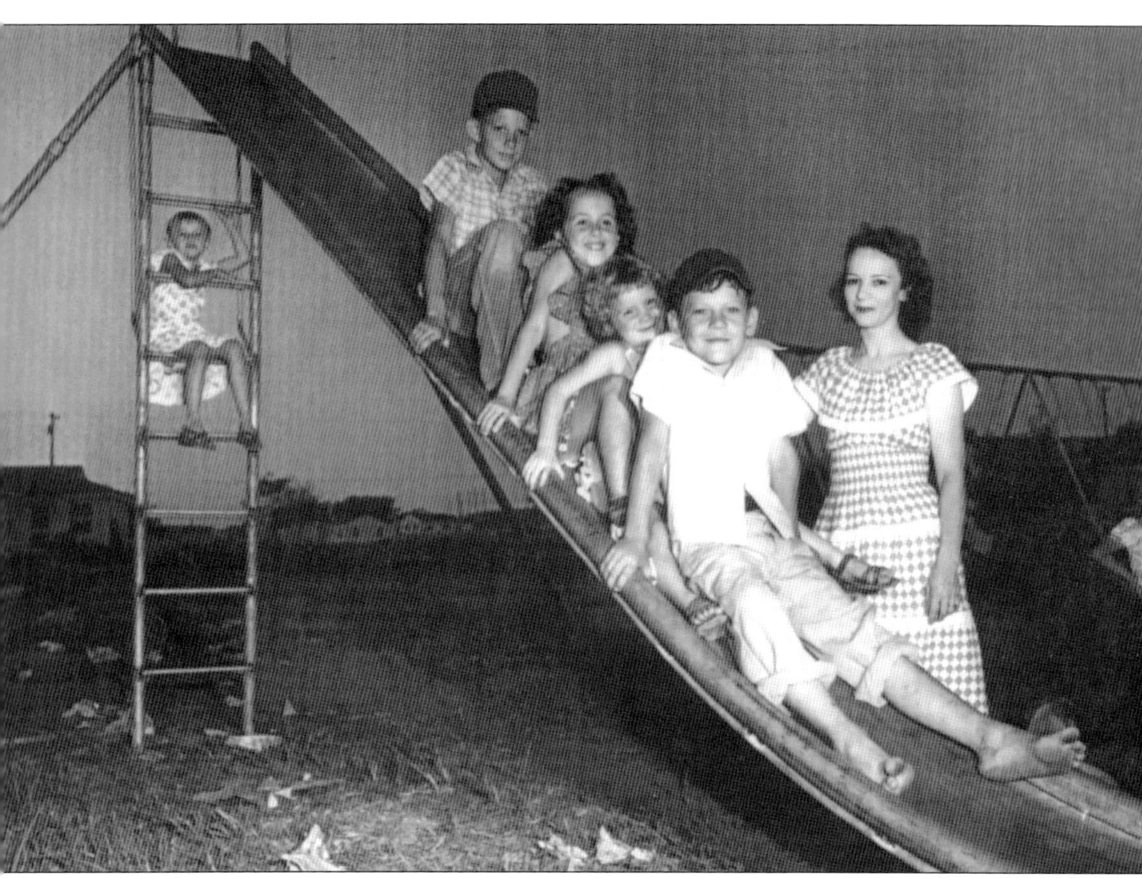

The River Oaks Garden Club opened a public playground at Greenbriar and Thurston Roads on September 6, 1947. On hand that day to try out the slide were, from top to bottom, Billy Gault, Dianna Elliott, Bonnie Newman, and Wade Paschal. Standing is Mrs. H.C. Riepe, president of the River Oaks Garden Club. (Courtesy of the River Oaks Historical Society.)

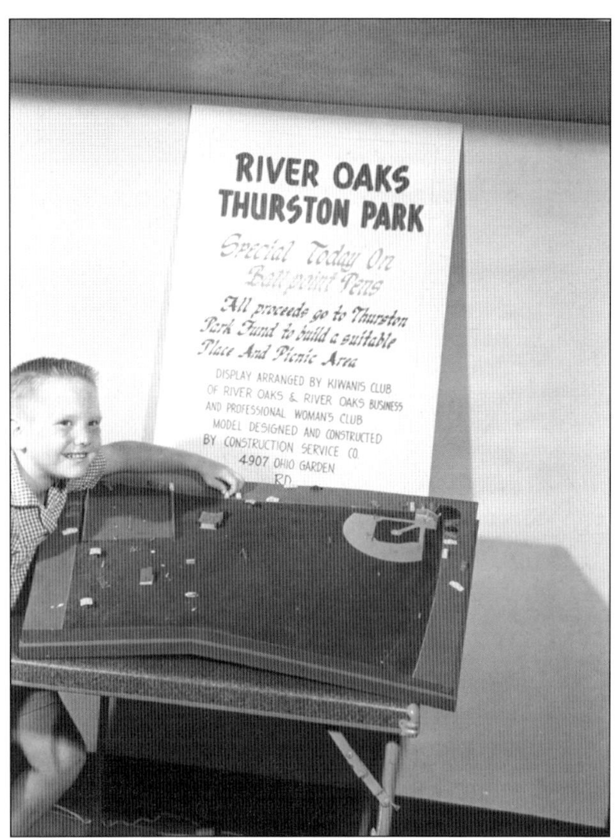

To the right, Thomas Spurlock, six-year-old son of Mr. and Mrs. J.R. Spurlock of 5508 Thomas Lane in River Oaks, looks at a model of the new River Oaks Thurston Park in a picture dated January 7, 1958. The young Spurlock grew up to be a noted musician, pictured below. Spurlock established himself as a musician playing for Fort Worth native Delbert McClinton in the early 1970s. He later went on to tour and record with numerous artists, including Robert Earl Keen, Highway 101, Rodney Crowell, and George Jones. Spurlock moved to Nashville in 1986 and set up a studio in converted train cars near Union Station. In the mid-2000s, Spurlock relocated to Austin where, in addition to his production work, he owned and operated a Thai food trailer. Spurlock played steel guitar. He passed away in November 2021. (Both, courtesy of the *Fort Worth Star-Telegram* Collection, University of Texas at Arlington Libraries.)

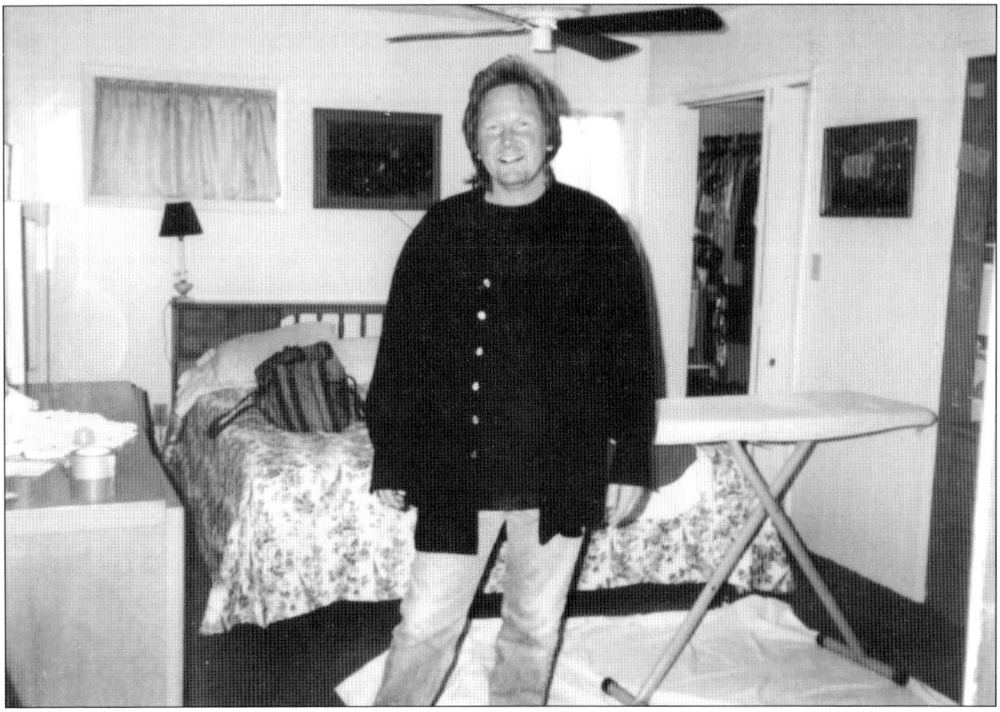

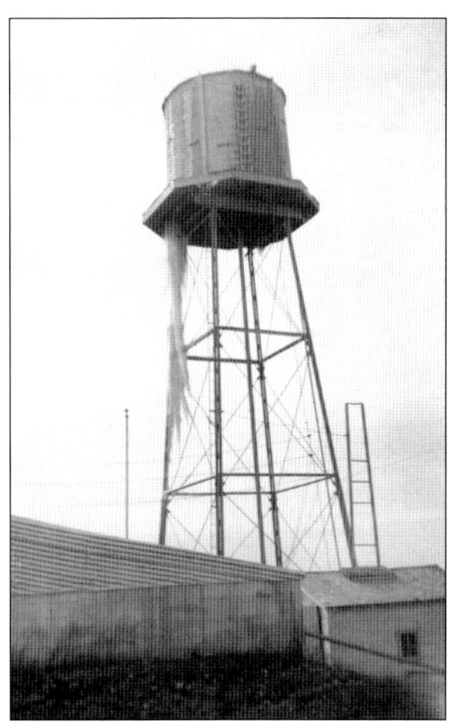

The original water tower for the city of River Oaks was located at the corner of Skyline Drive and Boicourt Street. Notice the frozen water streaming down the side of the tower. River Oaks has struggled with its drinking water and wastewater systems for almost the entirety of the city's history. (Courtesy of the *Fort Worth Star-Telegram* Collection, University of Texas at Arlington Libraries.)

Members of River Oaks, White Settlement, and West Side Lions Clubs journeyed to Brownwood and intervening points to publicize the 1953 Southwestern Exposition and Fat Stock Show. Standing from left to right are Glen Calhoun of the White Settlement Lions Club; Dr. H.G. Buxton, West Side Lions Club; C.C. Makarwich, River Oaks Lions Club; and J. Harrold Evans, West Side Lions Club, trip chairman. Makarwich, a native of Poland, was a 59-year resident of the city of River Oaks. (Courtesy of the *Fort Worth Star-Telegram* Collection, University of Texas at Arlington Libraries.)

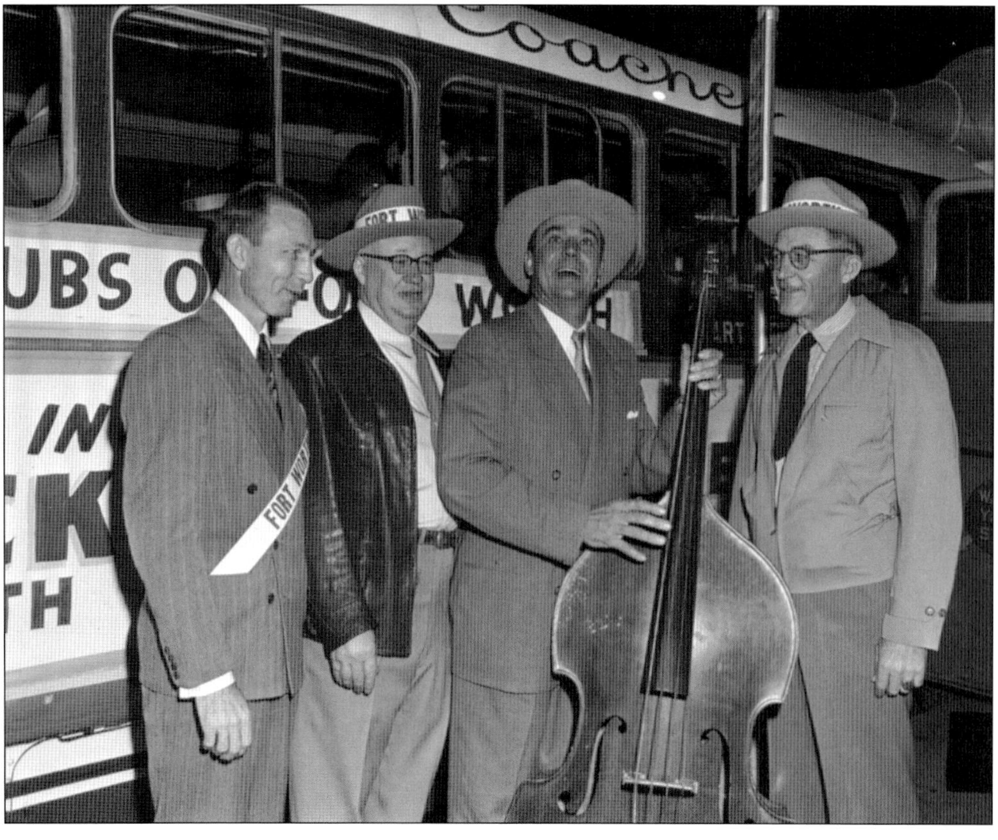

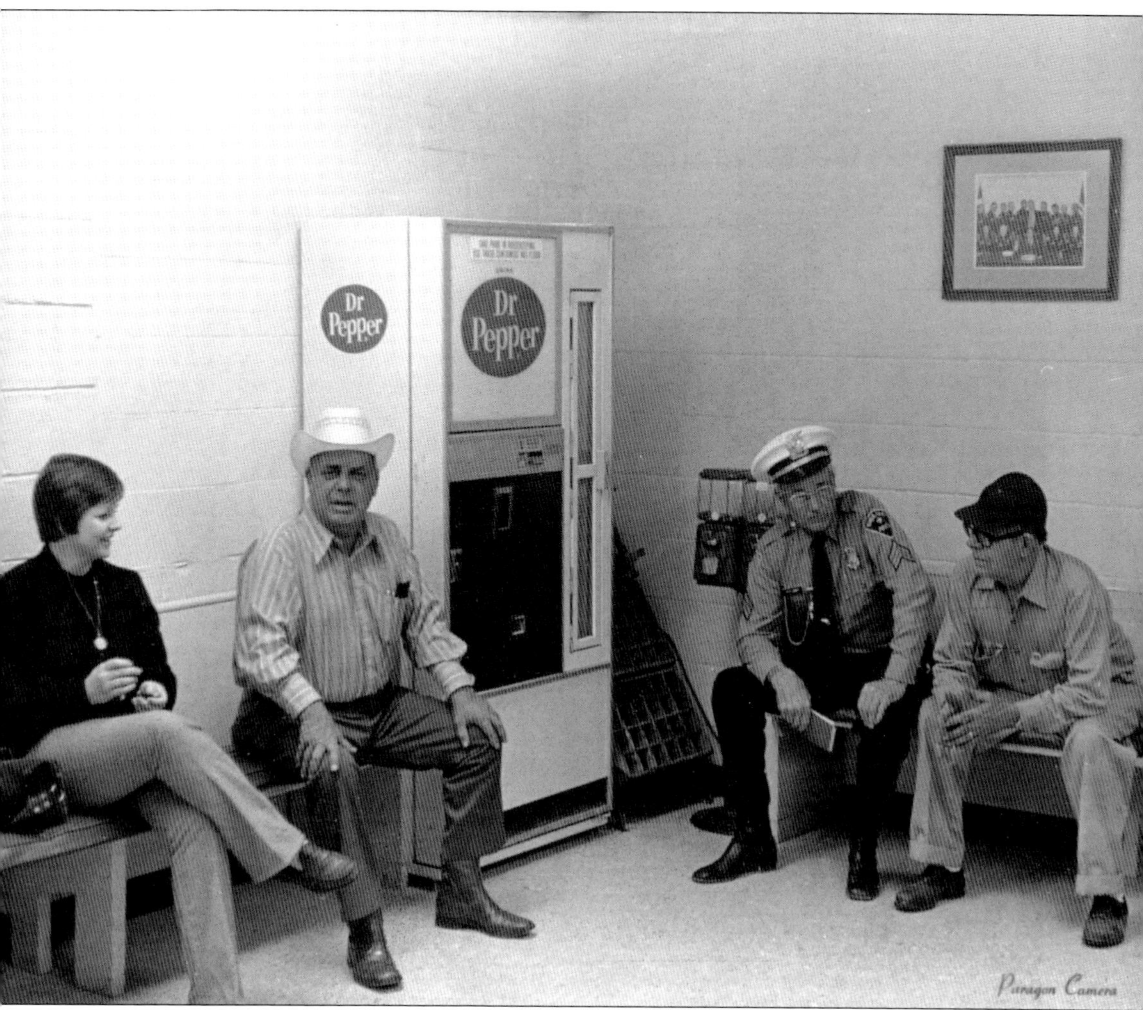

From left to right, Joe Martin, Fire Chief A.T. Huffines, Sgt. Paul Bray, and Assistant Fire Chief M.M. Weddle enjoy a break in this undated photograph taken by Sgt. Joe Martin. The River Oaks Volunteer Fire Department was organized in October 1946. Up until 2013, nearly all the volunteer personnel lived in the city and responded from their homes when alarms sounded or in later years calls came across their pagers. The River Oaks Fire Department is now a career fire service organization providing fire and rescue services to the citizens of River Oaks and surrounding communities. The River Oaks Fire Department has a rich history as a volunteer organization for many decades. The transition to a full-time career department took place in October 2019. The department now has 12 full-time professional firefighters divided into three shifts of four personnel. (Courtesy of the River Oaks Historical Society.)

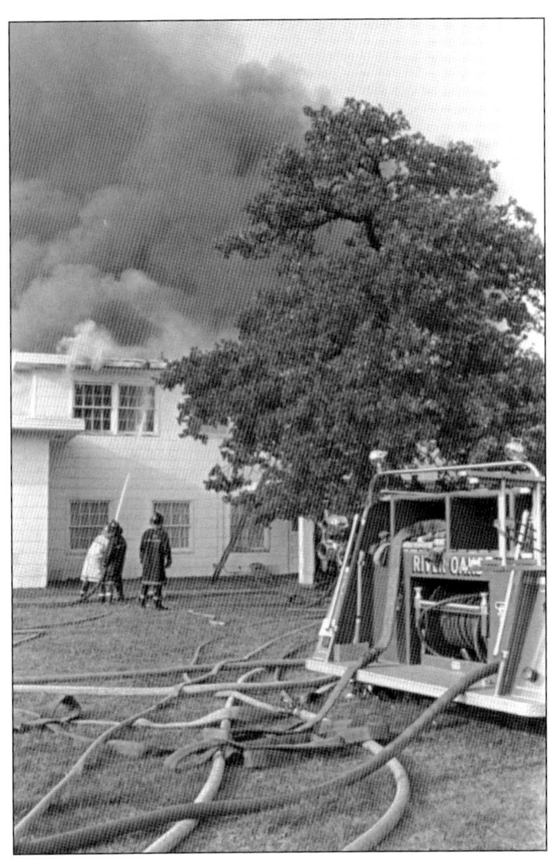

On September 20, 1973, the River Oaks YMCA caught fire. The blaze was described in the *Fort Worth Star-Telegram* as a "very hot fire." In addition to the River Oaks Fire Department, four other local fire departments responded to the scene. Three firefighters were overcome by smoke and were hospitalized, but none were seriously hurt. This is one example of the smaller local volunteer fire departments cooperating in emergencies. (Both, courtesy of the River Oaks Historical Society.)

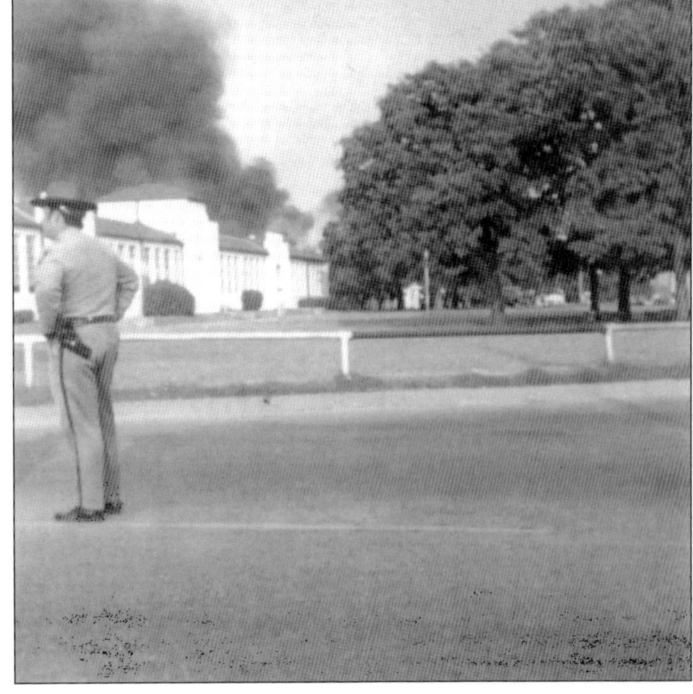

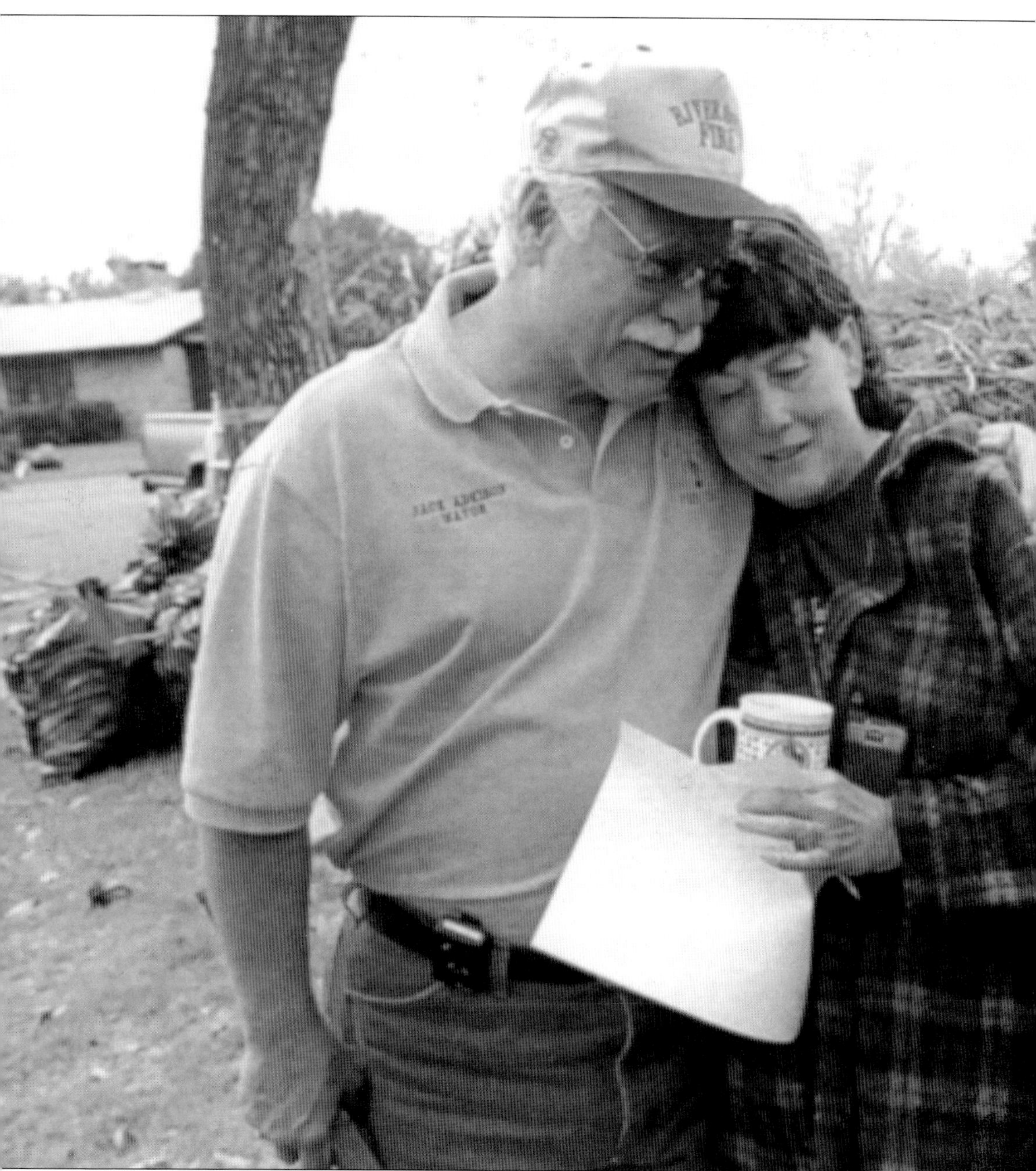

On the evening of March 28, 2000, a tornado touched down in River Oaks. The twister gained power, eventually becoming an F3 tornado, and ripped through River Oaks and Fort Worth. The storm damaged 266 homes across its 4-mile-long and 250-yard-wide path. Nine other tornadoes also occurred across North Texas. Jack Atkinson, the mayor at the time, noted that Adm. Craig McDonald, base commander of NAS JRB Fort Worth, contacted the city and offered immediate help. Even though the base had also sustained damage, Admiral McDonald offered manpower, fire trucks, and heavy machinery to help clear damage and rescue survivors, along with military police to curb any looting. This is one more example of the strong connection between the city of River Oaks and its military neighbors. (Courtesy of Jack Atkinson.)

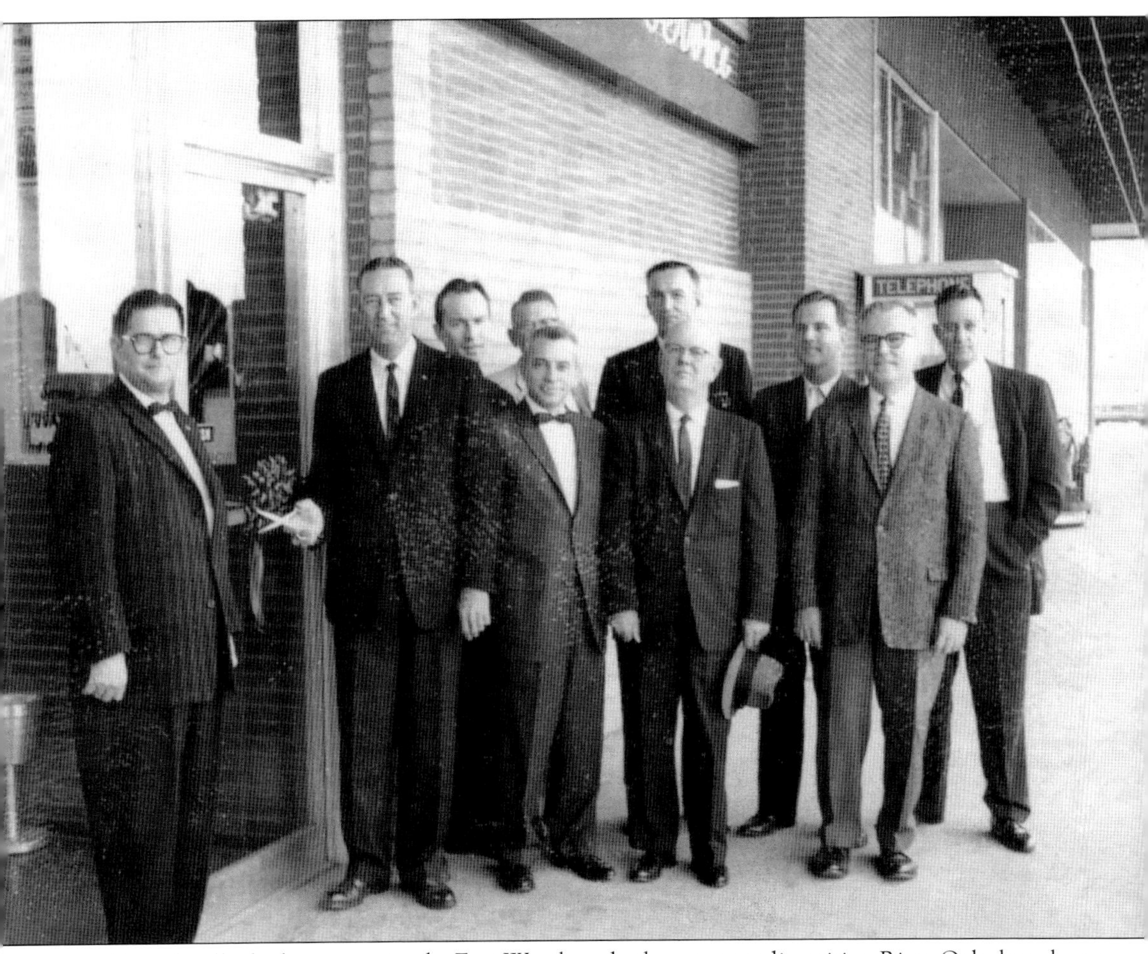

Being landlocked to expansion by Fort Worth and other surrounding cities, River Oaks has always shown great support for local businesses. One of the last remaining areas for economic growth was vacant land east of River Oaks Boulevard near Jacksboro Highway. The Fair Oaks Shopping Center was opened in 1952. One of the anchors of the center was Wyatt's Cafeteria. Pictured here is the manager of Wyatt's (far left), and next to him is Mayor Bob Blevins seen cutting the ribbon. (Courtesy of the *Fort Worth Star-Telegram* Collection, University of Texas at Arlington Libraries.)

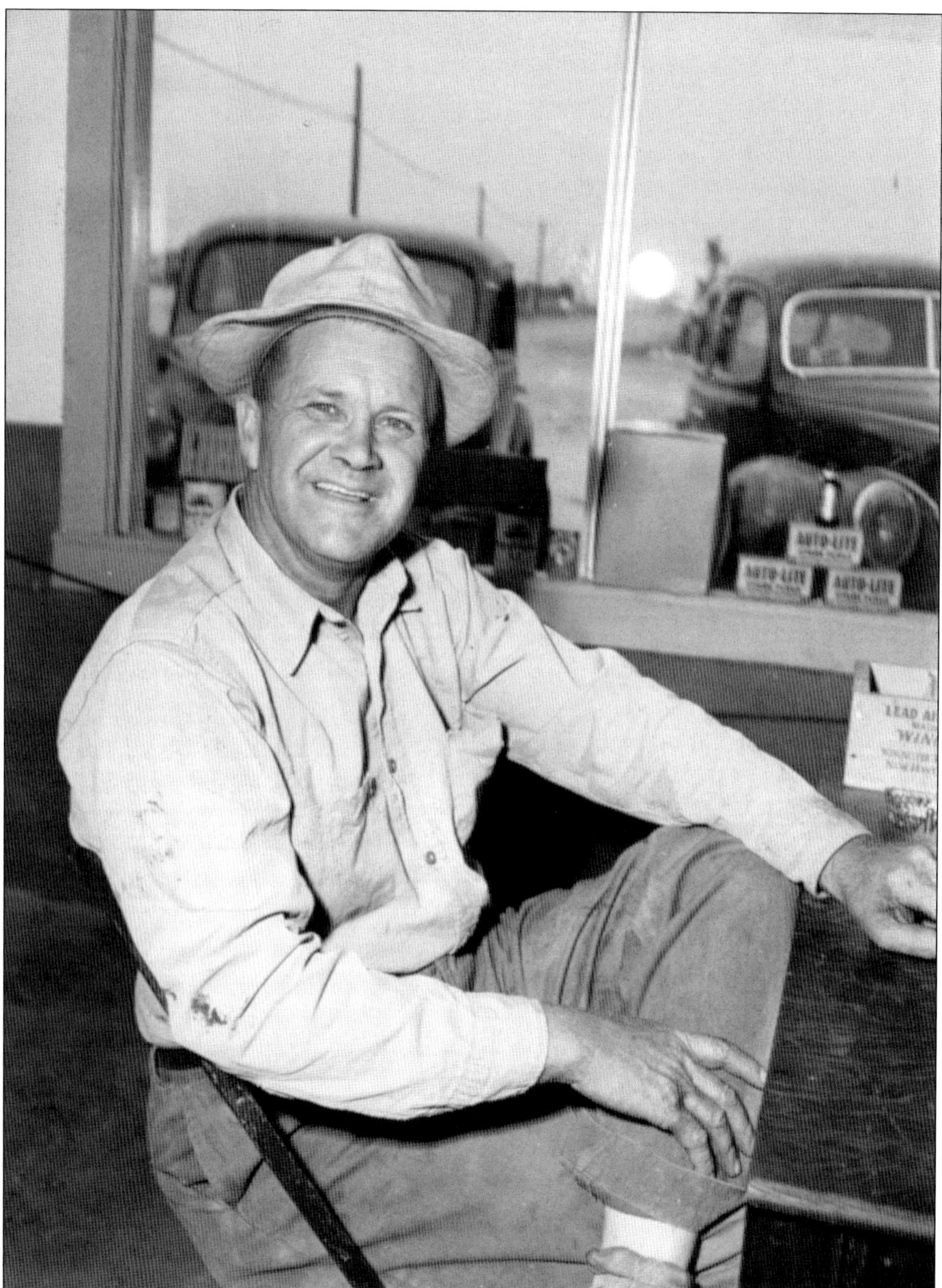

They say all politics is local, and that is especially true in small-town politics. The city of River Oaks has a long history of local businessmen and -women virtually donating their time—the present-day mayor and city council are paid less than $10 per meeting. Roy Adams is pictured in 1946 after he was elected alderman. Adams was a plumbing contractor. He polled 96 votes to his opponent's 37. (Courtesy of the *Fort Worth Star-Telegram* Collection, University of Texas at Arlington Libraries.)

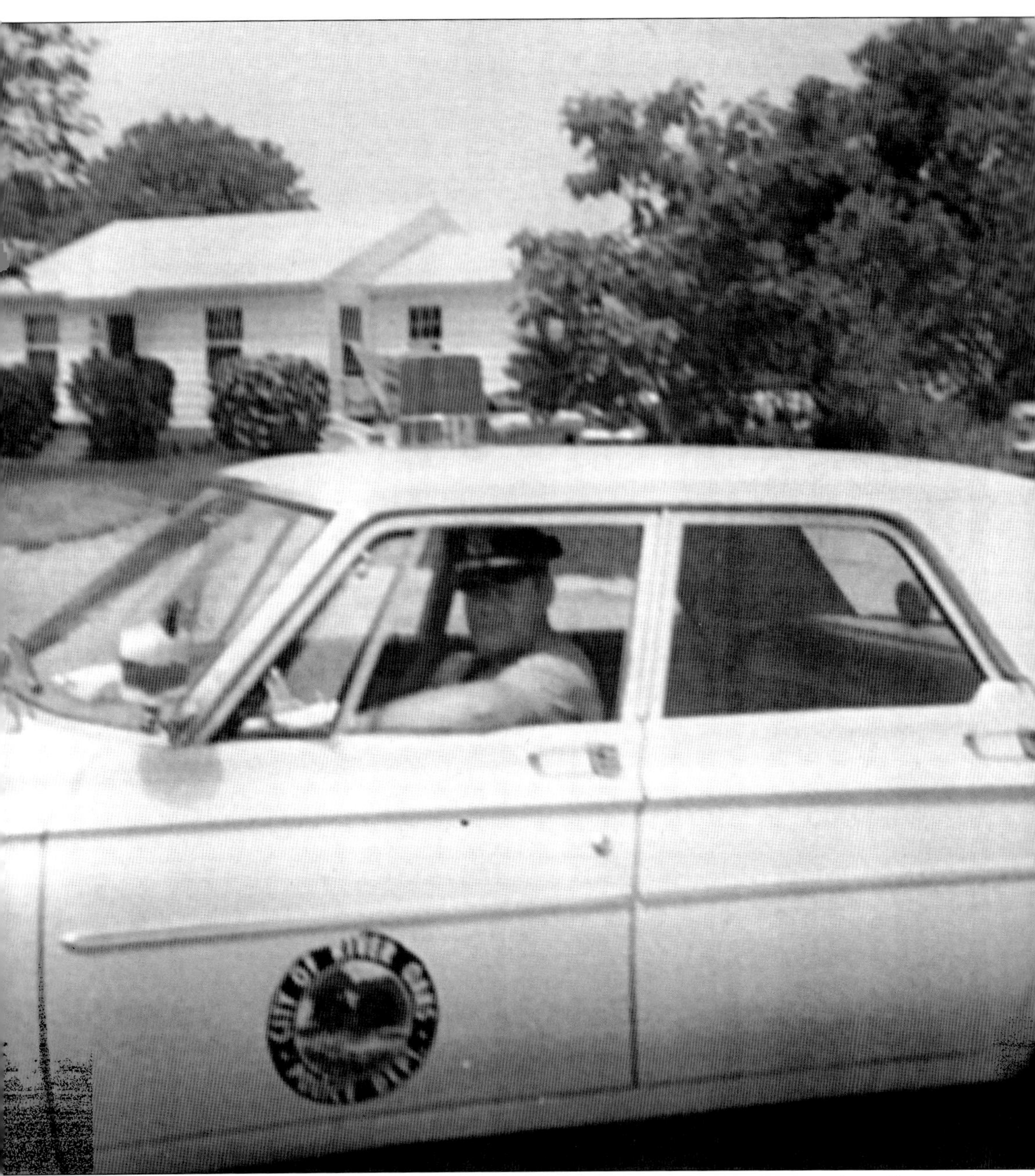

On May 7, 1946, the board of aldermen officially changed the name of River Oaks Village to the city of River Oaks. A little more than a year later, on April 1, 1947, Ordinance No. 58 created the River Oaks Police Department and the office of police chief. Early police car radios could only receive; they could not transmit and were unreliable. Whenever a call came to the station, the dispatcher would turn on a light over the outside door to the police station, indicating there had been a call. Officers would make frequent trips past the station to see if the light was on. (Courtesy of the River Oaks Historical Society.)

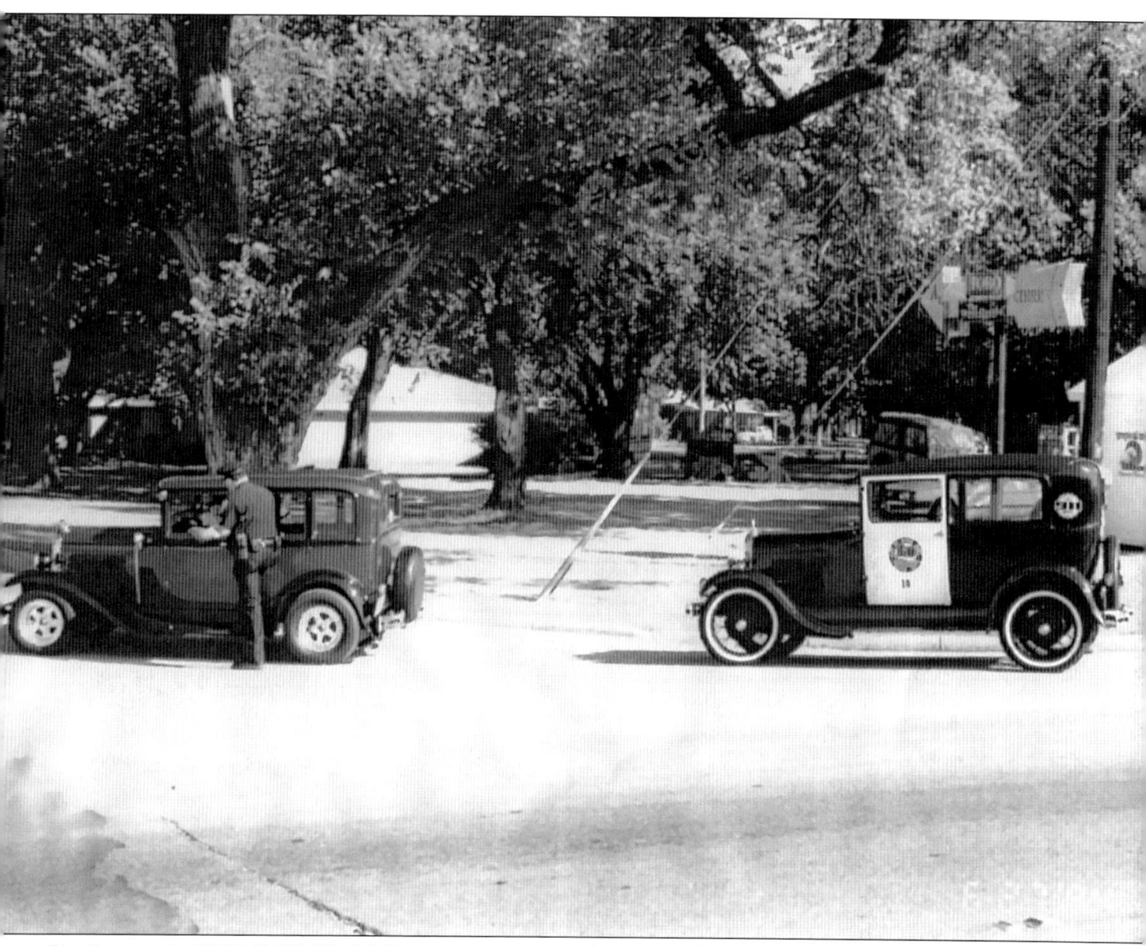

On August 1, 1990, D.W. "Dub" Bransom was named River Oaks chief of police. Chief Bransom was an avid antique car enthusiast and used his Ford Model A Tudor police car to represent the department. "Car 10," as it was called, had been restored to its original condition and was the oldest working police car in the nation. Car 10 was used for patrols, police surveillance, transporting prisoners, and the DARE program and also appeared at numerous car shows. The picture above shows Car 10 making a "traffic stop." (Courtesy of Darren Houk.)

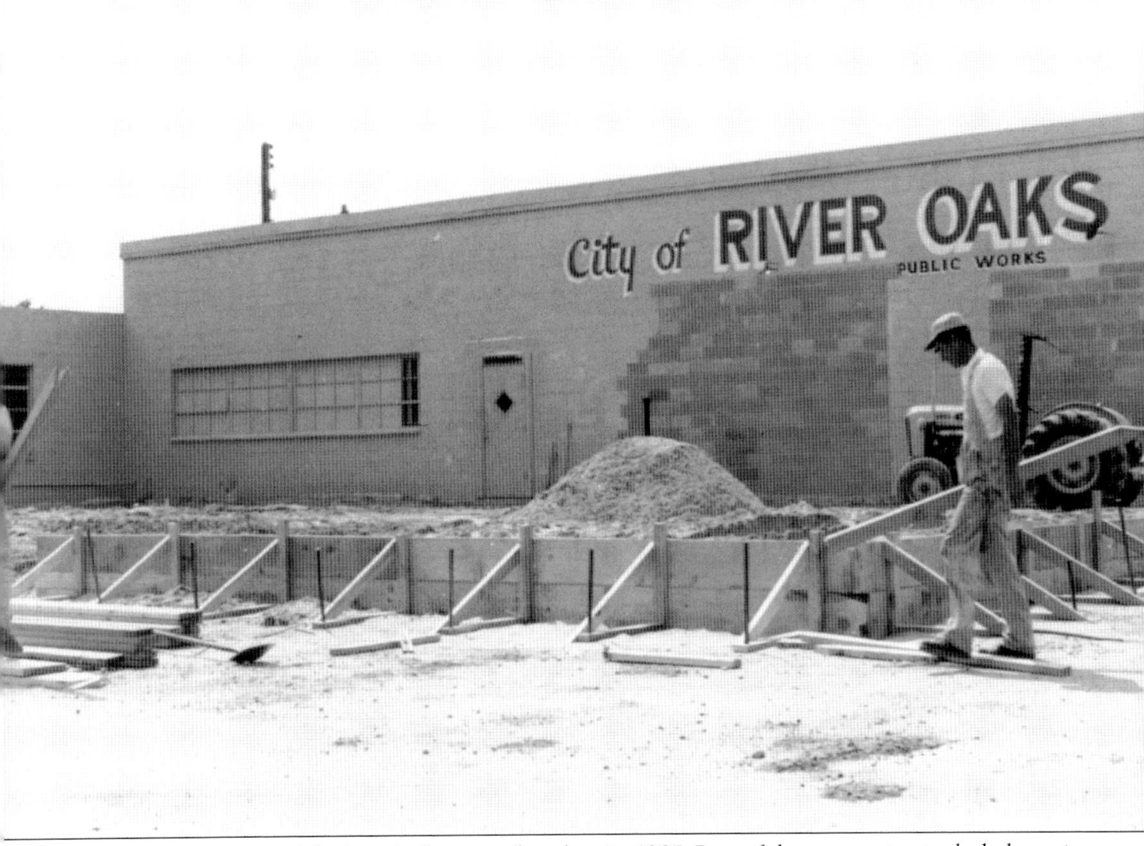

An extensive remodel of city hall was undertaken in 1987. Part of the renovation included moving the fire department bay doors to the northeast side of the building so the trucks would not be pulling out onto busy River Oaks Boulevard. The remodel was undertaken on a pay-as-you-go economic model so the city would not incur debt. (Courtesy of the River Oaks Historical Society.)

Seen at right, Dorothy Grace Harris was crowned Queen of River Oaks Fire Department in November 1945. In October 1958, Janice Fancher, the 18-year-old daughter of Mr. and Mrs. R.O. Fancher of 4917 Almena Road in River Oaks, represented the River Oaks Volunteer Fire Department in the Tarrant County "Miss Flame" Contest, pictured below. Janice was a freshman at Texas Christian University in Fort Worth. Events such as beauty pageants were used to spark community involvement and support for the city and police and fire departments. (Both, courtesy of the *Fort Worth Star-Telegram* Collection, University of Texas at Arlington Libraries.)

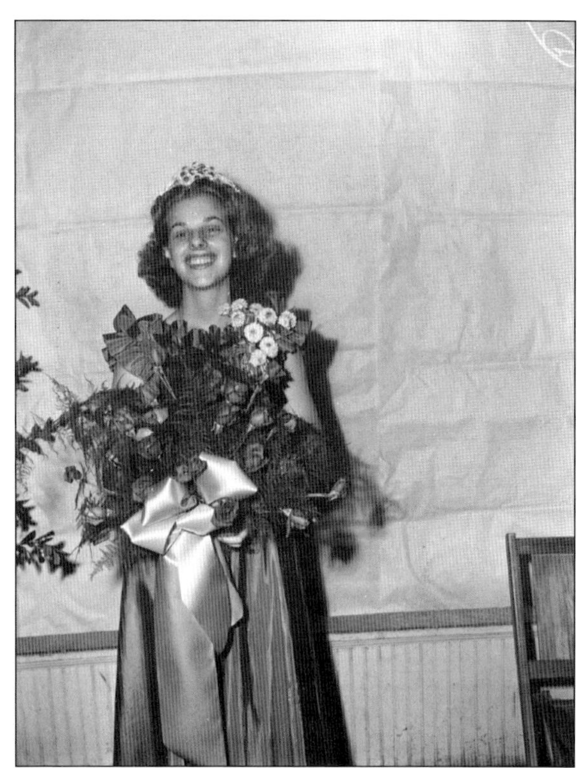

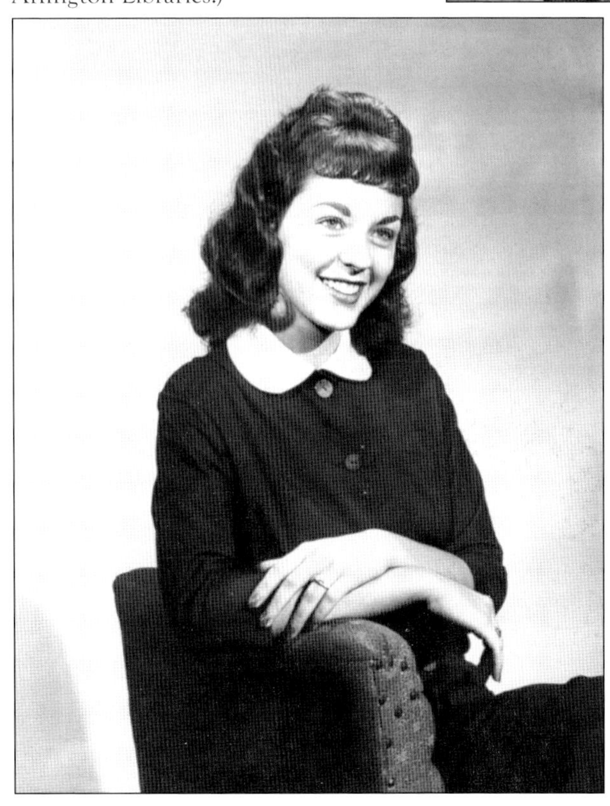

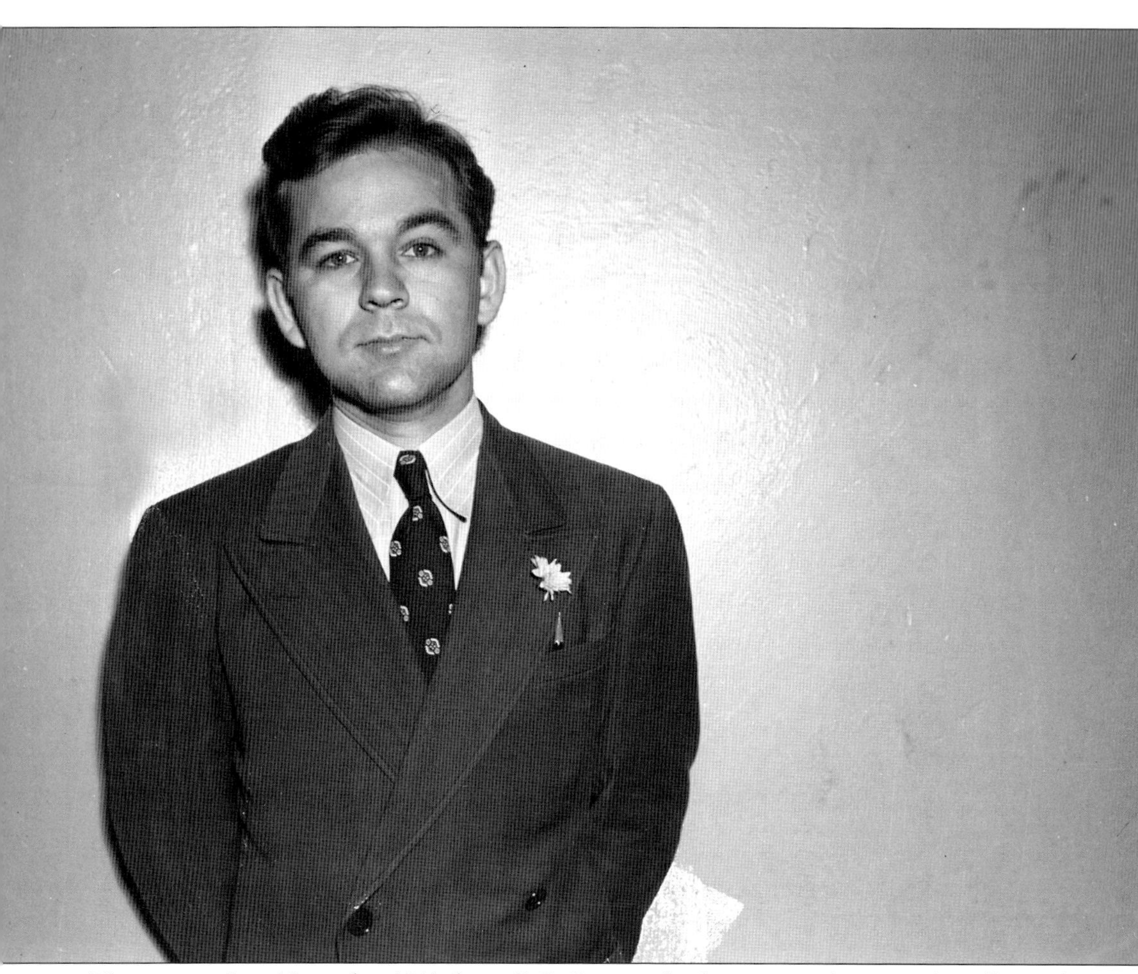

This picture from November 1941 shows D.D. Barron, the first mayor of River Oaks Village. The aldermen of the new River Oaks Village held their first official meeting in December in the home of the new mayor to outline policies and discuss plans for ordinances. The village charter was expected to be ready, and the oaths were administered to the officers. (Courtesy of the *Fort Worth Star-Telegram* Collection, University of Texas at Arlington Libraries.)

Neighborhood kids stopped playing on a rainy Wednesday afternoon just long enough to help unload some books for the expanded Castleberry River Oaks Library, scheduled to open on Friday, August 7, 1953. Vanilah Barton, the driver of the bookmobile of the Tarrant County Free Library, is assisted by, from left to right, James Clark, Sharon McKay, Bobbie Turner, and Marilyn Riepe, all students of the Castleberry Independent School District. (Courtesy of the *Fort Worth Star-Telegram* Collection, University of Texas at Arlington Libraries.)

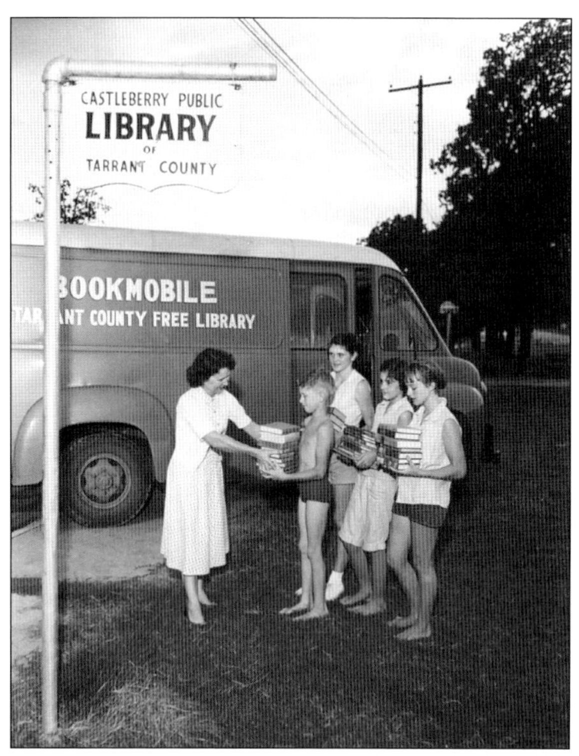

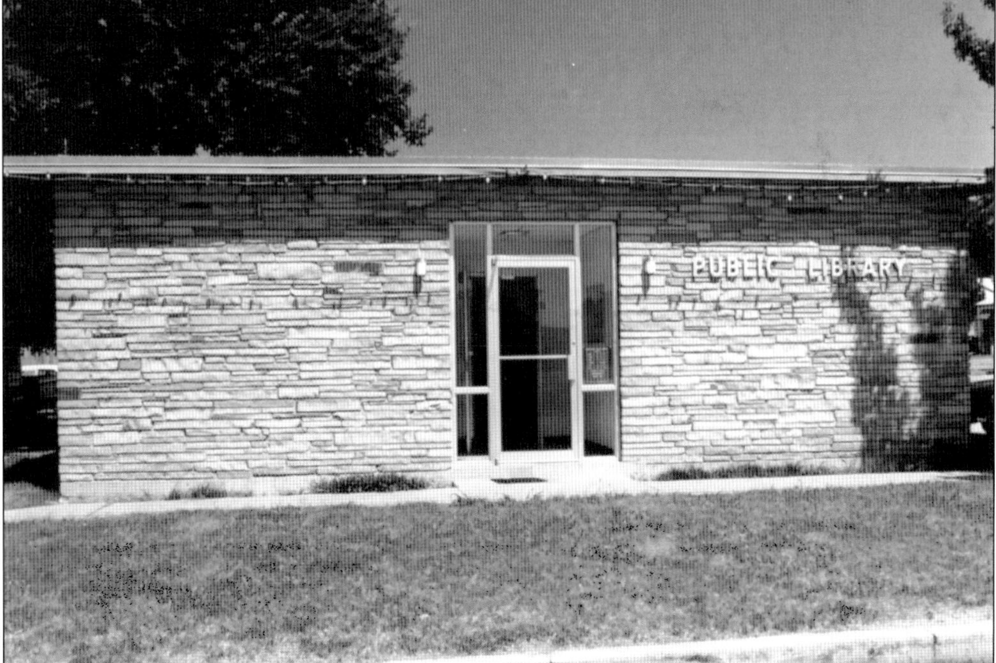

The old library is pictured here before the new city hall complex was erected. This building was incorporated into the new complex and exists today. The library was closed on October 1, 2020, due to the monetary constraints of operating a high level of essential services throughout the city. (Courtesy of the River Oaks Historical Society.)

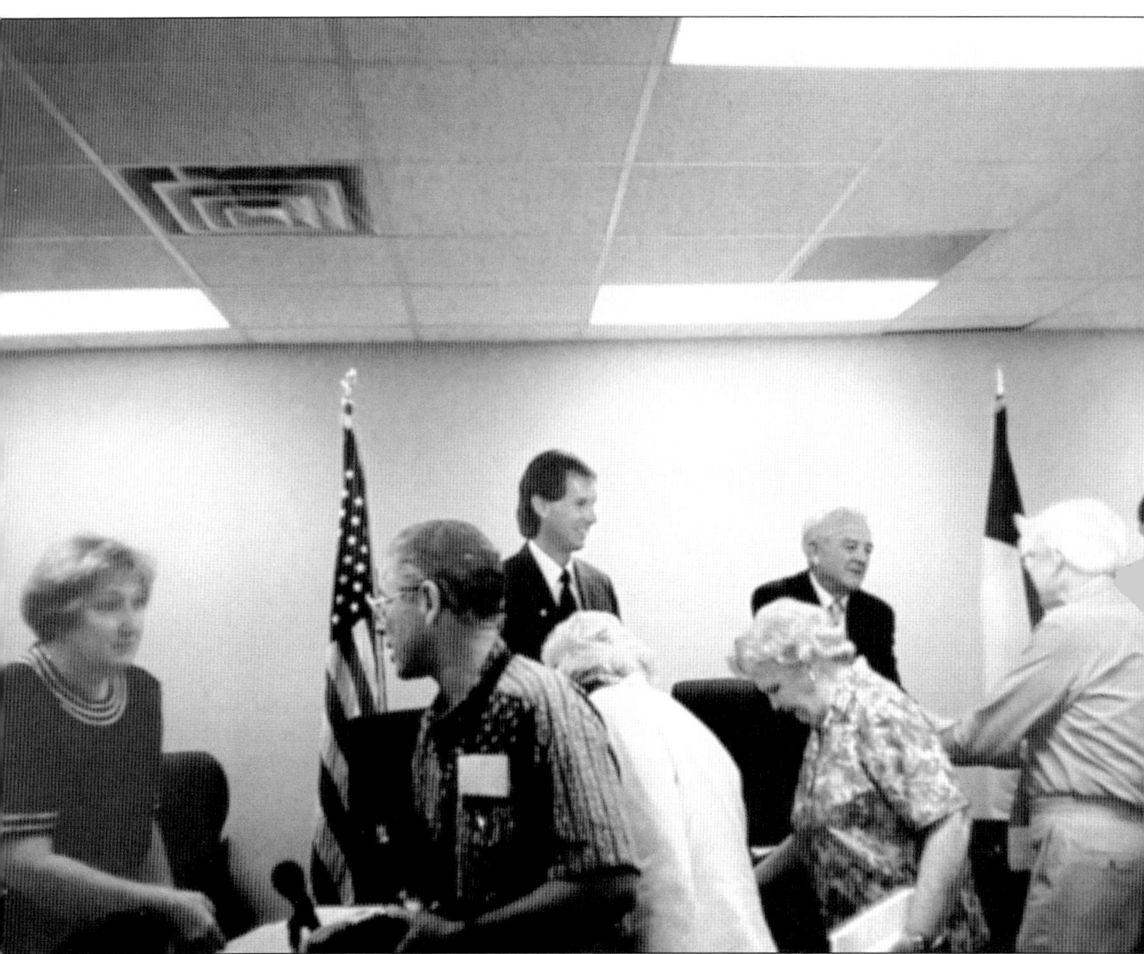

In 1995, Shirley Wheat was the first woman ever elected to the city council in River Oaks. Wheat is a lifelong resident and has always been active in her volunteer work and service to the city. She served one term on the city council and has been codirector of the City of River Oaks Event Center for many years. (Courtesy of the River Oaks Historical Society.)

Three

Schools and Churches

River Oaks being a small, mostly residential community has allowed the city to focus on the needs of its citizens. Two of the most important needs of any community are the education of the children and tending to the spiritual needs of all citizens.

The roots of the Castleberry Independent School District (CISD) stretch back to 1898, when the State of Texas certified the first school as a common school district. It was known as the Marine School No. 3. May Manning was the school's first teacher. A three-room brick structure was erected in 1919, and the name was changed to the Castleberry Common School District in honor of Zack and Fanny Castleberry, who provided well water to the school. The area grew rapidly in the next decade, and by 1932, another room was added to the schoolhouse. A new two-room frame building was added in 1934, and an additional one-room building was erected in 1936. Irma Marsh was CISD's first superintendent. She served the district from 1924 until 1972. The middle school is named in her honor. Matching bonds, Works Progress Administration projects, and other federal programs enabled the district to expand as necessary, including the erection of a large main building in 1938. Air Force personnel, aircraft mechanics, and their children arrived at nearby Carswell Air Force Base during World War II, and the school district expanded to accommodate them. In the 1950s, local high school students were transferred to the Fort Worth Independent School District. When Fort Worth announced in 1956 its intent to charge tuition for the education of Castleberry students, the Castleberry School District became independent and added a high school to its facilities. Today, CISD serves over 3,700 students and encompasses seven campuses.

River Oaks has 11 churches inside its borders. A wide variety of denominations including Baptist, Methodist, Catholic, Christian, and Nazarene tend to the spiritual needs of the city. Trinity Baptist is the oldest church continually serving the city, having been established in 1912.

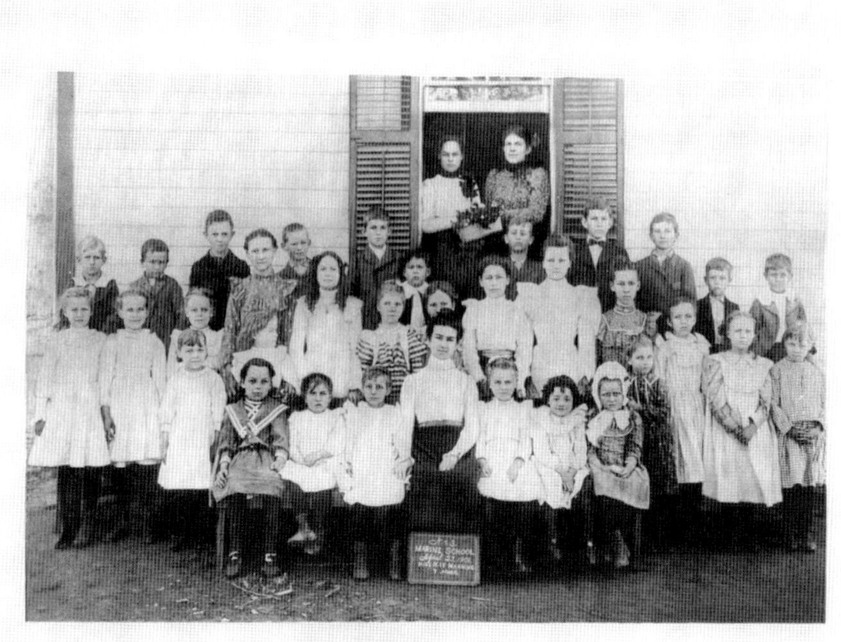

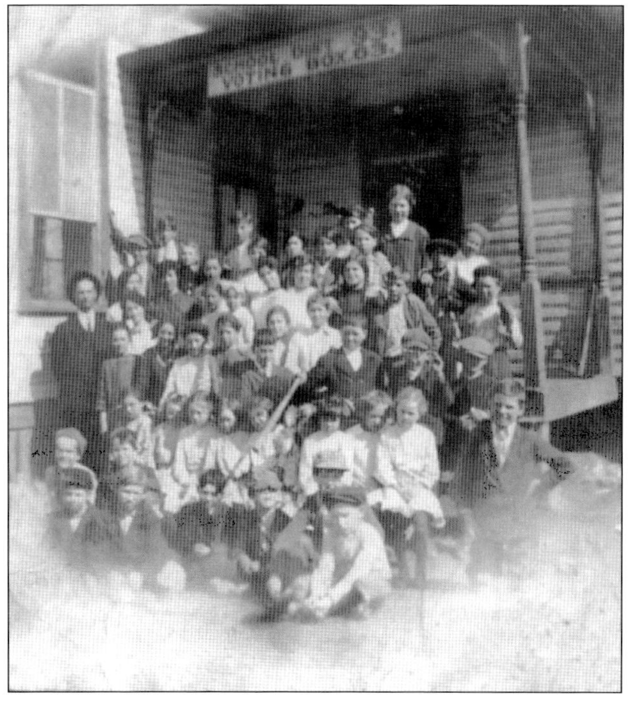

The forerunner of the Castleberry Independent School system was known as the Marine School No. 3. Certified by the State of Texas as a common school district in 1898, Marine School No. 3 was housed in a small frame structure erected on land given by local resident Ike Vinchinor. In 1902, a second room was added, and the school was known as Rosen Heights School No. 2 from that time until 1919. Above is the earliest known photograph of the school, taken on April 25, 1901. The teacher is May Manning. The only identified child is Grady Isbell, second row from the top, first boy on the right. The picture at left of School District 93 is undated. (Above, courtesy of the River Oaks Historical Society; left, courtesy of Linda Claridge.)

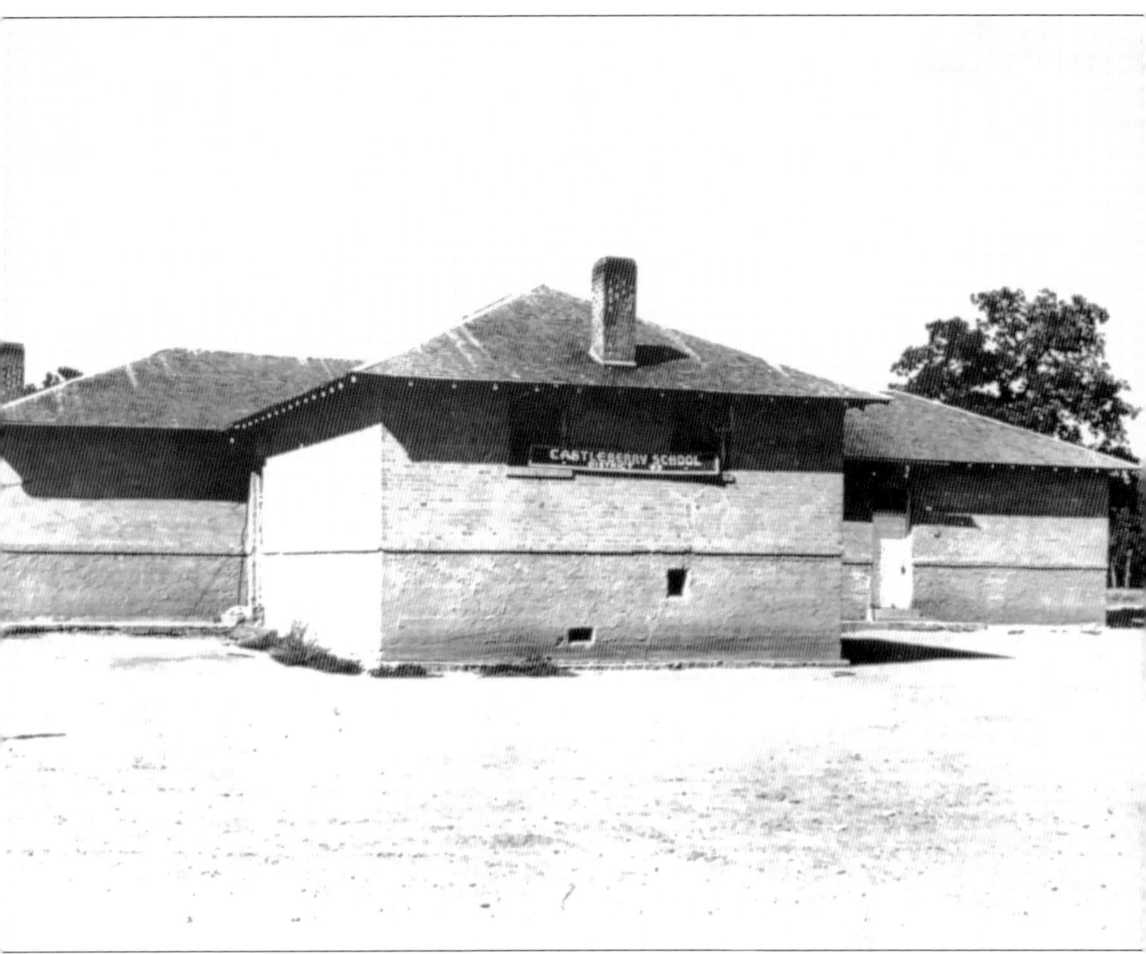

Castleberry School District 95 was built around 1919. The date of the photograph is unknown. The three-room brick building was erected at a cost of approximately $6,000, quite a sum for the time. The building was named after "Uncle Zack" Castleberry, who furnished water from their well for school purposes. (Courtesy of University of North Texas Libraries, the Portal to Texas History.)

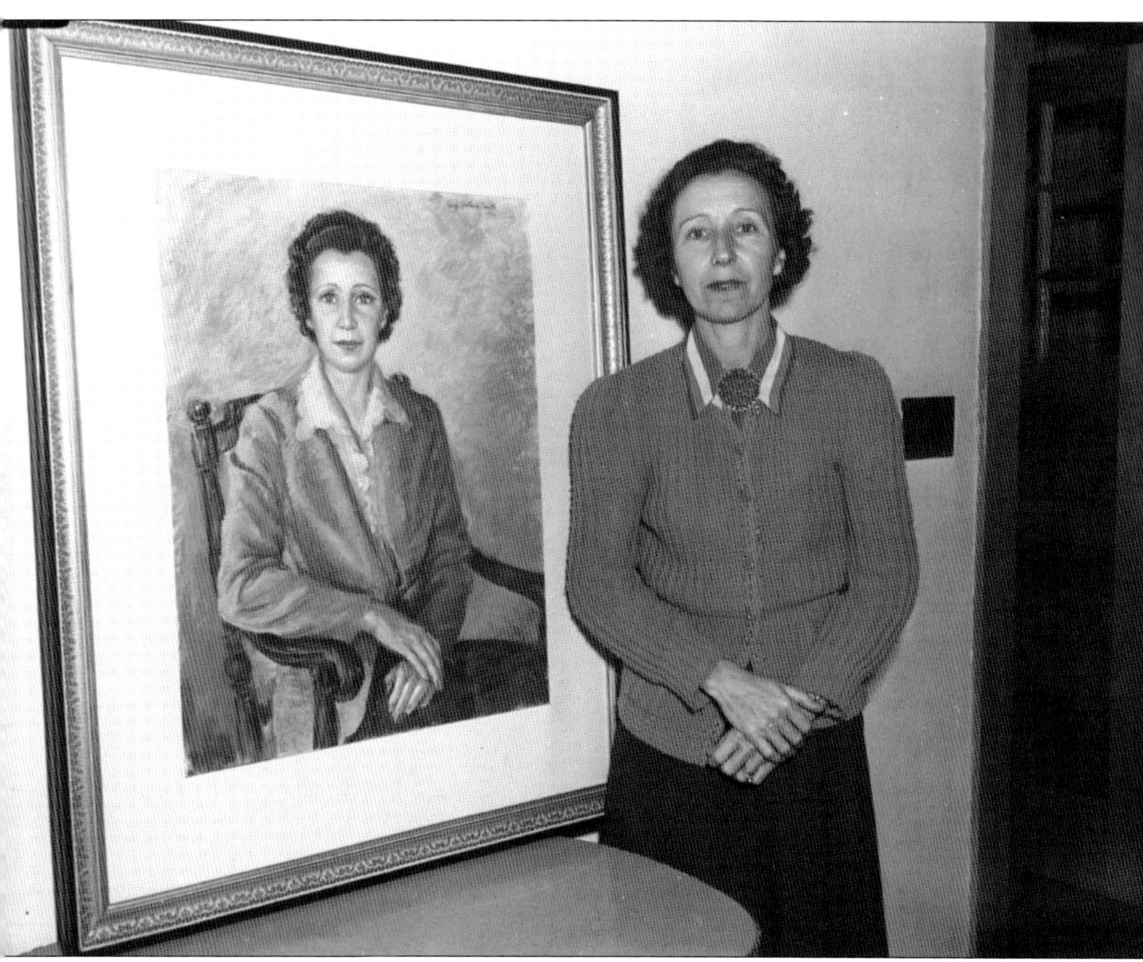

Irma Marsh was the longtime superintendent of the Castleberry School District. Marsh was a lifelong area resident. She was a graduate of North Side High School and received her bachelor's degree in education from Texas Wesleyan College, now Texas Wesleyan University, in 1939. She earned her master's degree in administration from Texas Christian University in 1941. Marsh became the Castleberry School superintendent in 1958 after teaching at Castleberry since 1924. She retired from CISD in 1972. Marsh was a member of River Oaks Methodist Church. In 1971, she was named Outstanding Administrator by the Texas Classroom Teachers Association. The City of River Oaks had an Irma Marsh Day, and the Zonata Club named her Woman of the Year for 1959–1960. Marsh died on February 10, 1987, at the age of 86. Irma Marsh Middle School is named in her honor for her many years of service to CISD. (Courtesy of the *Fort Worth Star-Telegram* Collection, University of Texas at Arlington Libraries.)

Seniors at Castleberry High School hoist a heifer cow to the roof of the high school building on May 31, 1962. It is doubtful this endeavor was a senior requirement for graduation, only a few weeks out at the time. Senior pranks were common practice until the time came when escapades such as hoisting heifers were deemed unsafe and an insurance liability. (Courtesy of the *Fort Worth Star-Telegram* Collection, University of Texas at Arlington Libraries.)

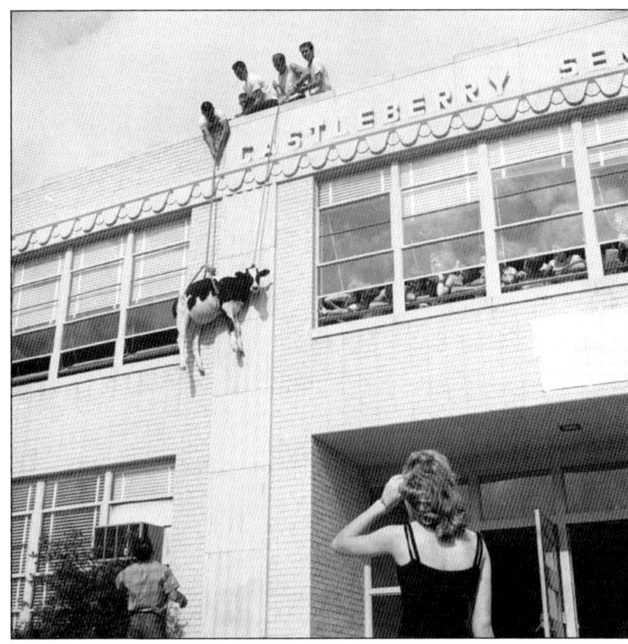

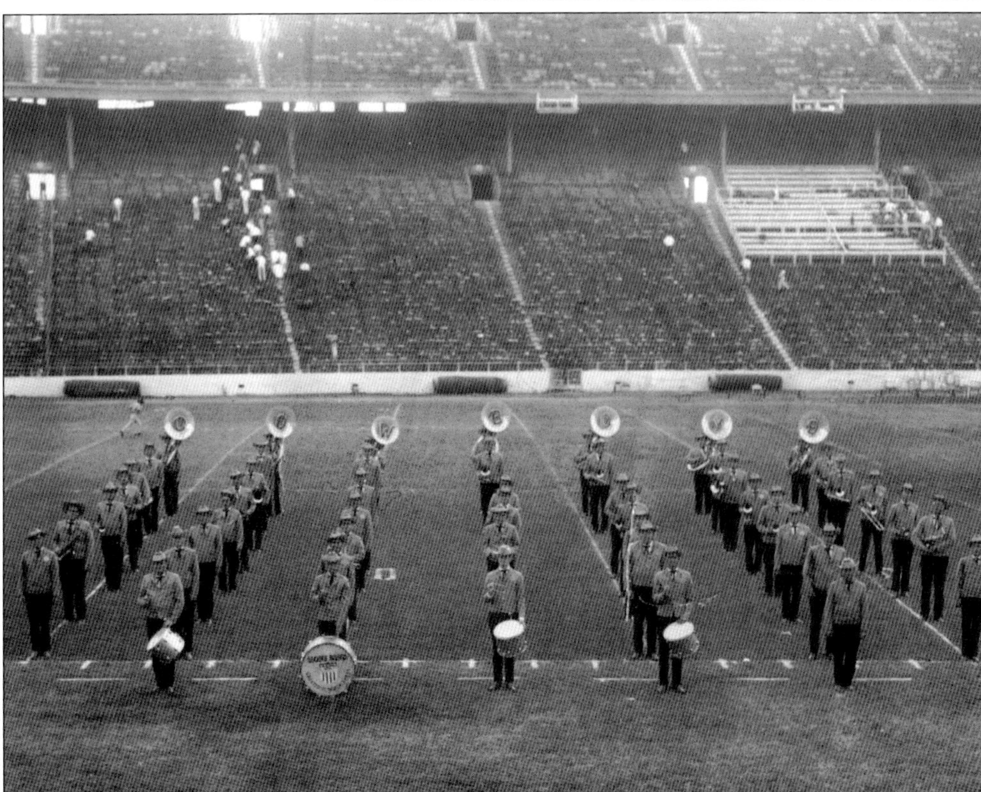

On November 21, 1965, the Dallas Cowboys lost a home game at the Cotton Bowl to the Cleveland Browns 24 to 17. Part of the halftime entertainment was a performance from the Castleberry High School marching band. (Courtesy of the River Oaks Historical Society.)

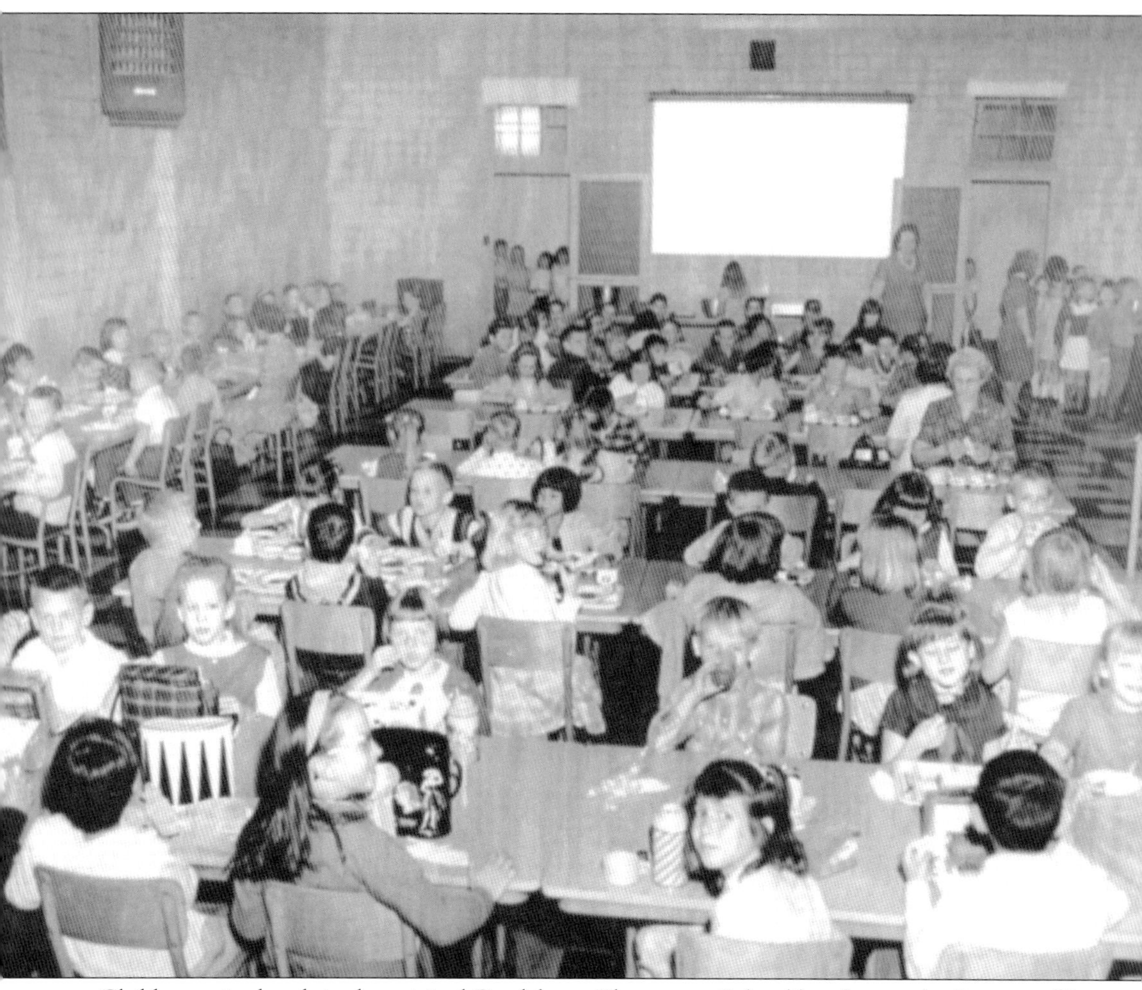

Children enjoy lunch in the original Castleberry Elementary School lunchroom/auditorium. The building was constructed in 1938 in the Art Deco style and expanded in 1945. After serving as an elementary school for 75 years, a new elementary building was constructed behind the property, and the original building was renovated to become the new administration building. Preserving the historical character of this early-20th-century building was a primary goal. (Courtesy of the River Oaks Historical Society.)

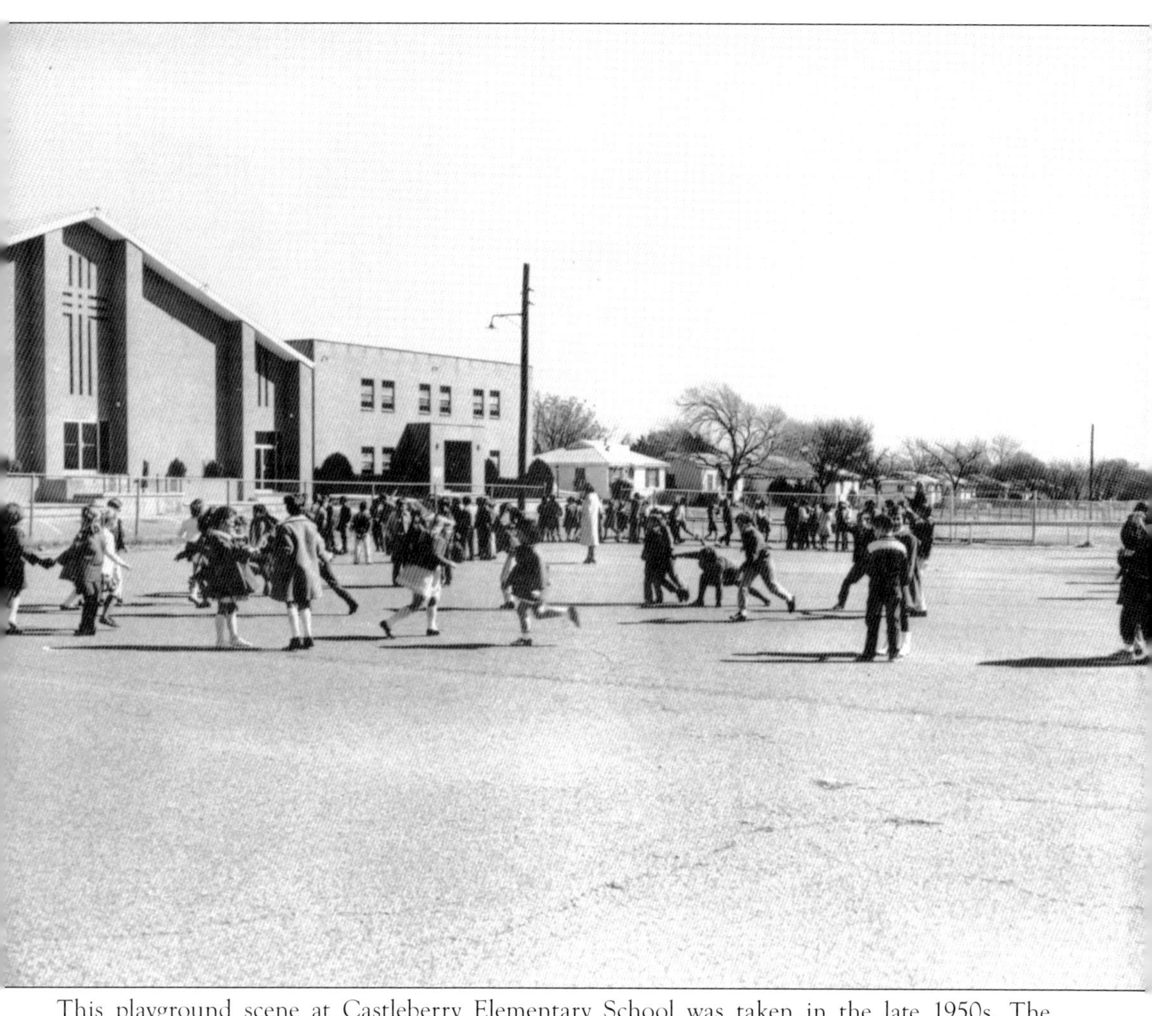

This playground scene at Castleberry Elementary School was taken in the late 1950s. The Castleberry Baptist Church, across the street on Tulane Avenue, is in the background. This school is now the CISD administration building, and a new elementary school has been built alongside is. The playground pictured is now a faculty and staff parking lot. (Courtesy of the River Oaks Historical Society.)

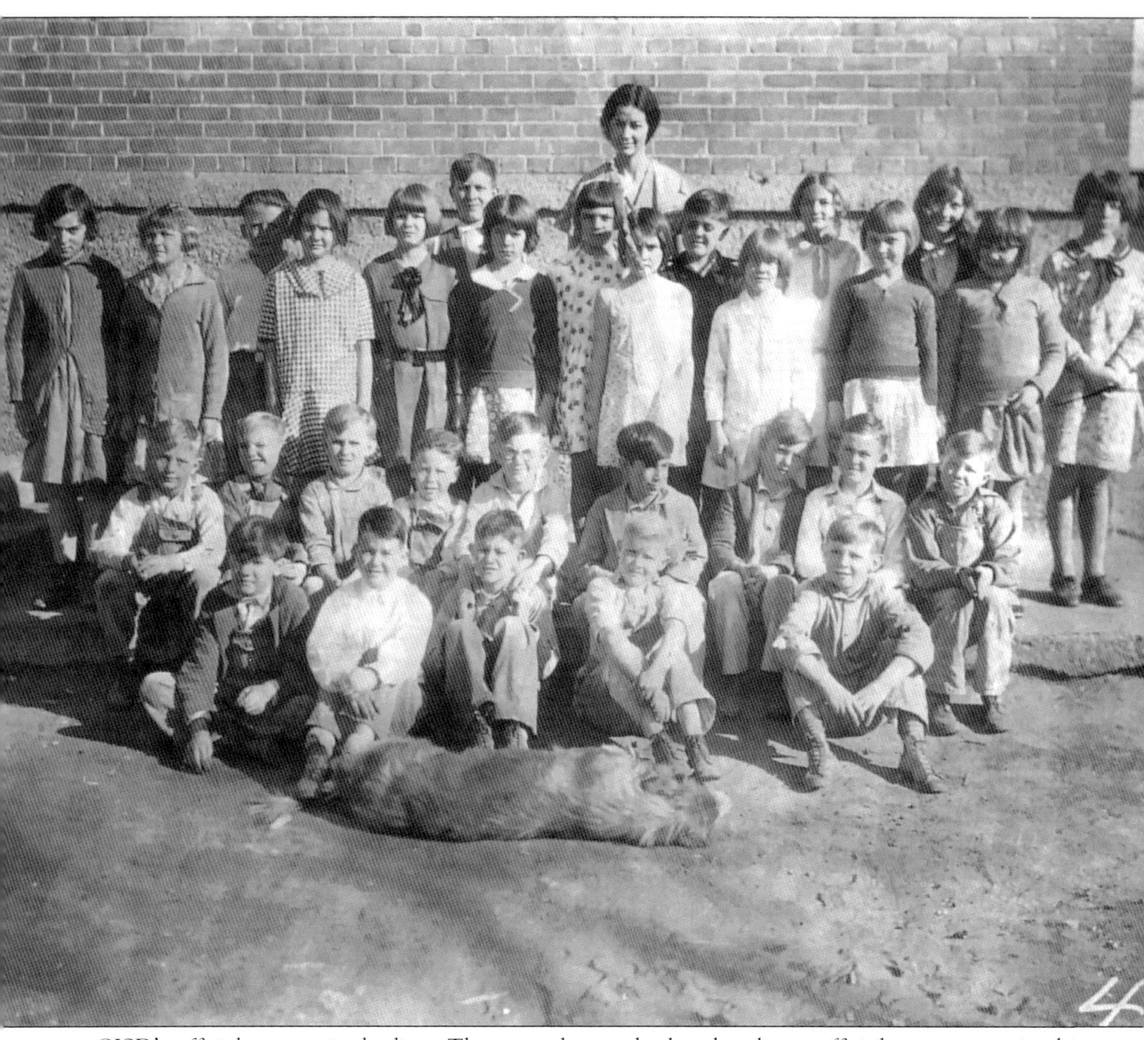

CISD's official mascot is the lion. There can be no doubt who the unofficial mascot was in this early, undated class photograph. Kudos to the photographer for getting the children and the dog to be still long enough to take this picture. Photography was much less forgiving at this time. (Courtesy of the River Oaks Historical Society.)

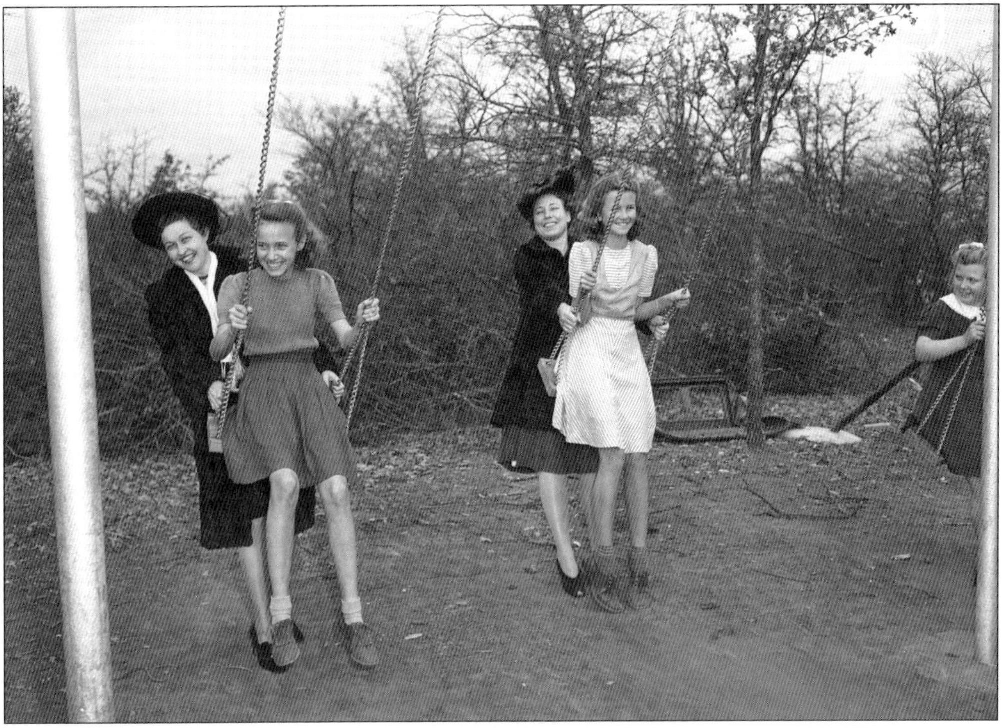

In this picture, taken in 1942, Castleberry school district parent-teacher association secretary Mrs. G.T. Crowley, on the left, is shown pushing Betty Bryant, while Louise Lynn is being given a push by Mrs. O.O. Strother, also of the association. CISD has always had the strong support of the community. (Courtesy of the *Fort Worth Star-Telegram* Collection, University of Texas at Arlington Libraries.)

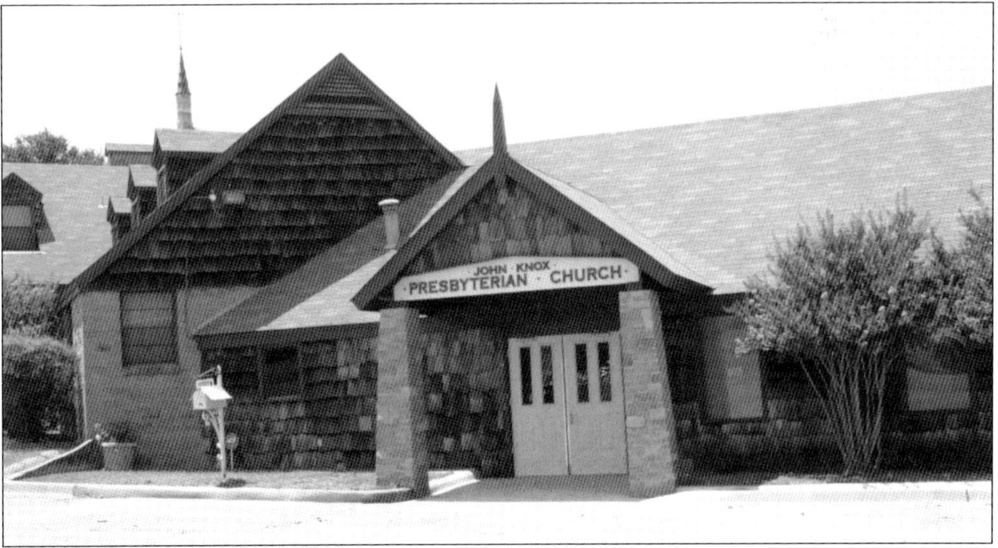

The first services of John Knox Presbyterian Church were held in a motion picture theater. In January 1947, there were enough people to officially organize a church. One hundred and forty-seven people signed their names to the original charter. Rev. Winston Bryant was called as the first pastor. (Courtesy of David and Shirley Bloomfield.)

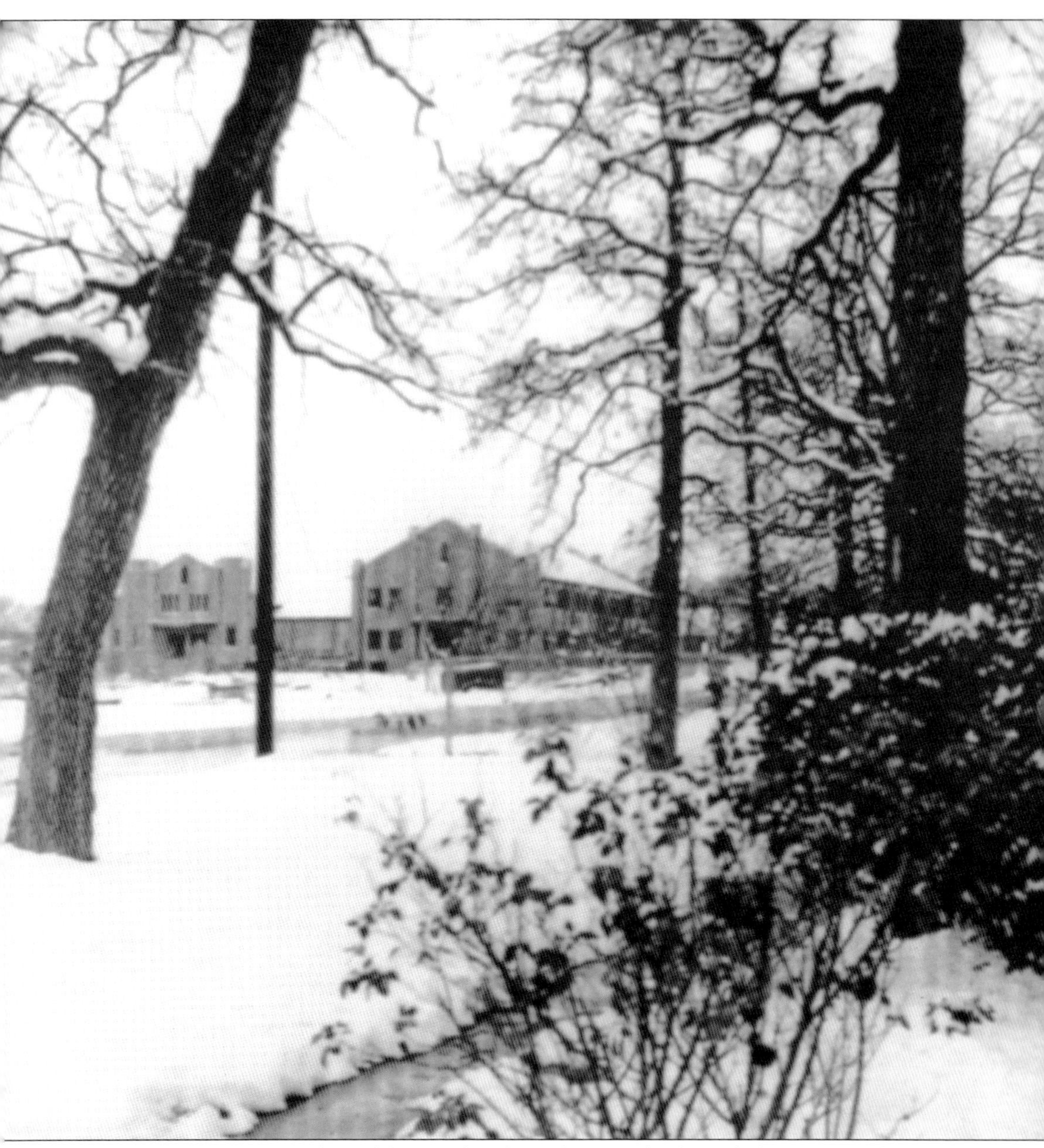

A beautiful snow-covered Castleberry Church of Christ peeks through the trees of Ohio Gardens in this undated picture. The church was formed in 1936. In 1951, construction began on a building at 1025 Merritt Street, and the church still meets there today. In 1953, the parallel wing (on the left) was added to the building to provide classrooms for Bible study. (Courtesy of the River Oaks Historical Society.)

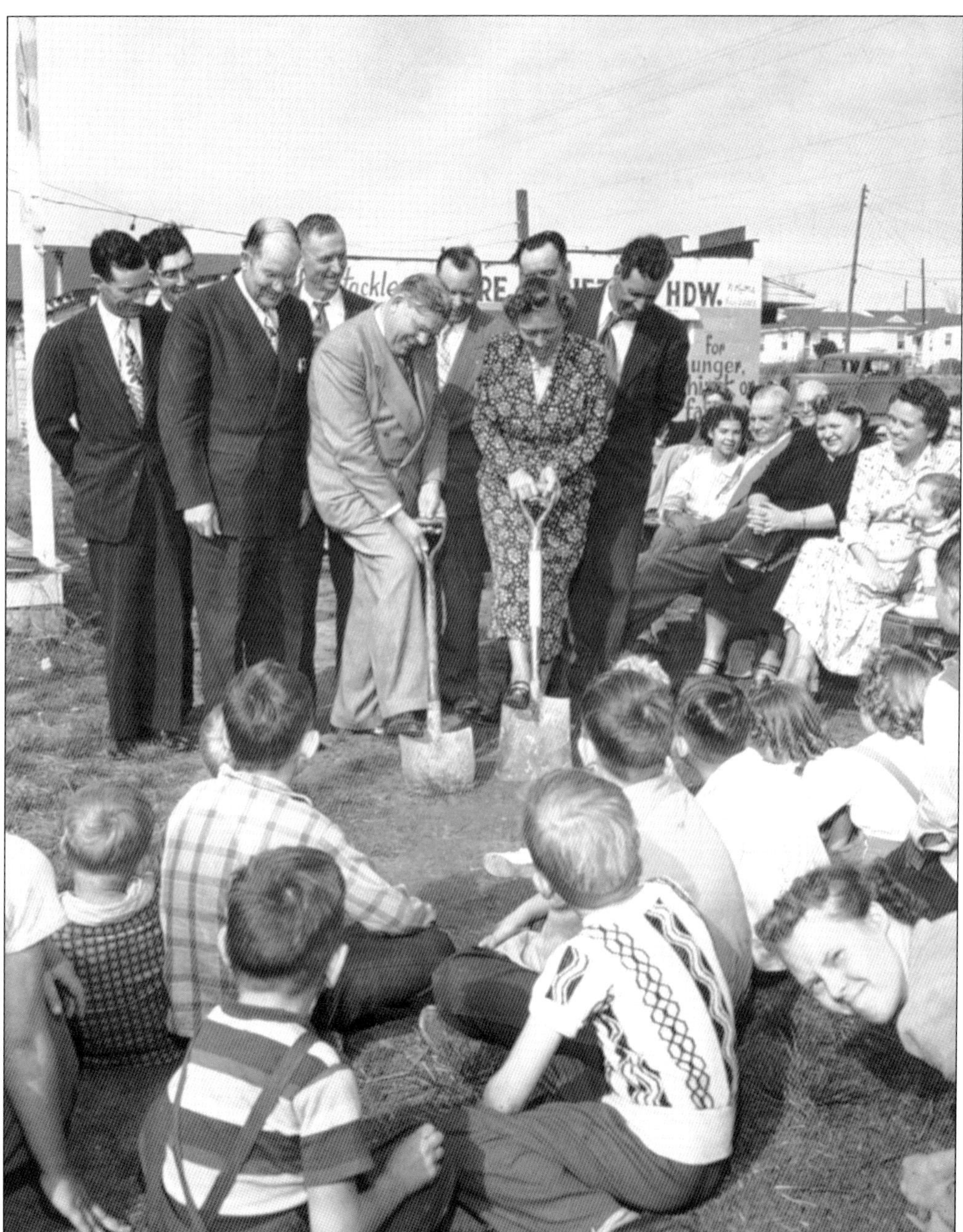

On March 6, 1950, Rev. O.B. Braune, pastor of the Rosen Heights Assembly of God Church, and Rev. Ollie Burns, pastor of the River Oaks Assembly of God Church, broke ground for the construction of a River Oaks church building at 1215 Roberts Cut Off Road. Looking on are, from left to right, Raymond Davis, River Oaks church trustee; Rev. Oda Stewart, pastor of the Fostepco Heights church and trustee; Arthur Sloan, associate pastor of the River Oaks church and trustee; Rev. R.H. Flippin, assistant pastor of the Bible study and prayer hall; D.E. Brannon, member of the building committee; and T.S. Haney, committee member and trustee. (Courtesy of the *Fort Worth Star-Telegram* Collection, University of Texas at Arlington Libraries.)

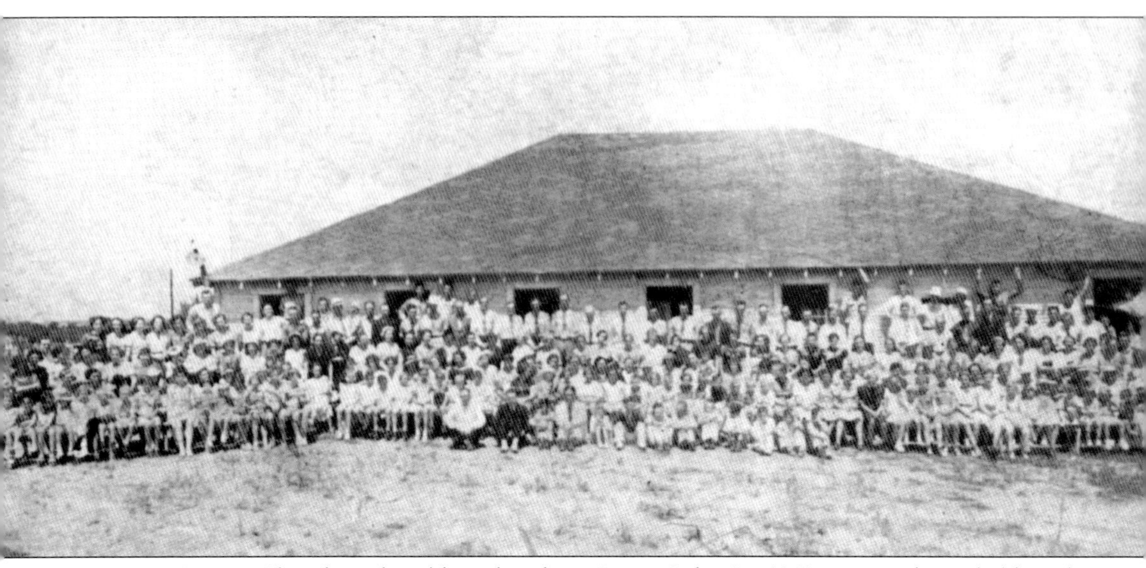

Trinity Baptist Church is the oldest church in River Oaks. In 1912, a revival was held at the schoolhouse. The preacher was Rev. William Park. A small group of eight people decided there was a need for a permanent church at the end of the revival. The group met at the home of Mr. and Mrs. McTeir on August 11, 1912, and organized the Trinity Missionary Baptist Church. Reverand Park became their minister. The building pictured was erected on Churchill Road in 1913 and burned in 1940. This picture is from the Easter service in 1927. Rev. Floyd Lefevers served the church for 17 years. Trinity Baptist Church has been serving the people of River Oaks for over 110 years. (Courtesy of the River Oaks Historical Society.)

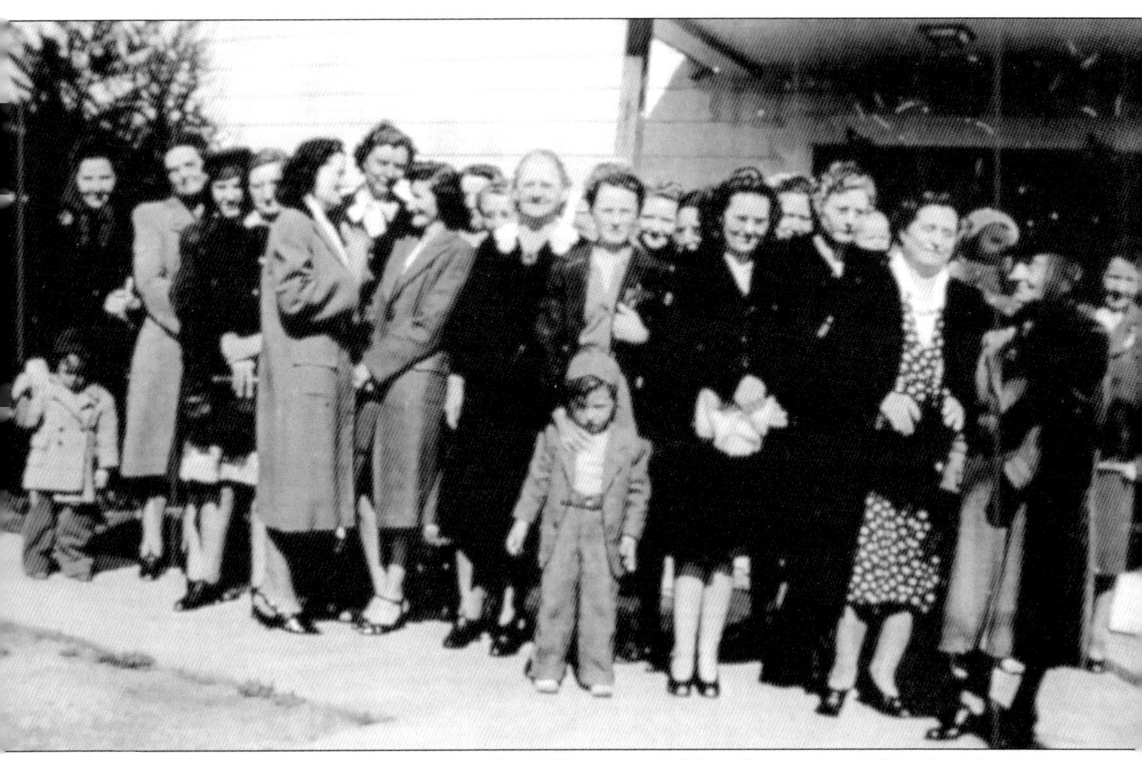

The first service in the Castleberry Church of Christ was held in September 1936. On March 5, 1936, a small group of people met in the home of Jewel Armstrong to discuss forming a new church. The first service was held three days later on March 8. A mere six months afterward, a building for the congregation was erected and in service. (Courtesy of the River Oaks Historical Society.)

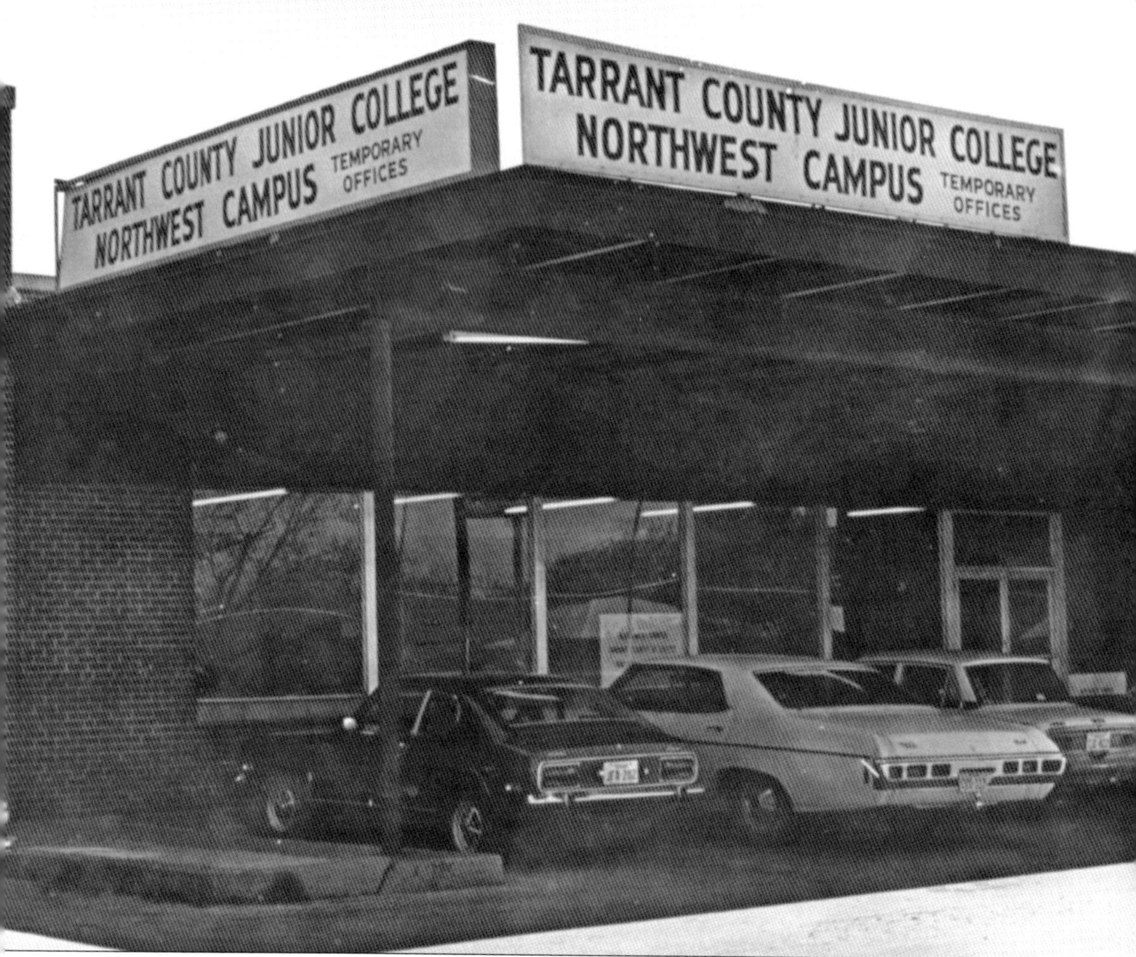

Temporary offices of Tarrant County Junior College Northwest Campus were briefly located in River Oaks in the Fair Oaks Shopping Center. The present Tarrant County College Northwest Campus is the nearest college to River Oaks. Many residents have furthered their education at the school. (Courtesy of the Tarrant County College District Archives.)

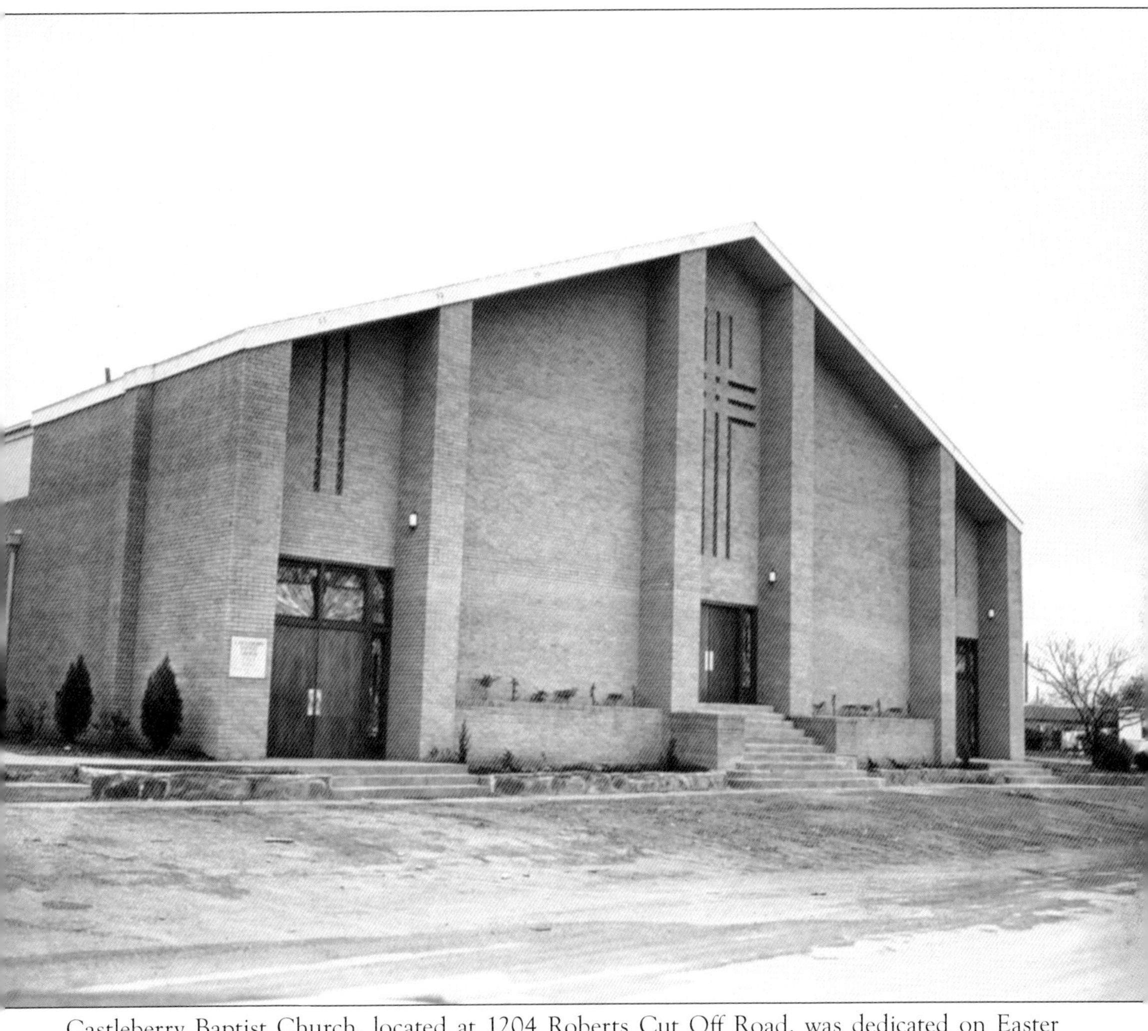

Castleberry Baptist Church, located at 1204 Roberts Cut Off Road, was dedicated on Easter Sunday, March 16, 1953. The pastor at the time was Rev. David A. Cavin. The church cost $100,000 to build. One Faith Church occupies the property today. (Courtesy of the *Fort Worth Star-Telegram* Collection, University of Texas at Arlington Libraries.)

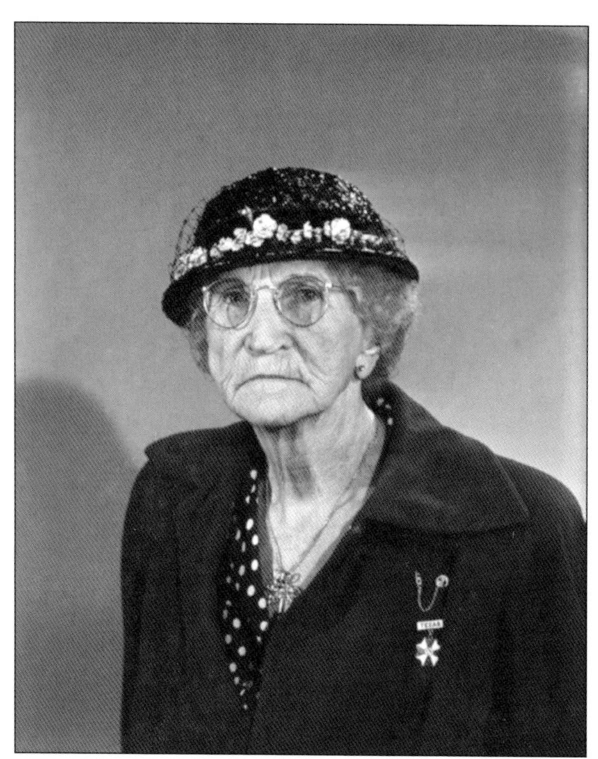

Like most churches, Castleberry Baptist Church had many varied outreach programs to benefit the community and the wider world. Mrs. Bill Blevins, better known as "mom" to airmen at Carswell Air Base, spent many years doing missionary work at the Air Force base. She visited the hospital, the stockade, dining halls, and club rooms on behalf of the school class at Castleberry Baptist Church. Her tireless outreach brought many airmen to attend the River Oaks church. This picture of Mrs. Blevins is from March 27, 1951. Rev. I.F. Foster was a reverend at Castleberry Baptist in 1953. He and his wife spent four years as missionaries in Japan. Below, Mrs. Foster is pictured wearing a kimono, and Reverend Foster is holding Japanese slippers. (Both, courtesy of the *Fort Worth Star-Telegram* Collection, University of Texas at Arlington Libraries.)

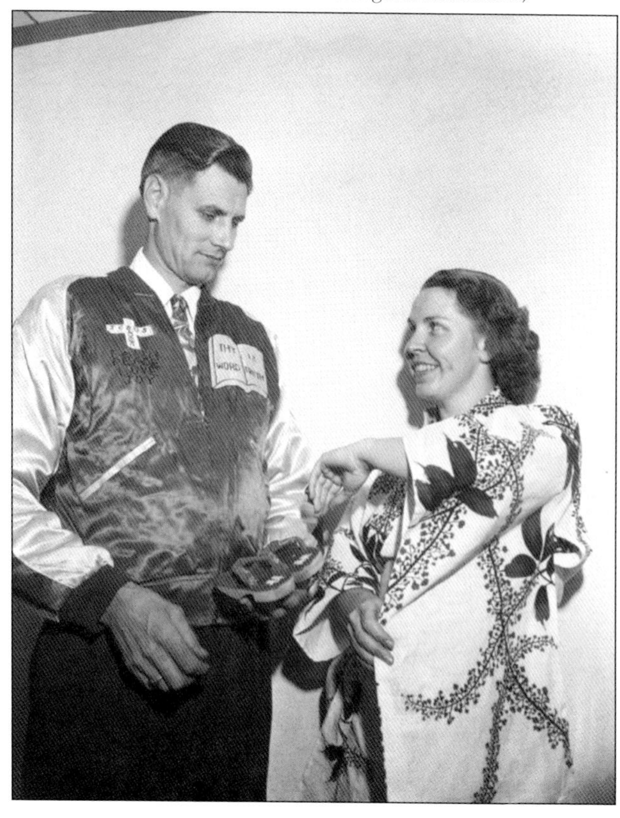

Council commissioner Herb Hilderbrandt (left) presents Scoutmaster Joe Waggoner a new charter while members of Boy Scout Troup 143 look on. The *Fort Worth Star-Telegram* morning edition dated June 9, 1950, reported the presentation was made at Castleberry Methodist Church. (Courtesy of the *Fort Worth Star-Telegram* Collection, University of Texas at Arlington Libraries.)

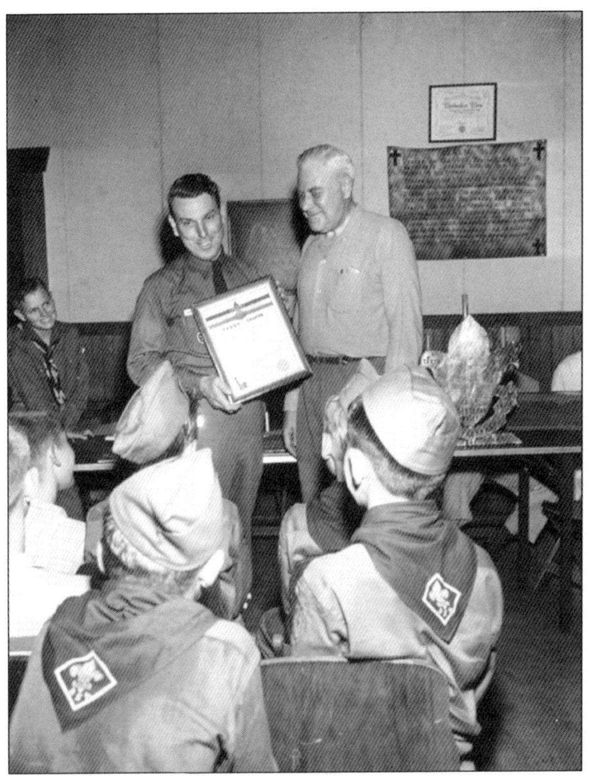

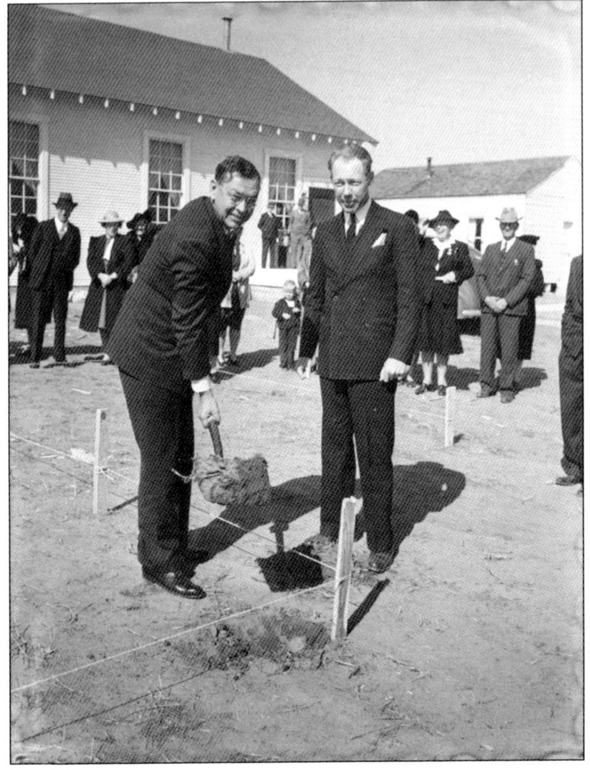

J.N.R. Score (left), president of Southwestern University, breaks ground for the new auditorium at Castleberry Methodist Church on Valentine's Day 1943. Rev. Carroll Thompson (right), pastor of the church, looks on. The Castleberry church was organized under the sponsorship of First Methodist Church when Reverend Score was pastor. The first service at Castleberry Methodist Church was held on Easter Sunday 1937. (Courtesy of the *Fort Worth Star-Telegram* Collection, University of Texas at Arlington Libraries.)

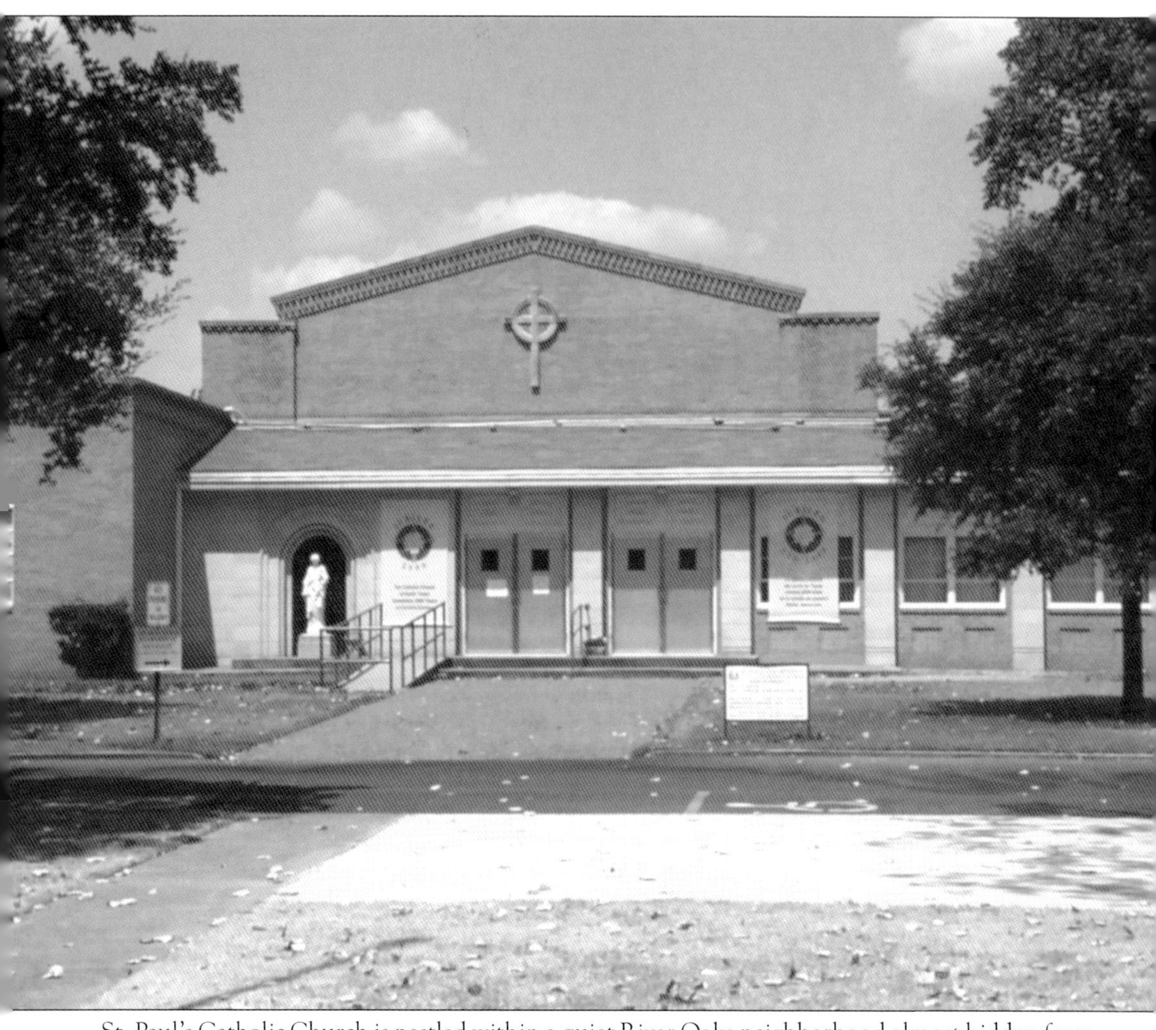

St. Paul's Catholic Church is nestled within a quiet River Oaks neighborhood almost hidden from view. The church was established in 1952, but the present church was not under construction until 1953. The first mass in the new building was held in August 1954 with the Reverend James P. Erbrick. (Courtesy of the River Oaks Historical Society.)

Four

The Heartbeat of the City

It would be a gross injustice to write about the citizens of River Oaks without first recognizing and remembering the countless men and women who have lived inside its city limits while honorably and bravely serving in the military at Tarrant Field Air Dome, then Carswell Air Force Base, which is now known as Naval Air Station Joint Reserve Base Fort Worth, and those who worked at Air Force Plant 4, originally used by Consolidated, then by Convair, and now by Lockheed Martin.

For as long as River Oaks has been in existence, the bomber plant and Carswell have had industrious, brave, and honorable men and women walking through their gates helping to defend the freedoms enjoyed in Texas and the United States, and many of those men and women left their duty at the end of each day and returned to their homes in the city of River Oaks. Their service and sacrifice will always be remembered, and their impact on the community remains to the present day.

The founding families of River Oaks are remembered with streets and parks named in their honor, and they will be mentioned throughout this book. However, as George Bailey said in *It's a Wonderful Life*, it is the regular folks who "do most of the working and paying and living and dying in this community," and that is true in every town, including River Oaks. The city is the wonderful oasis it is today largely due to the generations of regular folks who have worked and lived here, and a few of these men and women who have called River Oaks home have even gone on to carve their name nationwide. River Oaks boasts an International Motor Sports Hall of Fame member, several Pro Rodeo Hall of Fame members, an International Hot Rod Association Hall of Fame member, and one Olympian.

Of course, it is the neighbors and friends who raised their families in the 1.9-square-mile radius that is River Oaks that gave and continue to give the city its neighborly feel. There is only room here to mention a few of these men and women. The authors apologize to the many deserving folks who were left out due to space constraints.

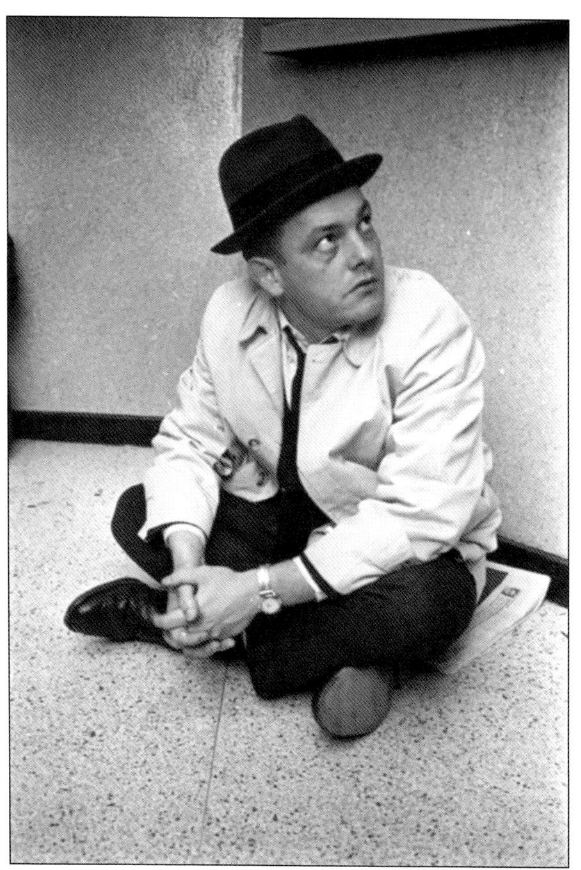

Longtime River Oaks resident Bob Schieffer worked for the *Fort Worth Star-Telegram* when Pres. John F. Kennedy was assassinated in Dallas. He is pictured here waiting for reports on the assassination in 1963. Among his more notable credits are as a CBS anchor, a *60 Minutes* contributor, and a *Face the Nation* moderator. (Courtesy of the *Fort Worth Star-Telegram* Collection, University of Texas at Arlington Libraries.)

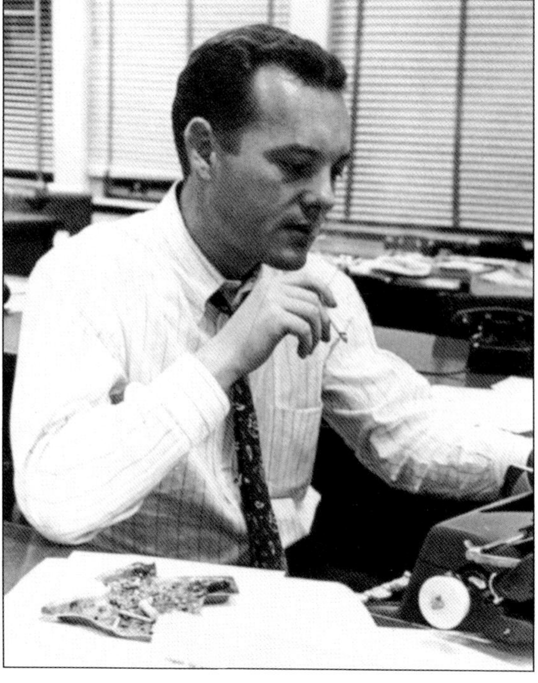

Bob Schieffer worked for the *Fort Worth Star-Telegram* until moving to CBS in 1969. He was born in Austin but grew up in River Oaks. Schieffer received a degree in English from Texas Christian University (TCU) in 1959. The College of Communication at TCU was renamed in Bob Schieffer's honor in 2013. (Courtesy of the *Fort Worth Star-Telegram* Collection, University of Texas at Arlington Libraries.)

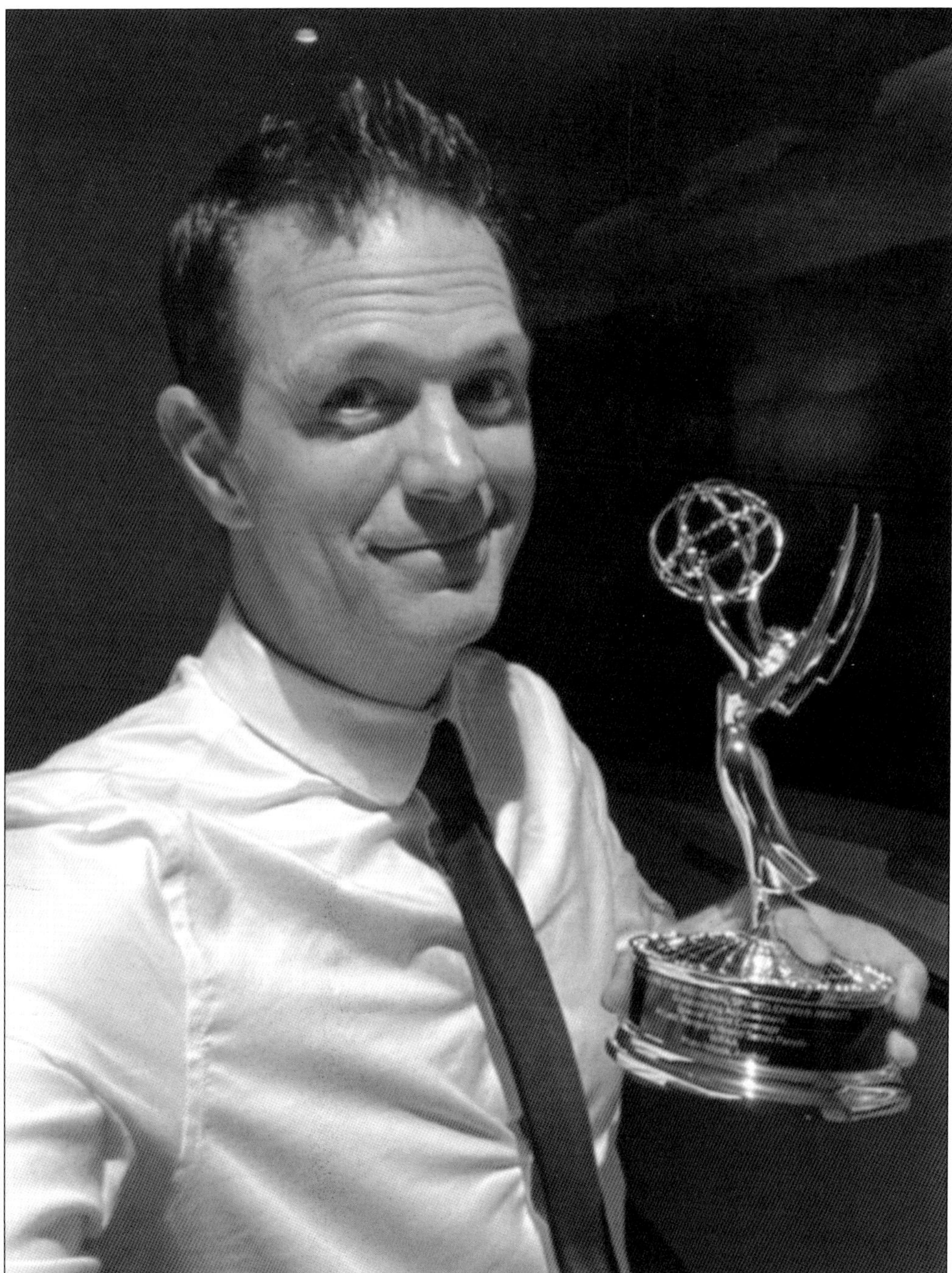

Marc Istook, son of homebuilder and race car driver Don Istook, is a three-time Emmy-winning anchor for Dallas ABC affiliate WFAA's morning news show *Daybreak*. Istook's first big break came at the age of 14 when he interviewed music legend Billy Joel for the *Fort Worth Star-Telegram*. He majored in radio/TV/film and journalism at TCU. His professional career began behind the scenes at ESPN, and his first job on camera was at KTEN, the NBC affiliate in Denison, Texas. Istook has worked for the Food Network, CNN, the BBC, the Speed Channel, and the TV Guide Network. (Courtesy of Don Istook.)

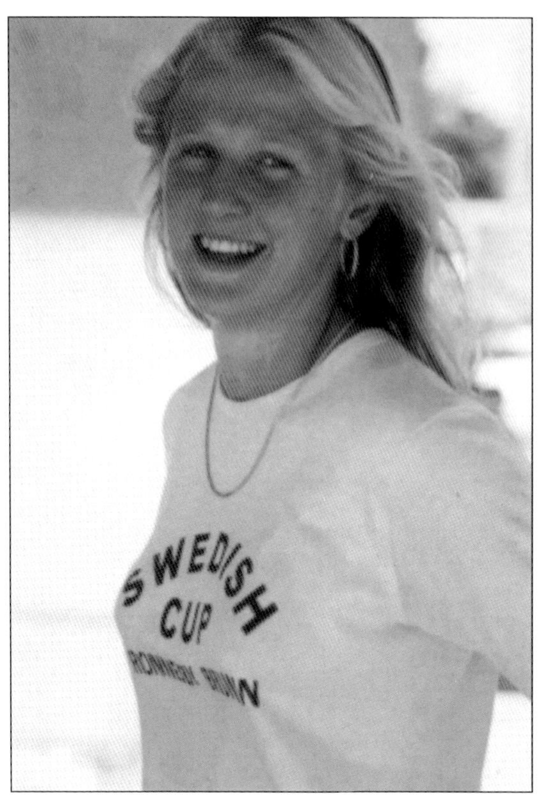

Christina Loock is a member of the Texas Swimming and Diving Hall of Fame (TSDHOF). She was undefeated in her high school. At Southern Methodist University, she was the first woman to earn a varsity letter in the Southwest Conference. Since there was no NCAA women's division, Loock competed against the men and finished third in the three-meter board in 1975. Christina Loock was coached and mentored by her father, Carl Loock (below), who was also a TSDHOF member. Carl moved his family to River Oaks in 1950. The family still owns their home in River Oaks. Carl worked as an engineer at Consolidated, Convair, and later General Dynamics. Christina Loock's older sister Vicki and her brother Cal are also members of TSDHOF. Christina Loock credits her mother's strong support for the family's diving success. (Left, courtesy of Christina Loock; below, courtesy of the *Fort Worth Star-Telegram* Collection, University of Texas at Arlington Libraries.)

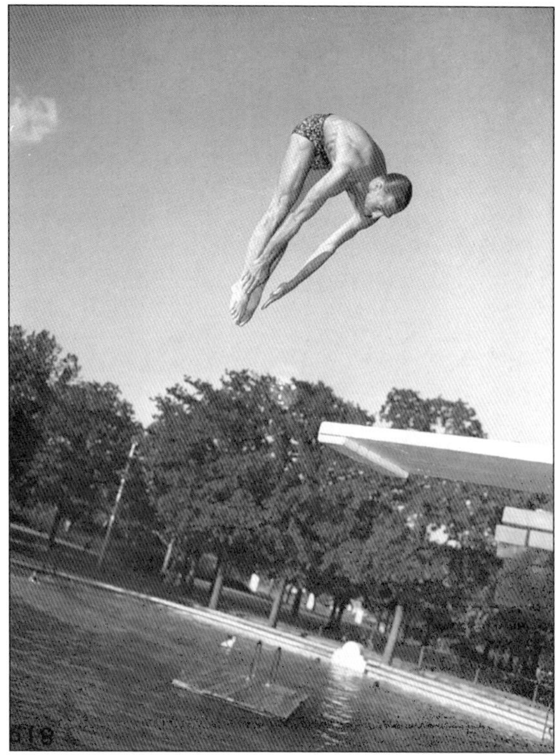

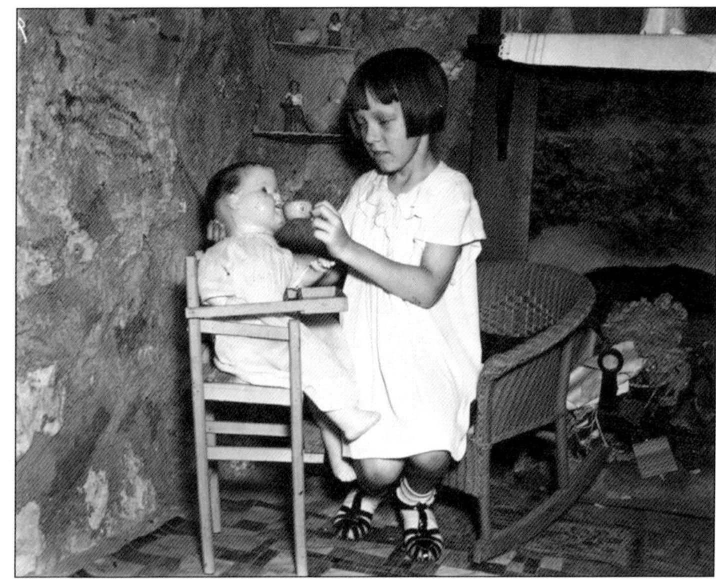

Minnie Marie Hoeflein, daughter of W.F. and Minnie Hoeflein, is seen here as a child playing in the home she helped her parents build starting in 1937 at 4309 Ohio Garden Road. The Hoeflein family built the home in their spare time and finally completed the residence in 1938. (Courtesy of the River Oaks Historical Society.)

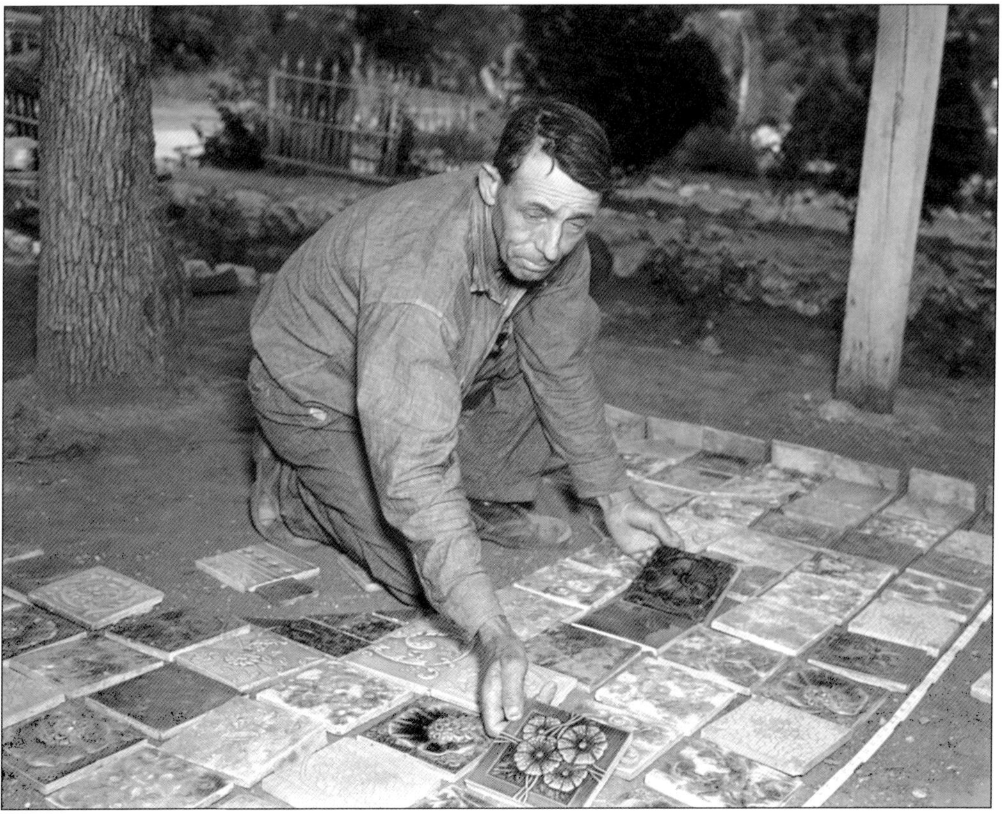

W.F. Hoeflein constructed the entire house with only the help of his family. He is seen here laying parts of the fireplace floor in June 1938. Hoeflein was likely to place anything in the concrete walls of his home. It is said the home contained glass, false teeth, petrified Indian feet, rusty scissors, and more. It was reportedly built for $600. (Courtesy of the *Fort Worth Star-Telegram* Collection, University of Texas at Arlington Libraries.)

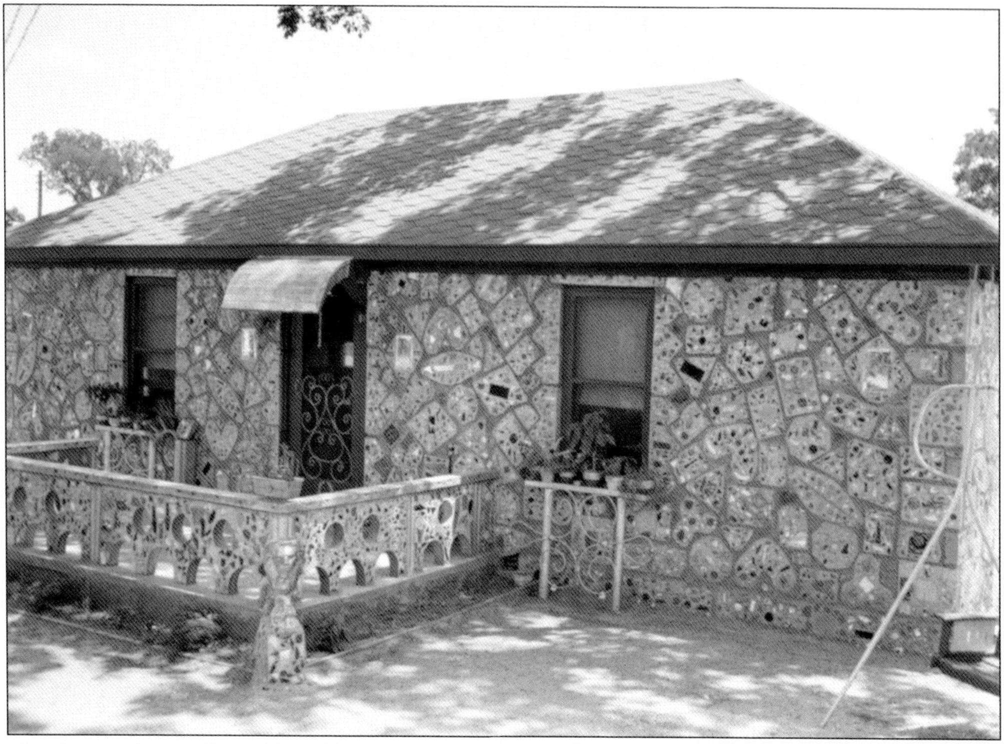

The famous River Oaks Glass House was once featured on *Ripley's Believe It or Not!* and for years operated as a museum to raise money for a local charity. It was severely damaged by flooding, and repairs were partially paid for by the Red Cross. One of the items destroyed in the flood was a baby pet alligator that reportedly died from catching measles from Minnie Marie Hoeflein. The gator was stuffed and kept near the pond in the backyard. The Red Cross did not pay to have the alligator replaced. Minnie Hoeflein was proud of the glass embedded in the wall of the glass house. These pictures are dated from 1938. Other unique items on the walls include mirrors, china, goat horns, hubcaps, and churn lids. (Both, courtesy of the *Fort Worth Star-Telegram* Collection, University of Texas at Arlington Libraries.)

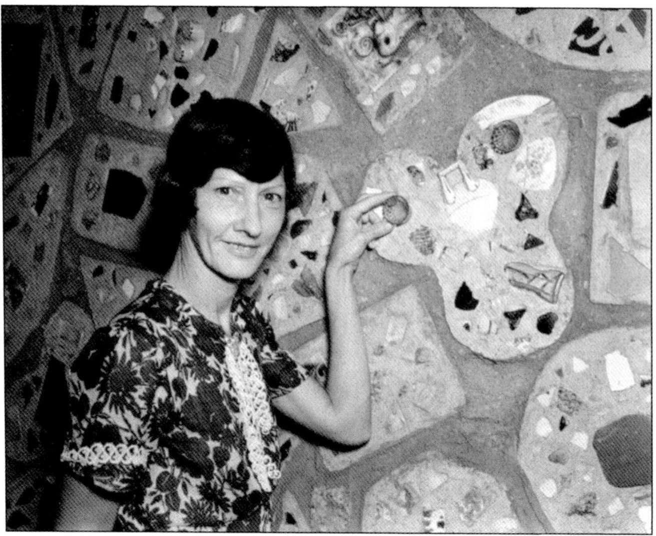

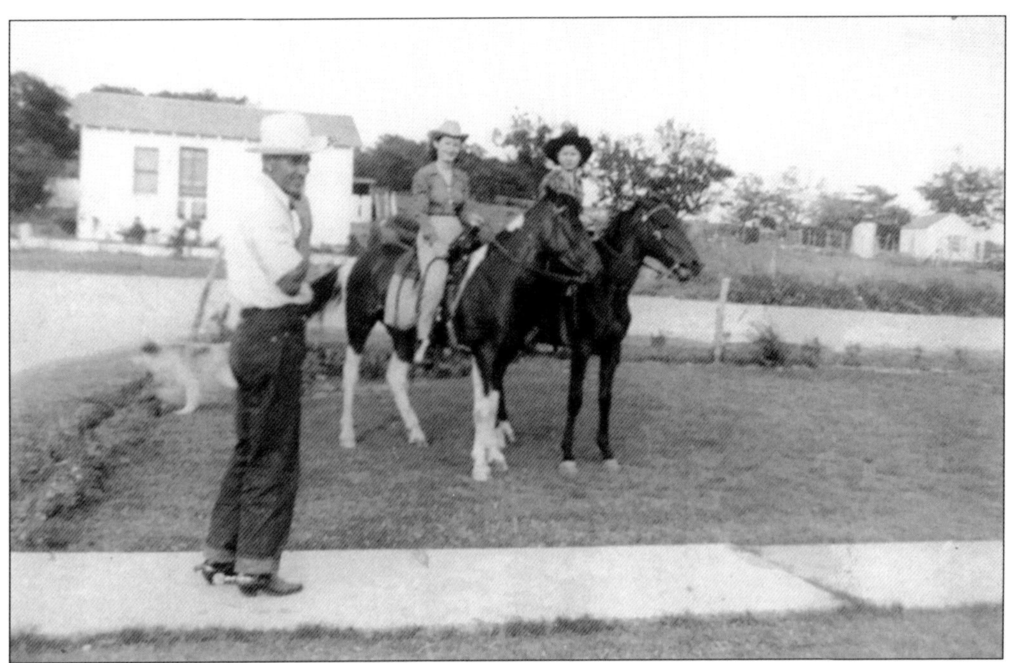

River Oaks, being almost entirely surrounded by Fort Worth, the 12th-largest city in the United States, and often being confused with one of the wealthiest neighborhoods in the country with the same moniker down in Houston, has always had to struggle for its identity. One thing the city of River Oaks has in common with that tony neighborhood in Houston is that both are in the great state of Texas. If there is one thing all Texans love, it is their horses. It would not be unusual to see a horse sauntering down any street in Texas, no matter how expensive or reasonable the price of houses in the neighborhood. The undated photograph above shows Lonzo Armstrong standing next to mounted Jewel Armstrong Kuykendal and Katherine Tucker on Yale Street in River Oaks. The image to the right proves one can never start too early getting a child acclimated to a horse-heavy culture. The young woman, child, pony, and location in River Oaks are unknown. (Both, courtesy of the River Oaks Historical Society.)

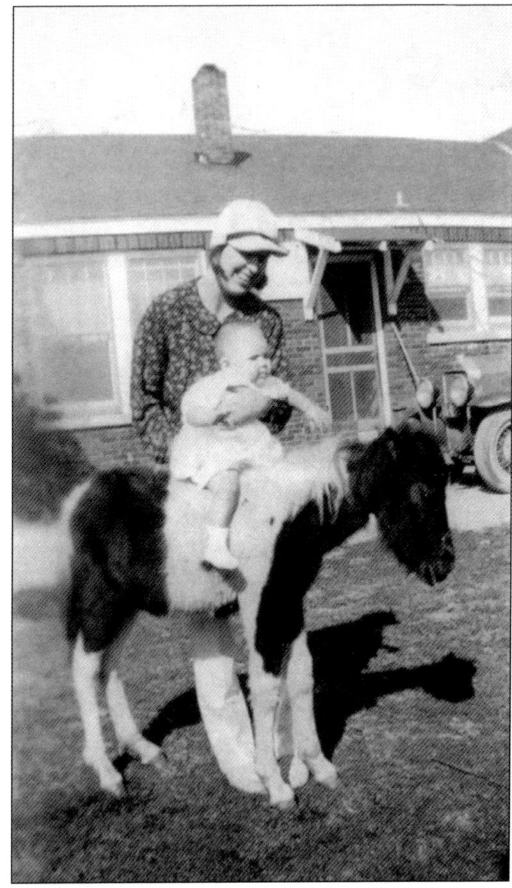

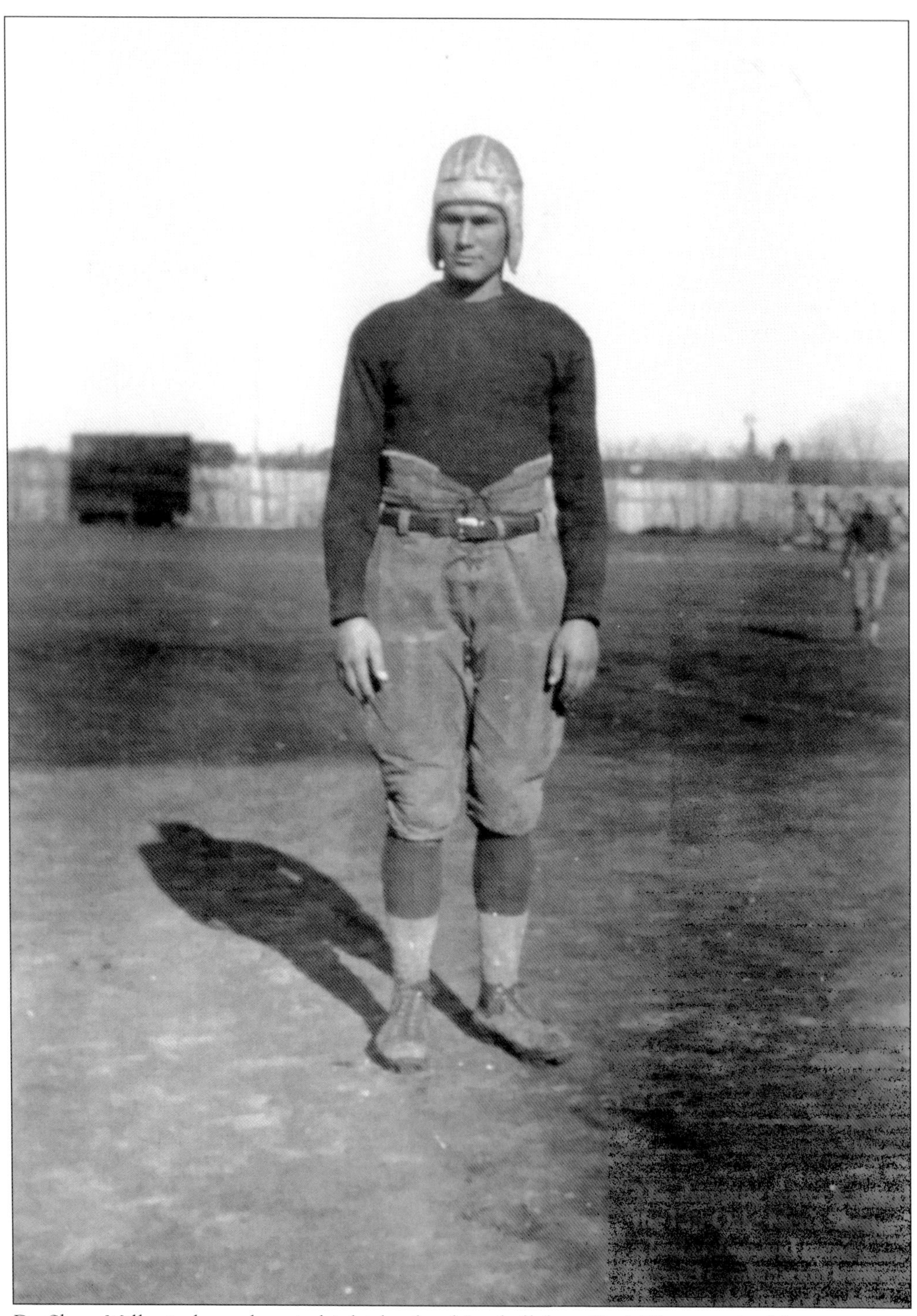

Dr. Sloan Miller is shown here in his high school football days. Dr. Miller practiced for many years in River Oaks. His home and practice were located at the intersection of Ohio Garden Road and River Oaks Boulevard. He was one of a group of doctors who founded Fort Worth Osteopathic Hospital. (Courtesy of the River Oaks Historical Society.)

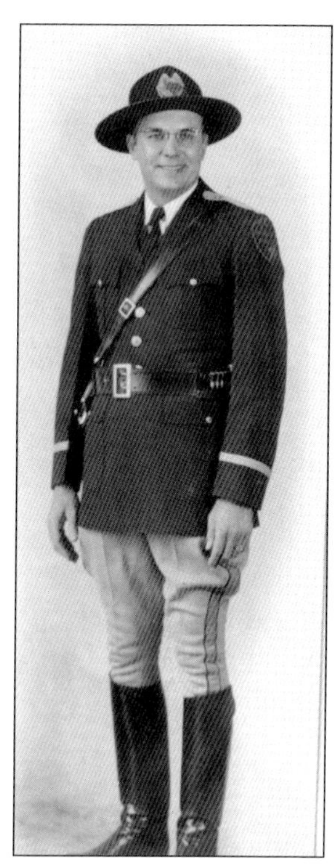

C.C. "Corky" Makarwich was born in Poland on December 16, 1912. He immigrated to the United States with his parents at 18 months. The family settled in Fort Worth. He graduated from Northside High School and went on to TCU. After college graduation, Makarwich joined the Texas Department of Public Safety (DPS) and was stationed in San Antonio. He resigned from the DPS, moved with his family to River Oaks, and went into the construction business. Makarwich was a member of the River Oaks United Methodist Church, River Oaks Masonic Lodge 1311, the Lions Club, and the volunteer fire department and served several terms on the city council. (Courtesy of the River Oaks Historical Society.)

Corky Makarwich (right) acted as the general contractor for the new headquarters building for Boy Scout Troop 143, located on the grounds of Castleberry Methodist Church. T.C. Molloy (foreground), business agent for Cement Finishers Union Local No. 34, poured the cement foundation. Also pictured is Joe Waggoner, Troup 143's Scoutmaster. The picture is dated September 16, 1951. (Courtesy of the *Fort Worth Star-Telegram* Collection, University of Texas at Arlington Libraries.)

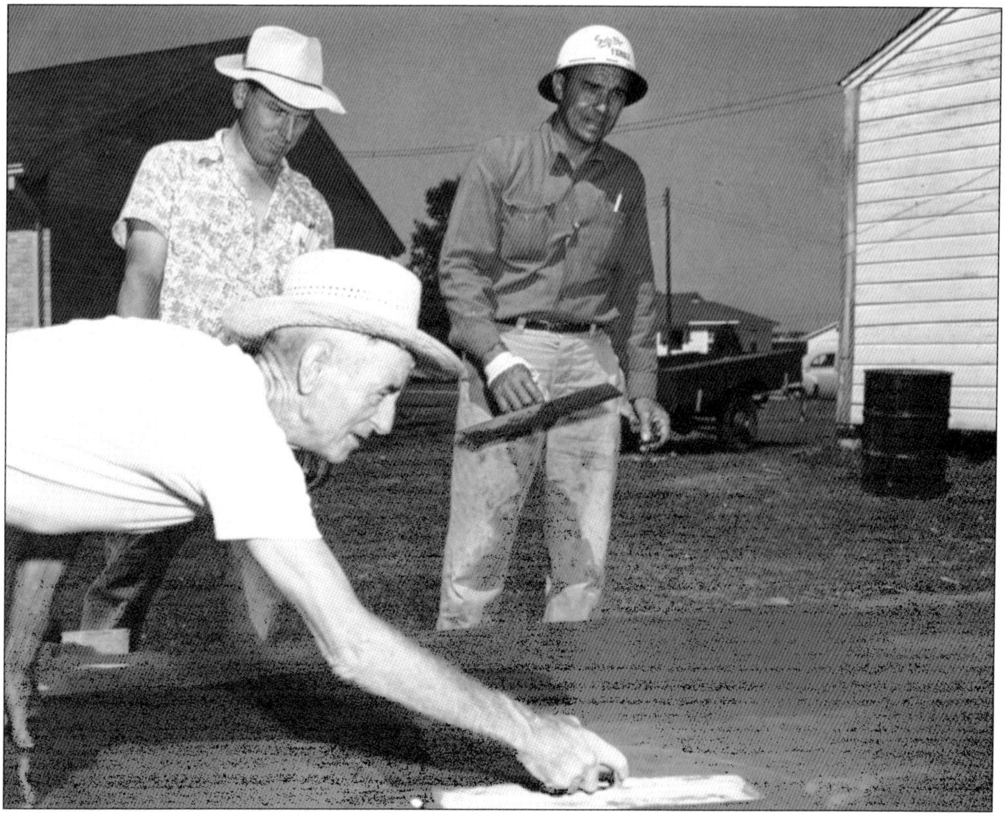

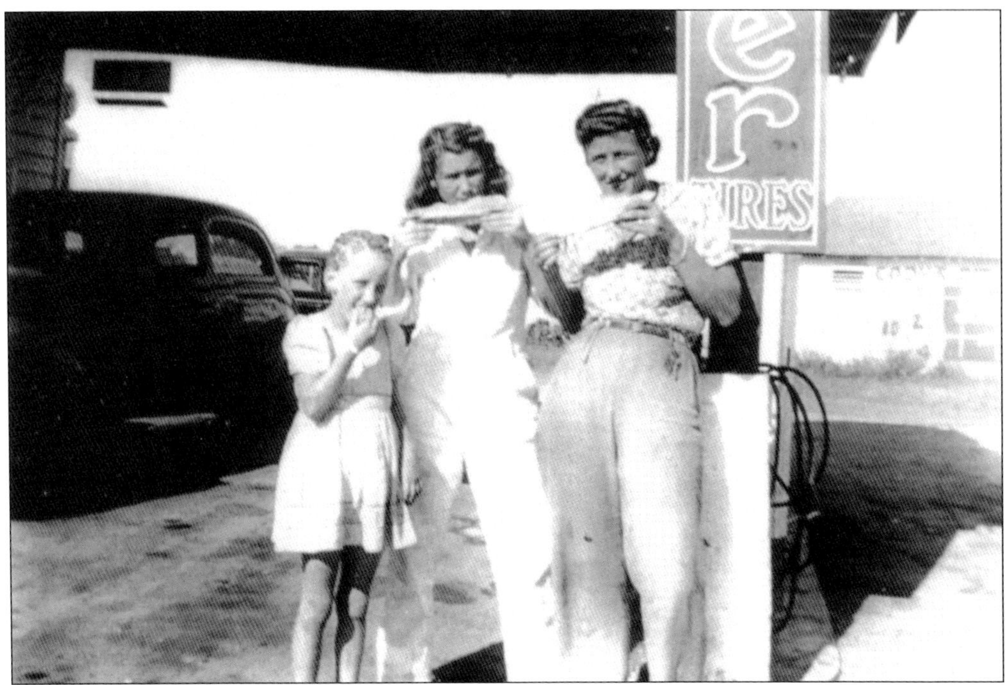

During the summer, when Texans are not riding horses, they like to keep cool by eating an ice-cold slice of watermelon. From left to right, Anita Mercer, Ola Nell Mercer, and Bessie Mercer are shown here enjoying a cold slice on a hot day in front of the Mercer Gas Station. (Courtesy of the River Oaks Historical Society.)

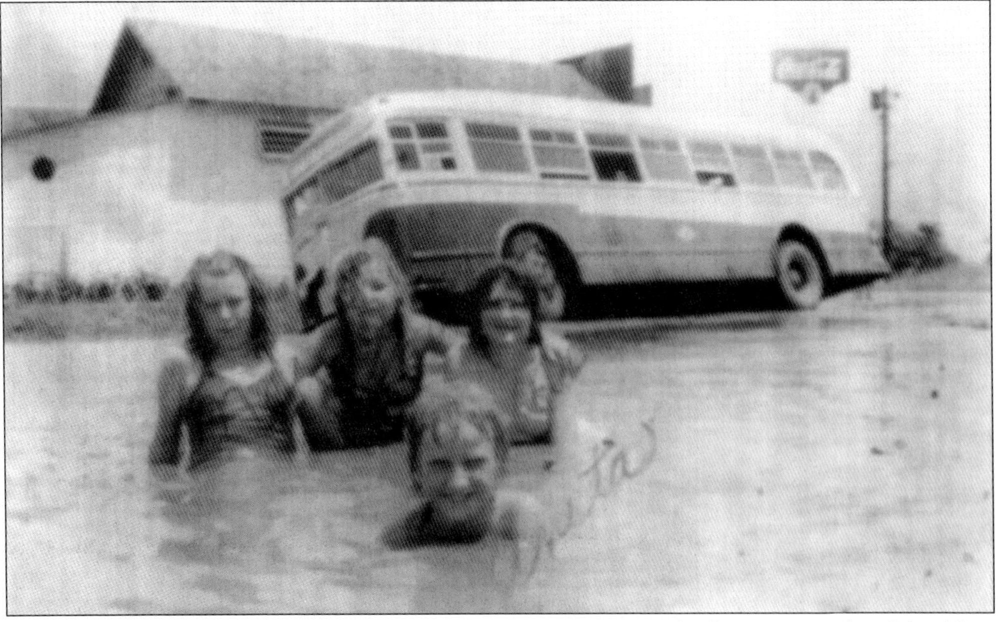

River Oaks suffered from severe flooding issues before coming under better control with building levees on the Trinity River. From left to right, younger residents Johnie Mercer, Shirley Hallum, Anita Mercer (front), and Norma Hallum often knew how to make the best of a bad situation. (Courtesy of Linda Claridge.)

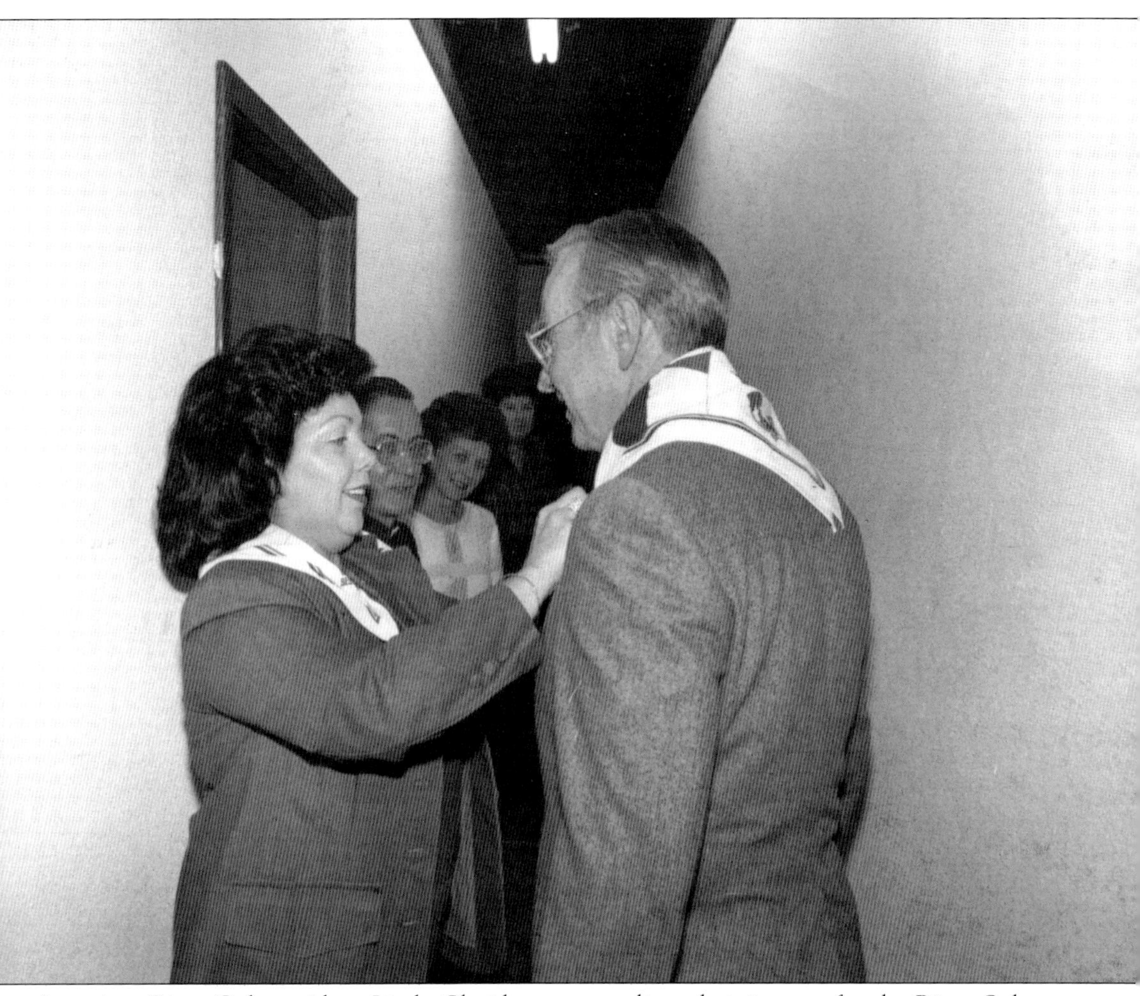

Longtime River Oaks resident Linda Claridge was a police administrator for the River Oaks Police Department. Before this job, she was a district manager for Sen. Bob Glasgow for almost 10 years. Here, she is seen assisting longtime Speaker of the House Jim Wright of Fort Worth. Claridge also was a decorated race car driver, winning over 40 races. (Courtesy of Linda Claridge.)

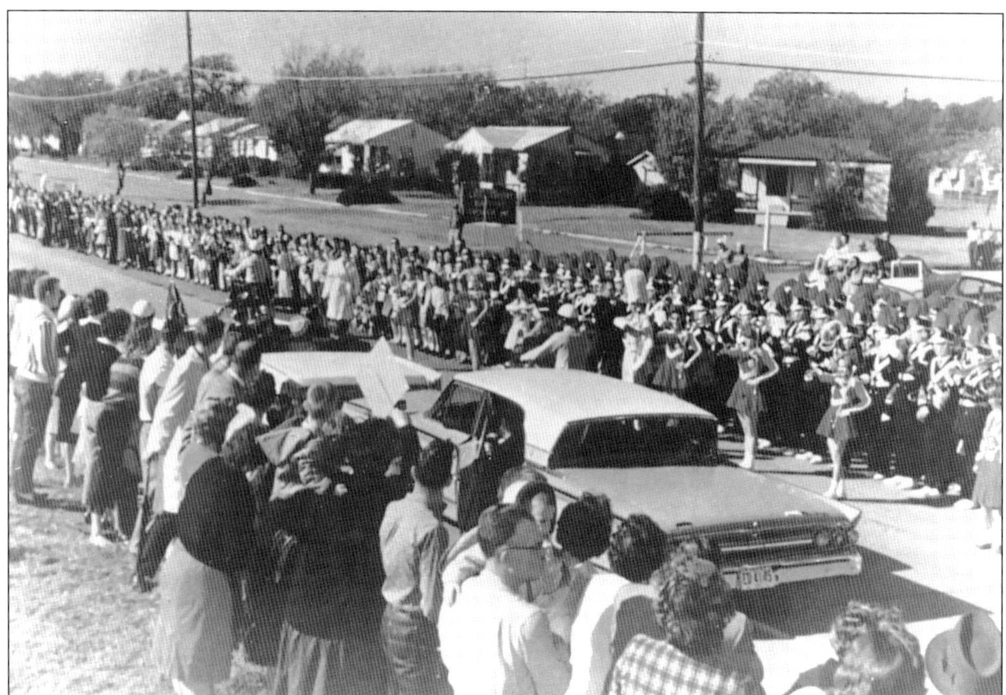

On the morning of November 22, 1963, Pres. John F. Kennedy, First Lady Jackie Kennedy, and Texas governor John Connelly left the Hotel Texas, now the Hilton, in Fort Worth and joined a motorcade traveling to Carswell Air Force Base for the short flight to Dallas on Air Force One. Kennedy spoke at a breakfast hosted by the Fort Worth Chamber of Commerce that rainy morning. The motorcade traveled down River Oaks Boulevard, where it seemed the entire city turned out to greet them. Kennedy had spent the day before speaking in San Antonio and Houston before ending the day in Fort Worth. In a matter of hours after these photographs, the president was assassinated on the streets of Dallas in front of the Texas Book Depository. (Both, courtesy of the River Oaks Historical Society.)

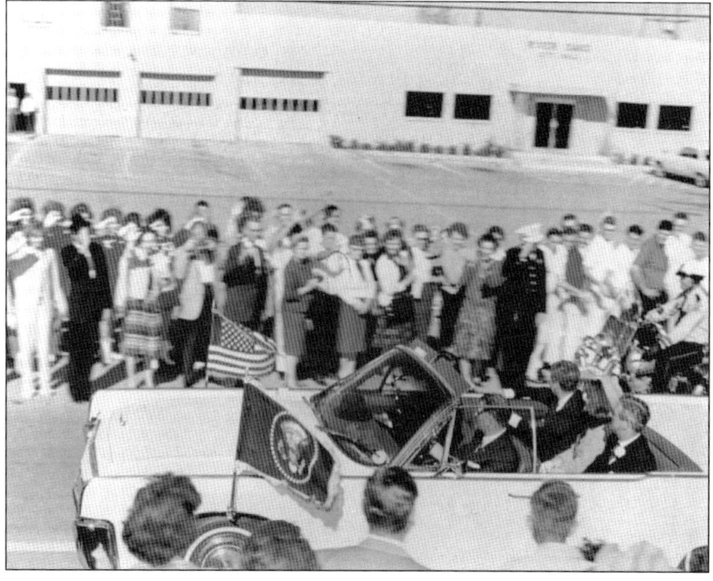

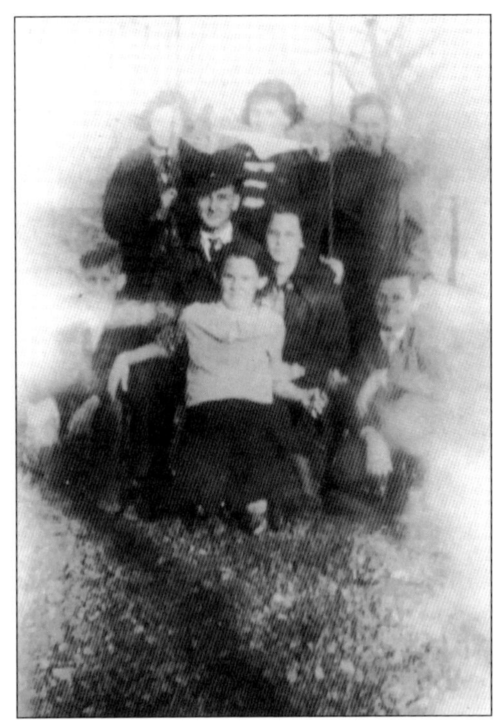

Small towns often build strong bonds. Even though River Oaks has an urban feel being surrounded by Fort Worth and other cities, the community is close-knit. Friendships formed in elementary school often last a lifetime. Labeled only "The Bunch," the undated photograph to the right shows eight young people who are obviously close since they are bunched up for the picture. Pictured below is the "Castleberry Mafia," who grew up in River Oaks in the 1940s and 1950s and attended local schools. They are not much of a crime syndicate, as one member is a pastor, one is an architect, and another is a retired schoolteacher. The group started in 1997 when two friends began meeting for coffee and grew to almost 50 members. The photograph is undated. (Right, courtesy of River Oaks Historical Society; below, courtesy of Randy Hooper.)

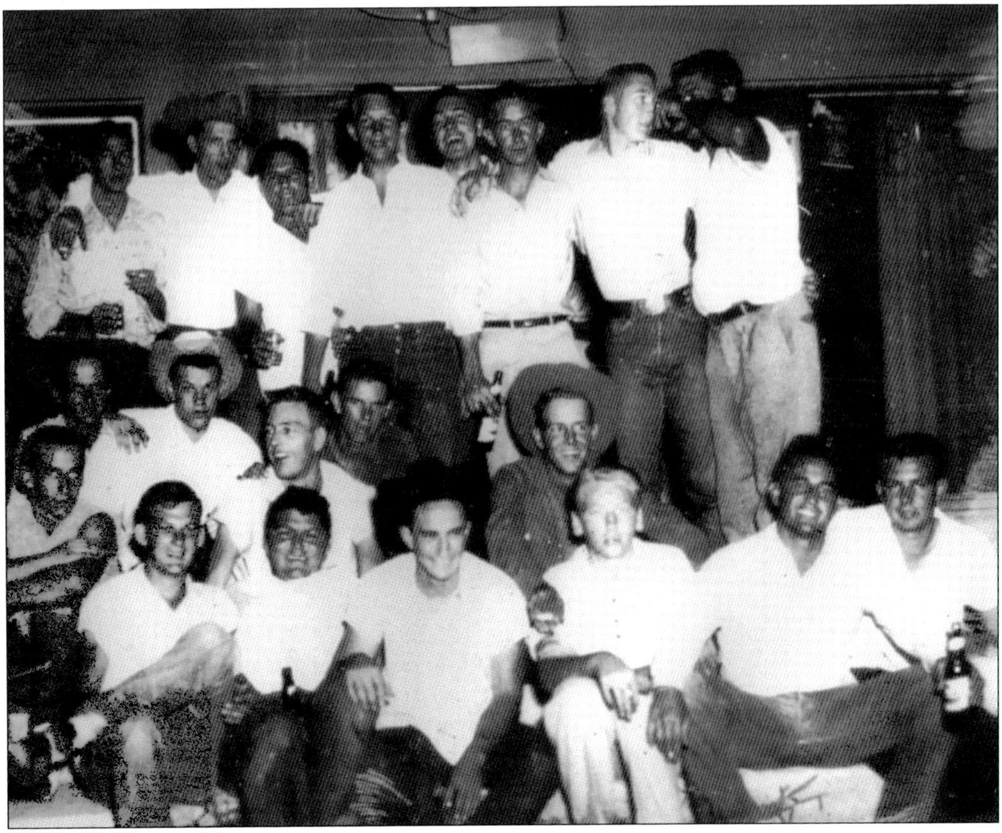

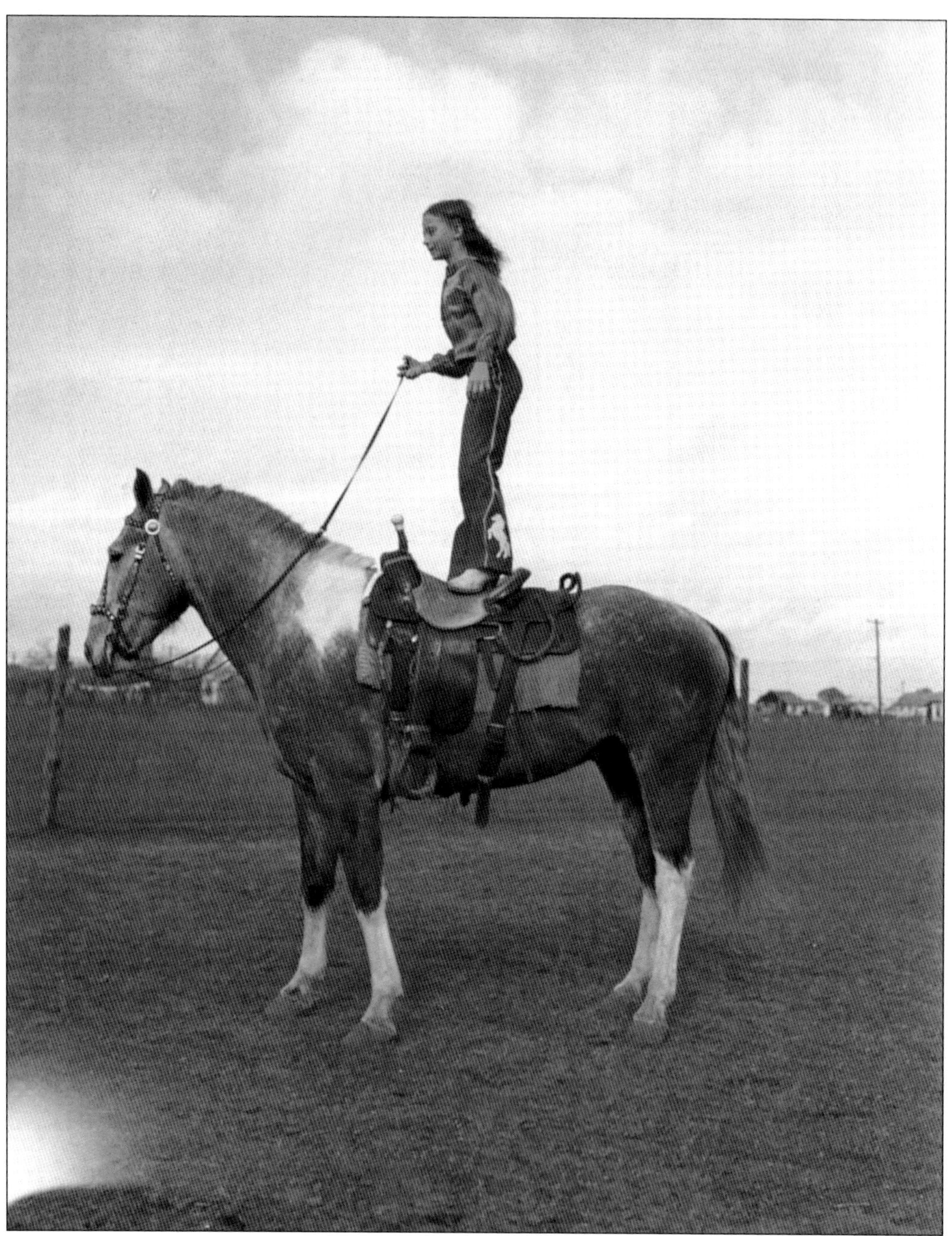

Mitzi Lucas Riley, the daughter of Tad Lucas, made her rodeo debut at the tender age of six. It is said she learned to ride before she could walk and performed in rodeos for over 20 years. In 1996, she was inducted into the National Cowgirl Hall of Fame. (Courtesy of the *Fort Worth Star-Telegram* Collection, University of Texas at Arlington Libraries.)

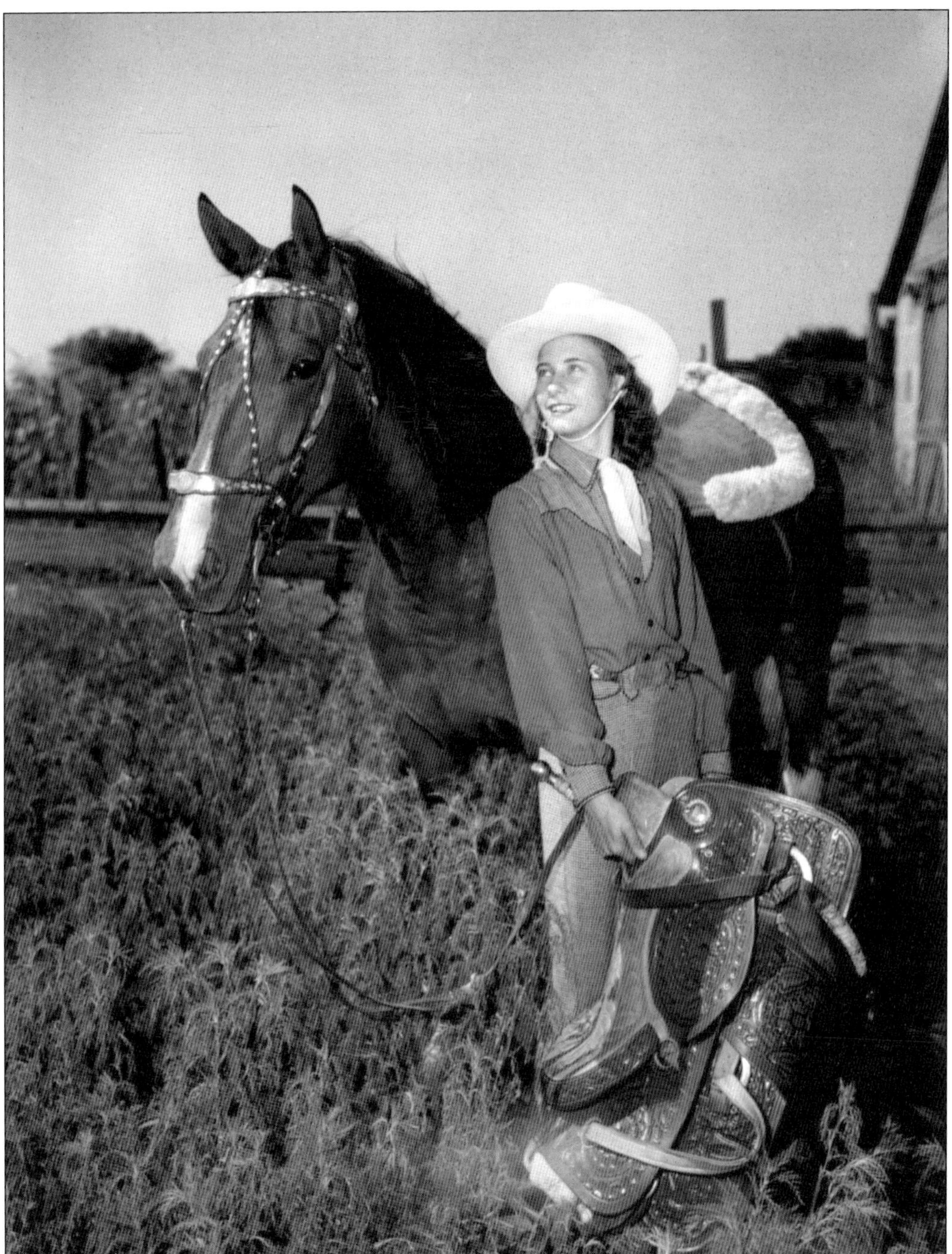

Mitzi Lucas Riley was born prematurely and weighed only two pounds, fourteen ounces at birth. In 1936, Mitzi performed at the Texas Centennial Celebration's Western pageant "The Last Frontier," produced by Billy Rose at the original Casa Manana location. In 1947, Mitzi married champion calf roper Lanham Riley and toured the country rodeoing. Mitzi retired as a rodeo star in 1954 to raise the couple's children. (Courtesy of the *Fort Worth Star-Telegram* Collection, University of Texas at Arlington Libraries.)

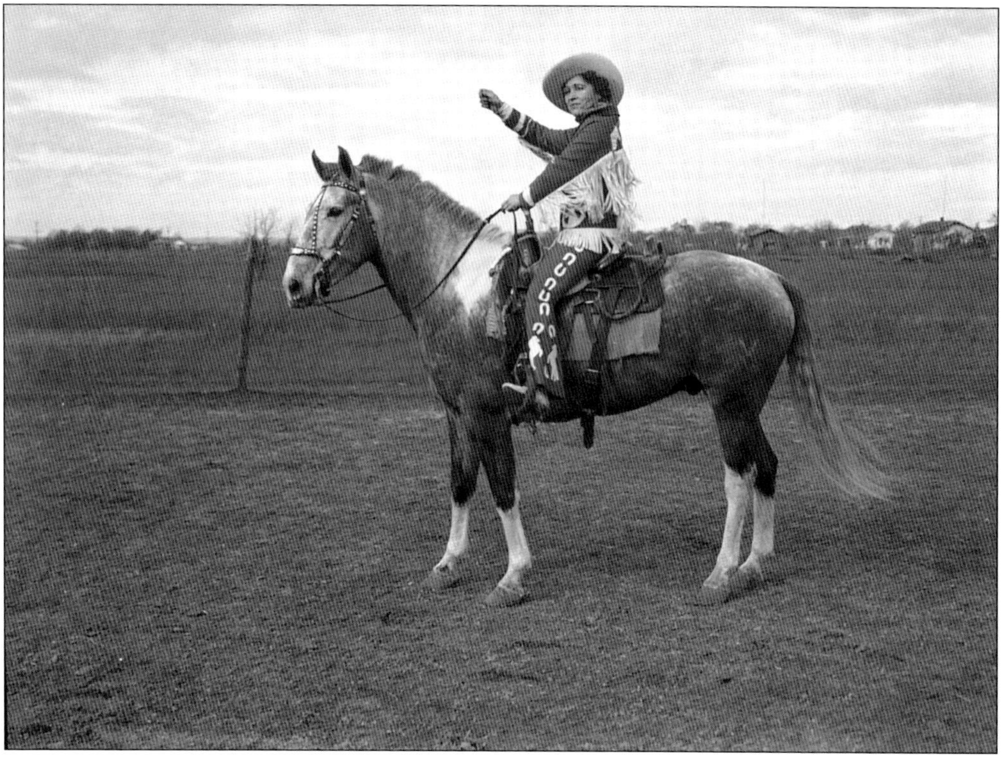

Tad Lucas, born Barbara Inez Barnes, gained the nickname "Tad" because she crawled and slithered around so quickly as a baby that her father called her tadpole. Tad met fellow rodeo cowboy James Edward "Buck" Lucas while competing in the Fat Stock Show in Fort Worth. The couple married in Madison Square Garden in 1924 while on their way to compete at Wembley Stadium in London. (Courtesy of the *Fort Worth Star-Telegram* Collection, University of Texas at Arlington Libraries.)

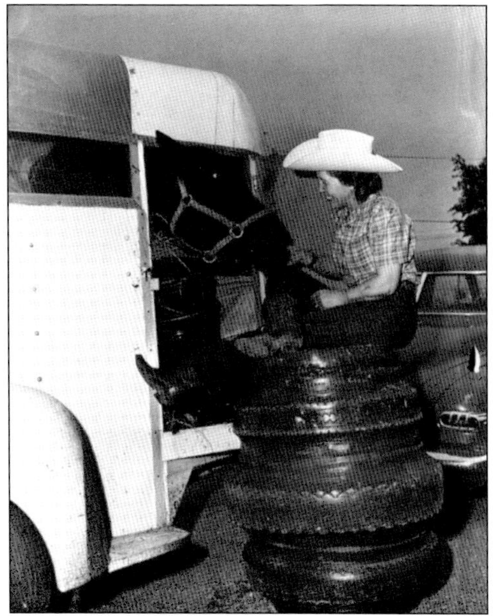

Tad Lucas performed at the Fat Stock Show and Rodeo in Fort Worth many times. Lucas loved performing and only retired in 1958 because her horse was getting old and she did not want to train a new one. Tad Lucas is the only person to be inducted into the National Rodeo Hall of Fame, the National Cowgirl Hall of Fame, and the Pro-Rodeo Hall of Fame. (Courtesy of the *Fort Worth Star-Telegram* Collection, University of Texas at Arlington Libraries.)

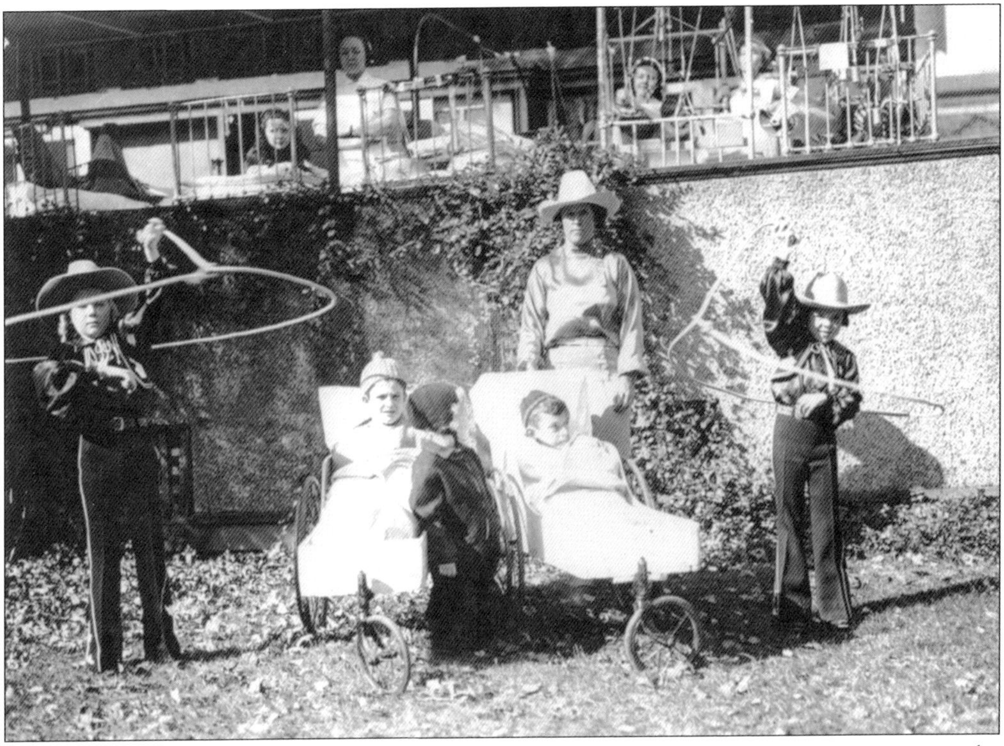

Velda Tindall Smith learned to trick ride at the age of 12 and gave her debut performance the following year to a crowd of 8,000 at Gilbert's Ranch Rodeo. Velda consistently placed high in trick riding, flat races, and relay races at major competitions like Cheyenne Frontier Days. As trick riding became less profitable, Velda began a career as a barrel racer and helped to form the Texas Barrel Racing Association. She served as president for five years and at the age of 54 won grand champion barrel racer at the 1964 Dallas Fair. Her husband, Louis Cleo Tindall, was an accomplished trick and fancy rider, holding the World's Champion title for 10 years. He met Velda Callahan Tindall at the Fort Worth Stock Show and Rodeo. The two were married in 1925 at the 101 Ranch in Marland, Oklahoma, where they performed for several years. In later years, Louis became involved in gambling and was shot in the driveway of his home in Fort Worth; he died several days later. (Both, courtesy of the River Oaks Historical Society.)

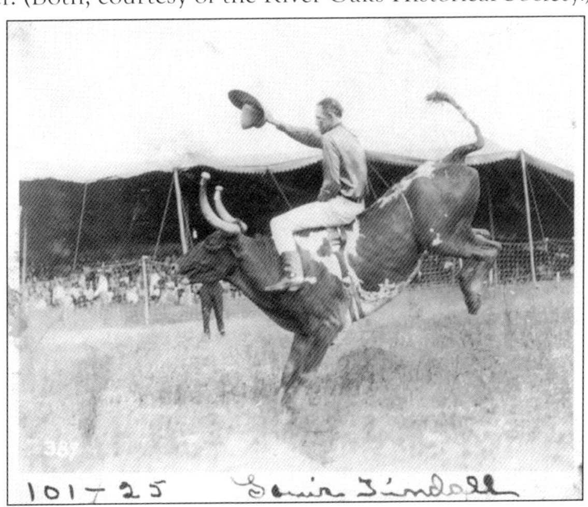

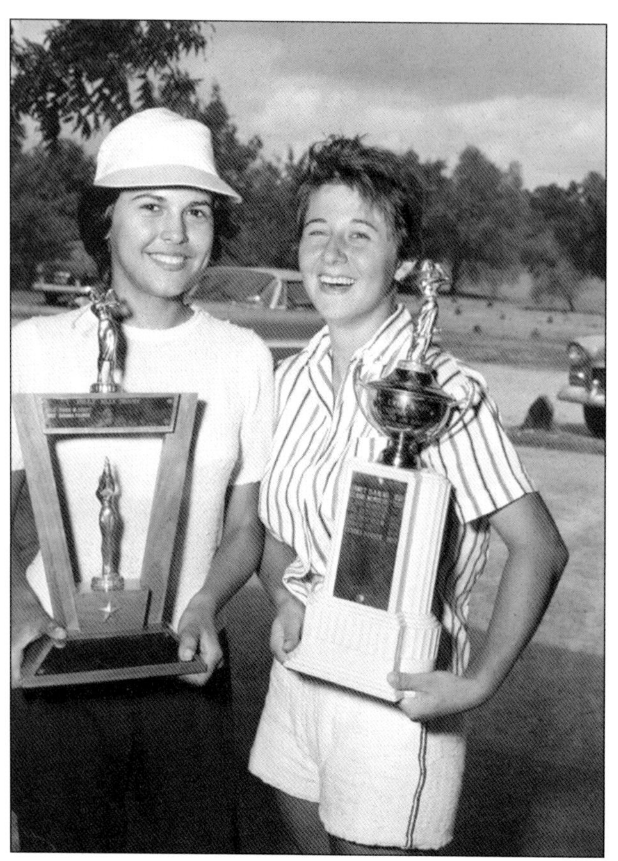

Sandra Palmer became a member of the LPGA Tour in 1964 and won 19 LPGA Tour events, including two major championships. She was inducted into the World Golf Hall of Fame in 2024. To the left, Sandra Palmer, pictured on the right, holds the winner's trophy after victory in the girl's junior tournament at Rockwood in 1958. She defeated Rachel Garza (left), who received the runner-up trophy. Palmer was born in River Oaks but grew up and first played golf in Bangor, Maine. She returned to Texas and attended North Texas State University, now the University of North Texas, where she was a cheerleader and homecoming queen. In 1961, Palmer was runner-up in the National Collegiate Championship. She was a four-time winner of the West Texas Amateur and won the Texas State Amateur in 1963. (Both, courtesy of the *Fort Worth Star-Telegram* Collection, University of Texas at Arlington Libraries.)

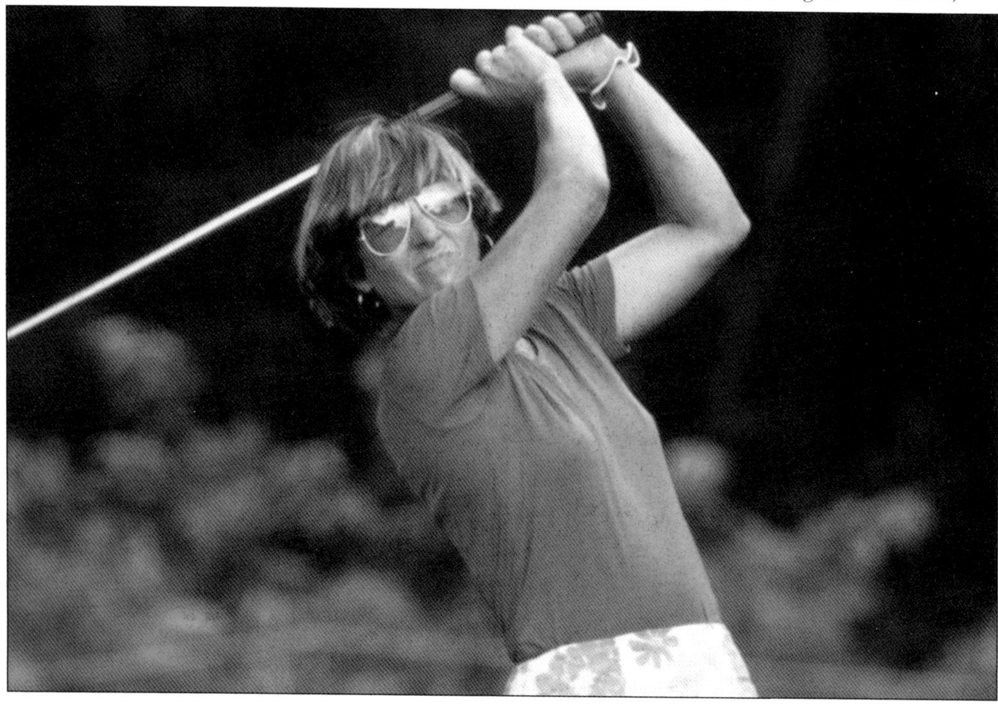

Johnny Rutherford met Betty Hoyer, a nurse, at the Indianapolis Motor Speedway in 1963 while taking his rookie test. The two married two months later and were a highly visible and inseparable couple throughout Johnny's racing career. Betty looked on from the pits when Johnny won his first Indy 500 in 1974, helping to end the superstition in American racing against allowing women in the pit area. Pictured here are Betty and Johnny Rutherford at the All Sports Celebrity Fashion Show benefiting the Cystic Fibrosis Foundation in October 1986. Below, Rutherford is pictured in the winner's circle at the Indy 500. Rutherford was also known as "Lone Star JR" and proudly wore a Texas decal on his racing helmet. During an Indy Car career that spanned more than three decades, Rutherford scored 27 wins in 314 starts. He became one of six drivers to win the Indianapolis 500 at least three times, winning in 1974, 1976, and 1980. Rutherford began racing on the streets and local tracks around River Oaks. Rutherford won in his first start at Daytona International Speedway, making him one of the youngest drivers ever to win a NASCAR points-paying race as well as only the sixth racer in history to win in their NASCAR debut race. (Right, *Fort Worth Star-Telegram* Collection, University of Texas at Arlington Libraries; below, courtesy of Jack Atkinson.)

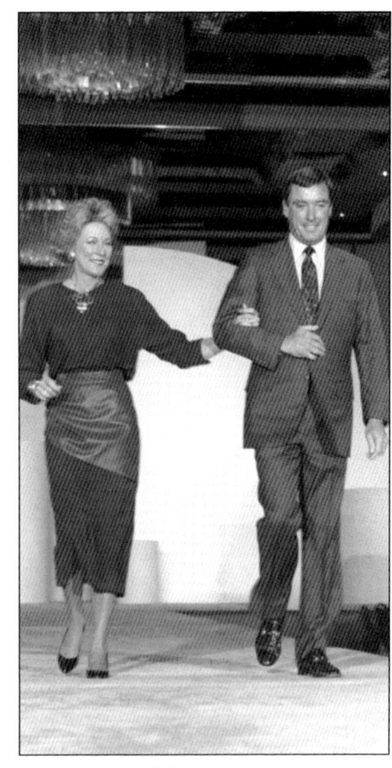

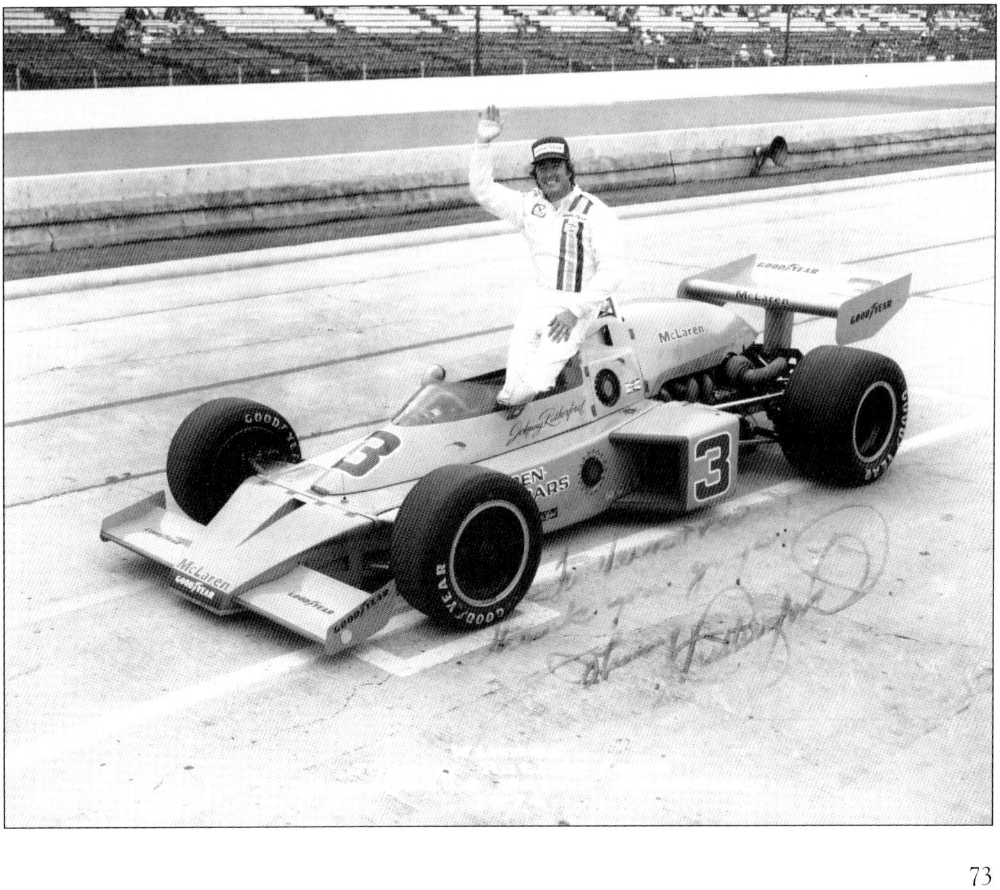

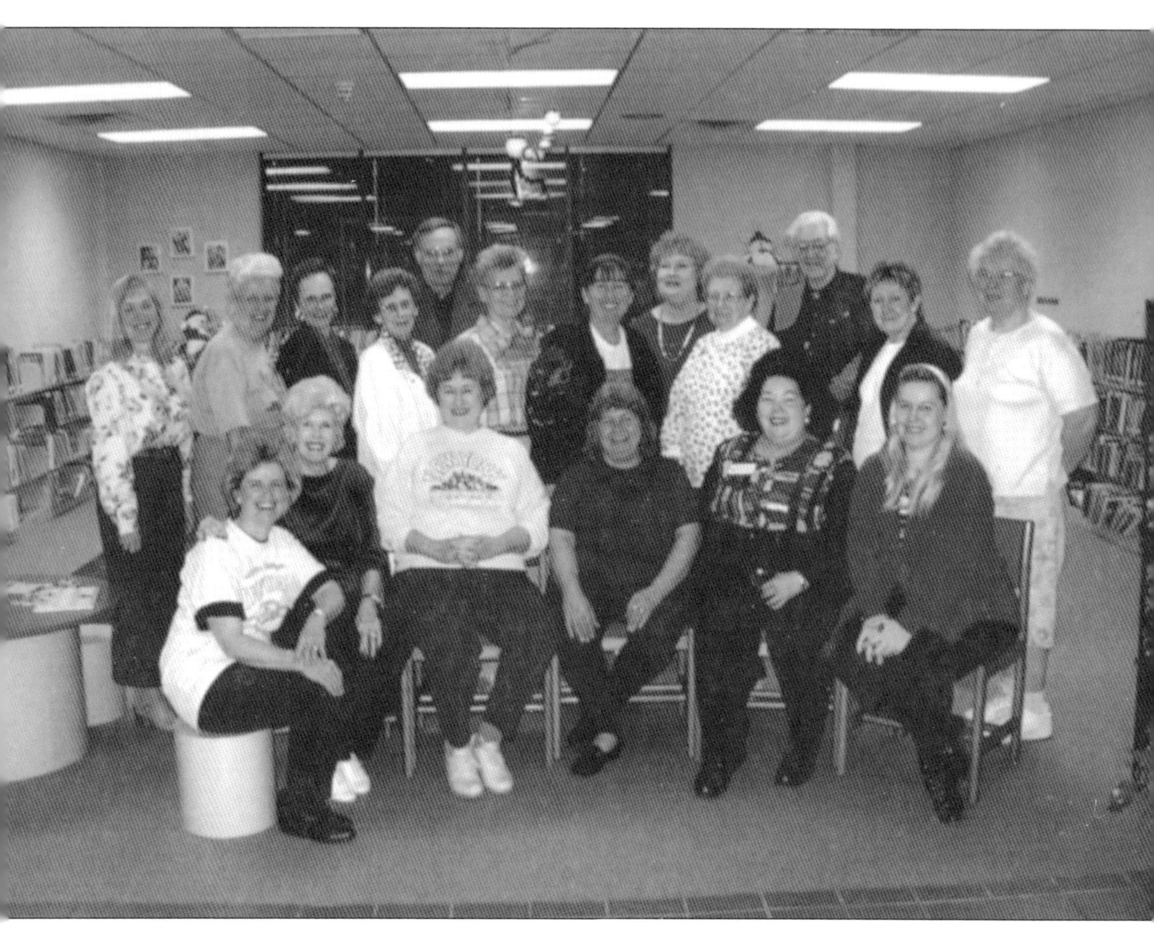

The city of River Oaks has always been a roll up your sleeves and get the job done type of city. When something important needs to be done, neighbors come together and get the job done. There is little to no room in city budgets for saving the city's rich history. The River Oaks Historical Society came together and began collecting bits and pieces of the city's history, and it continues to do so to this day. The first meeting of the River Oaks Historical Society was held on March 15, 1999. The first elected officers were, from left to right, (first row) Second Vice Pres. Shirley Bloomfield, Third Vice Pres. Billie Gregory, Treasurer Peggy Holland, Pres. Mary Earwood, First Vice Pres. Linda Claridge, and Sec. Sherry Dast; (second row) Sarah Biles, Dorothy Callaway, Sue Ann Hayley, Georgia Walker, Duane E. Hayley, Orene Estes, Barbara Throne, Bernie Stone, Katherine Wilson, Dub Ray, Shirlie Wheat, and Mary Karle. (Courtesy of Linda Claridge.)

Five

Entertainment

Over its 75-year history, the citizens of River Oaks have had a wide variety of options for entertainment. When drive-in theaters were popular, River Oaks had bookend drive-ins on either side of River Oaks Boulevard and one indoor theater midway in between. All three are gone today due to soaring land prices and the consolidation of theater chains. One of the most unique swimming holes in the entire state of Texas, however, is still thriving after almost 100 of existence. The city of River Oaks is bordered on one side by the infamous Jacksboro Highway, home of some of the most notorious speakeasies and gambling nightclubs in Texas. Though one of these questionable nightspots was located in the city limits, every town has a few local beer joints, and River Oaks was no exception. One of the most famous and historically significant dance halls in the world of music gave birth to Western swing on the edge of River Oaks.

While primarily a bedroom community, the city has taken great pride in building and maintaining city parks (see chapter two) for the public's enjoyment. Over the decades, the city has had a wide variety of cafés and restaurants serving up staples like barbeque and chicken-fried steaks and ethnic foods ranging from Mexican to Italian to Mediterranean dishes. Fraternal organizations such as the Lions Club and Freemasons, along with other community service and nonprofit organizations, have a long history of service to the city. Of course, with the West Fork of the Trinity River winding its way around the city and Lake Worth a short distance away, fishing and water activities have always been just outside residents' back doors. The city of River Oaks is a small town nestled up close to the 12th-largest city in the United States. This geography, while sometimes limiting, also offers its citizens the advantage of living a slower, small-town pace while still enjoying the amenities and entertainment opportunities of a metropolitan area. Of course, with Air Force Plant 4 and an Air Force base as neighbors, there were and are almost always entertaining and interesting birds in the sky.

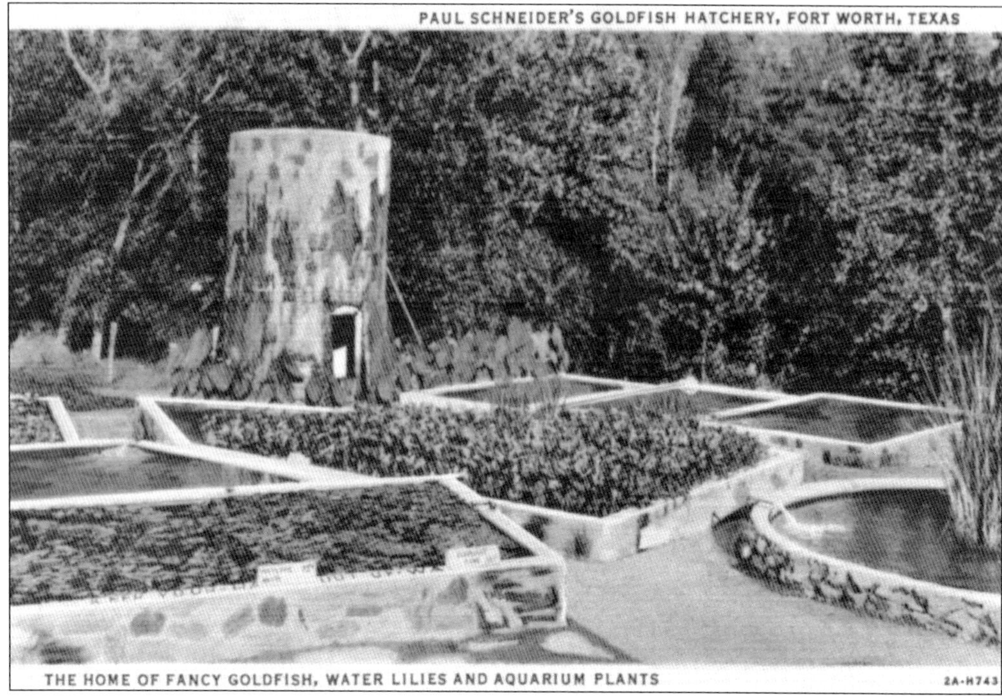

Burger's Lake has been a fixture on the edge of River Oaks since the 1920s. Traveling salesman Hugo Burger bought Paul Schneider's Goldfish Hatchery in 1929, and Burger's Lake was born. Burger made improvements to the swimming pond Schneider built by adding sandy beaches, diving boards, and a grove of pecan trees to the bur oaks, cottonwoods, and sycamores already on the property. This improvement was a hit, and families have been flocking to the resort ever since. (Both, courtesy of Burger's Lake.)

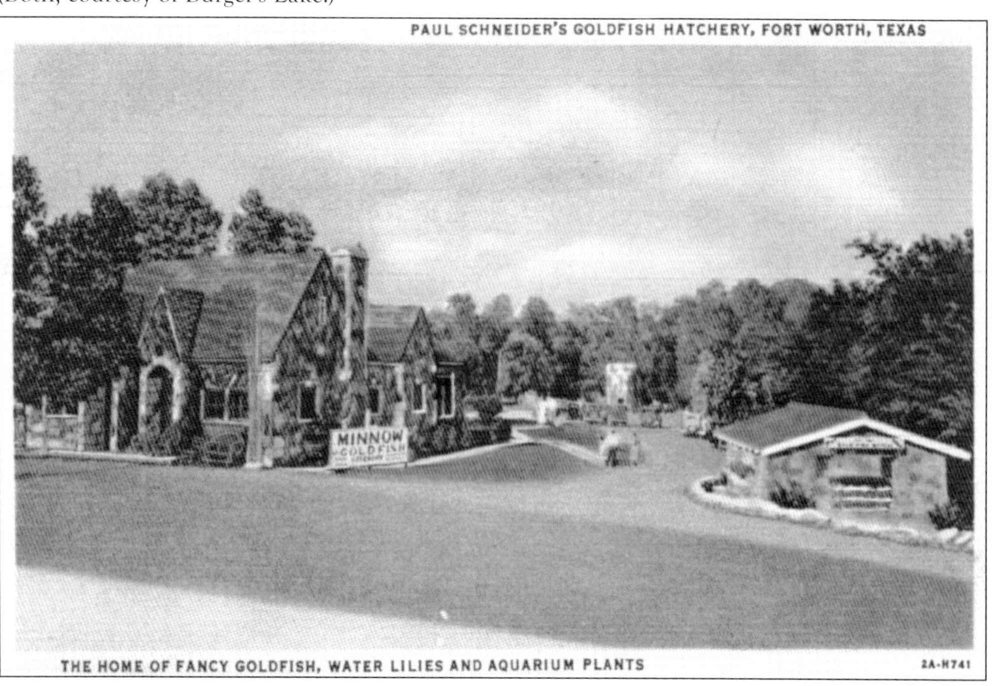

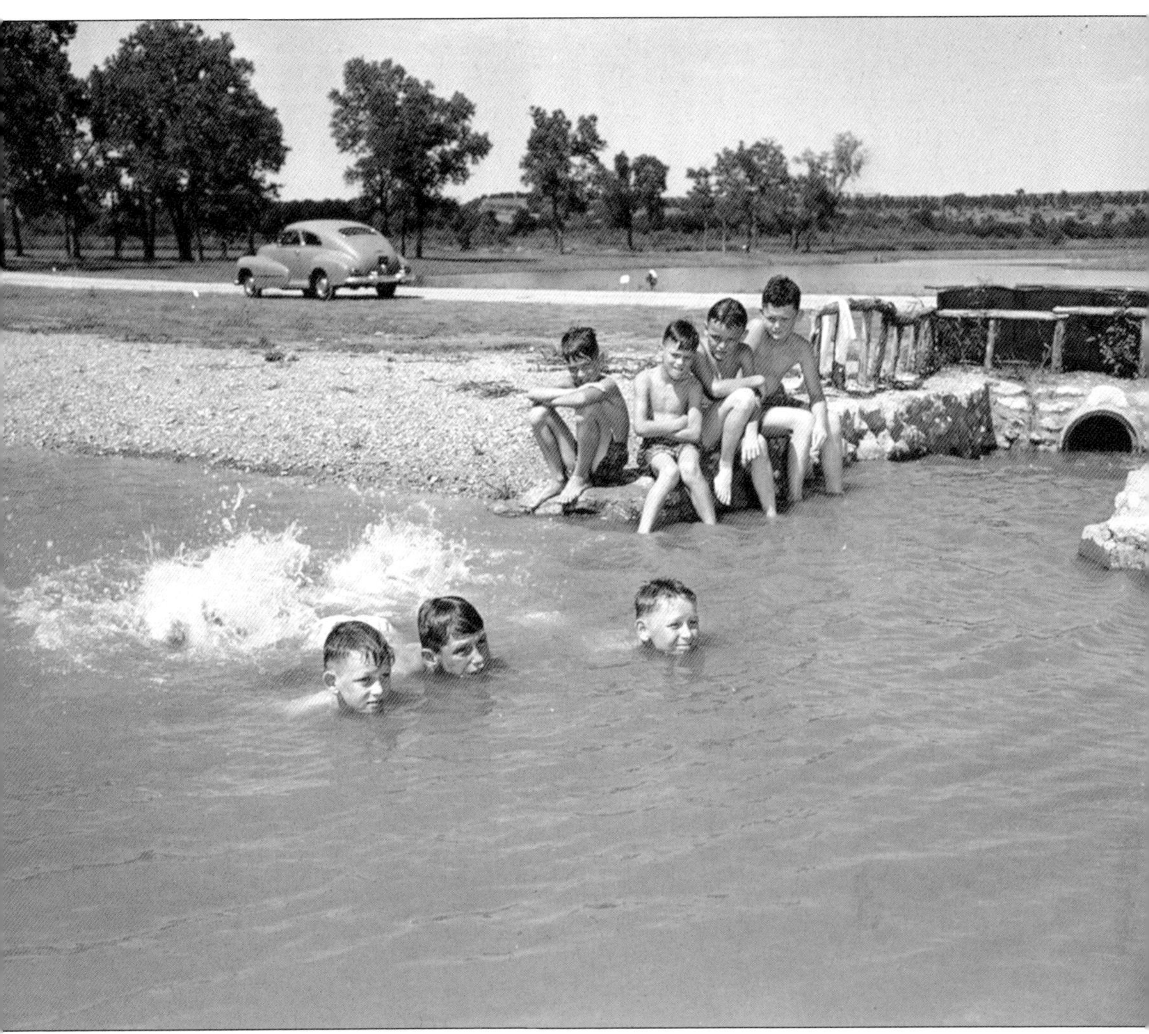

Located on the edge of River Oaks, YMCA Camp Carter has been serving the youth of Tarrant County since 1948. Amon Carter Sr. is widely considered the area's greatest supporter. Early on, he served on the YMCA board and laid the cornerstone of the Downtown Fort Worth YMCA in 1924. When his son Amon Carter Jr. was 10 years old, he visited a YMCA camp in nearby Weatherford, Texas, and had a great time. The senior Carter decided Fort Worth needed such a camp and began acquiring land and funds. The 350-acre camp has a lake, a swimming pool, rope course, basketball and volleyball courts, an equestrian center, archery ranges, a rifle range, and athletic fields. (Courtesy of the *Fort Worth Star-Telegram* Collection, University of Texas at Arlington Libraries.)

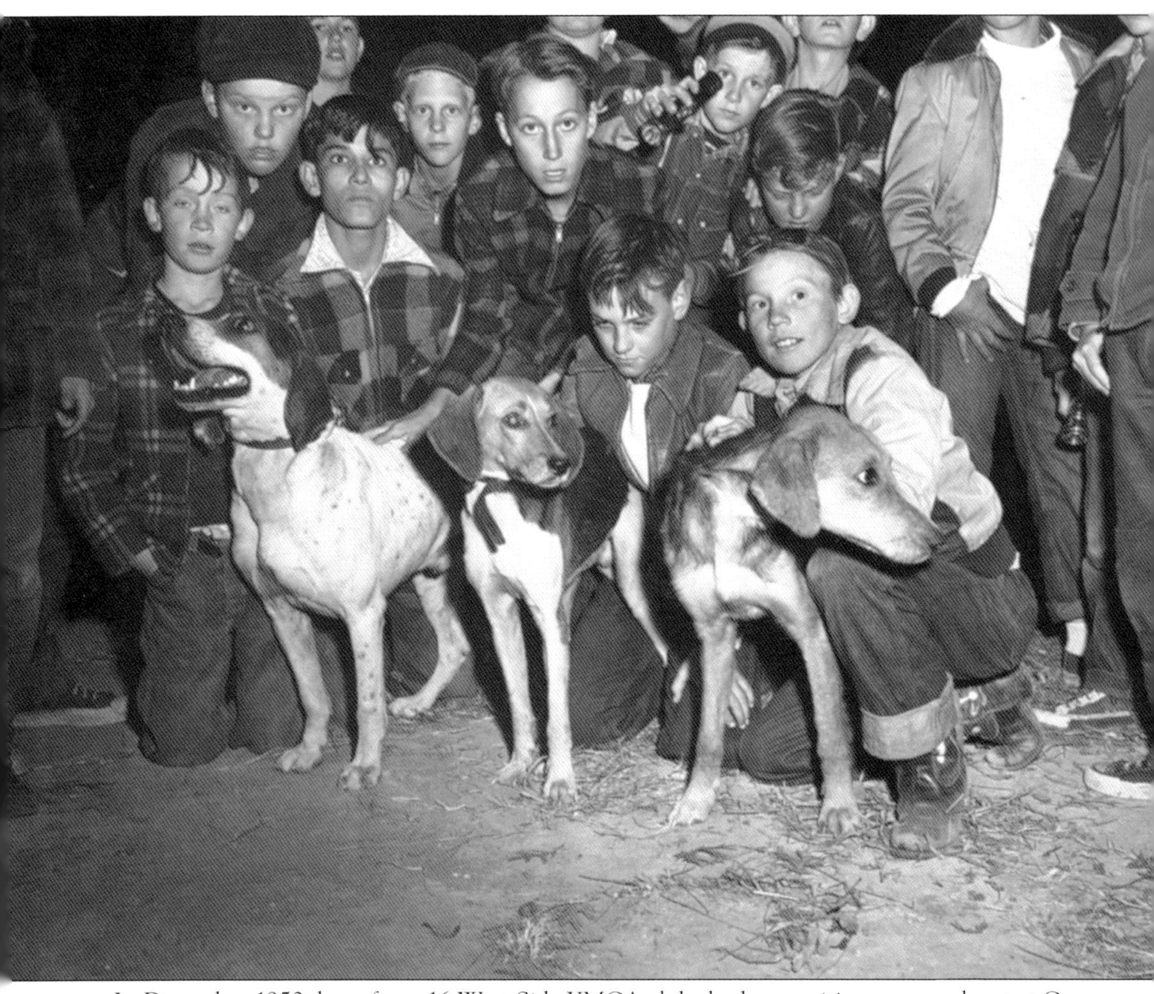

In December 1950, boys from 16 West Side YMCA clubs had an exciting possum hunt at Camp Carter. Today, Camp Carter offers a range of activities for youngsters ranging from canoeing to archery, horseback riding, and more. It is not clear when possum hunting was taken off the list, but it is no longer an option. (Courtesy of the *Fort Worth Star-Telegram* Collection, University of Texas at Arlington Libraries.)

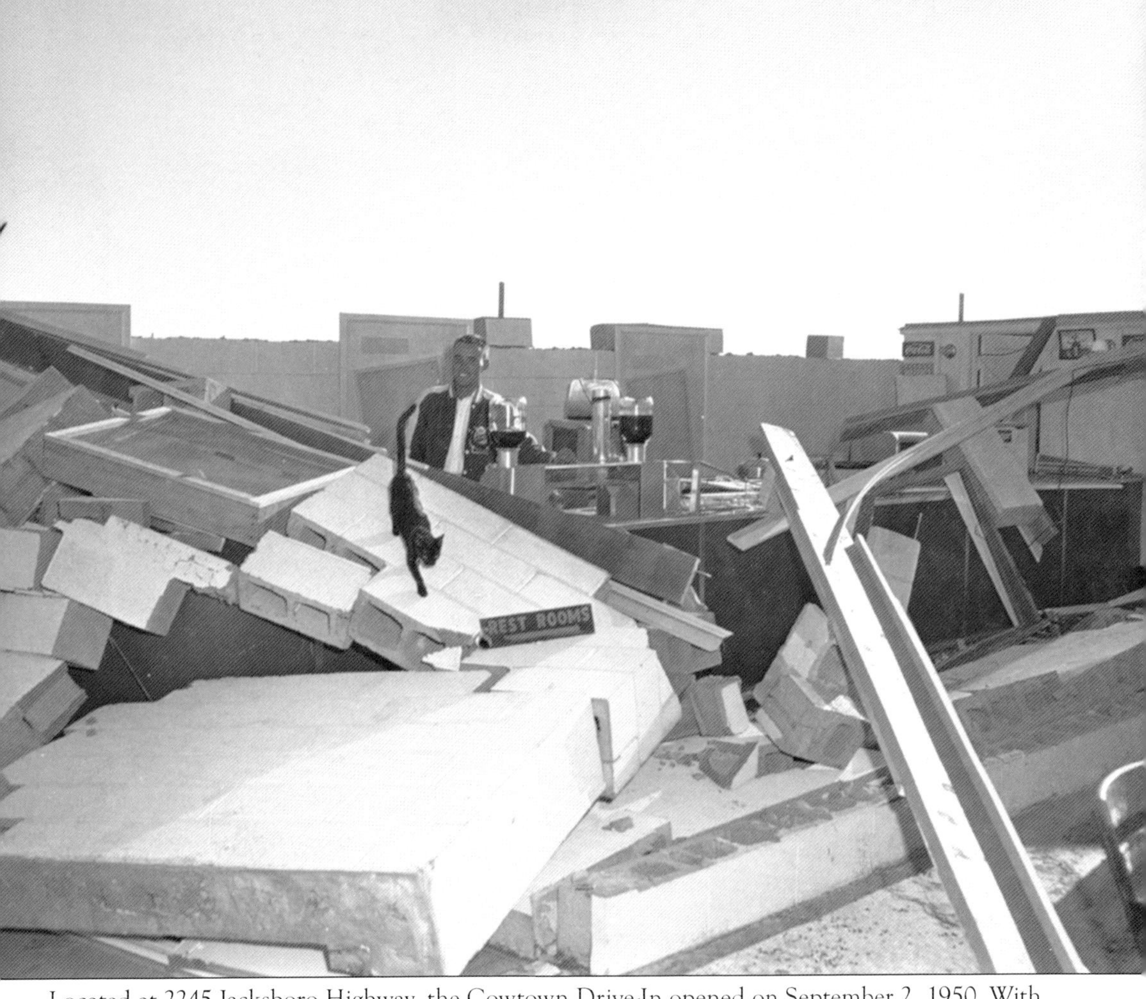

Located at 2245 Jacksboro Highway, the Cowtown Drive-In opened on September 2, 1950. With a capacity for 950 cars, the Cowtown featured a children's playground and in-car heaters. Mostly screening third-run movies, the opening night feature was the Gregory Peck Western *The Gunfighter*. On opening night, moviegoers were greeted at the ticket office by young ladies dressed as cowgirls in full Texas regalia. After a series of openings and closing in the mid-1960s, the Cowtown finally shuttered in 1984. (Courtesy of the River Oaks Historical Society.)

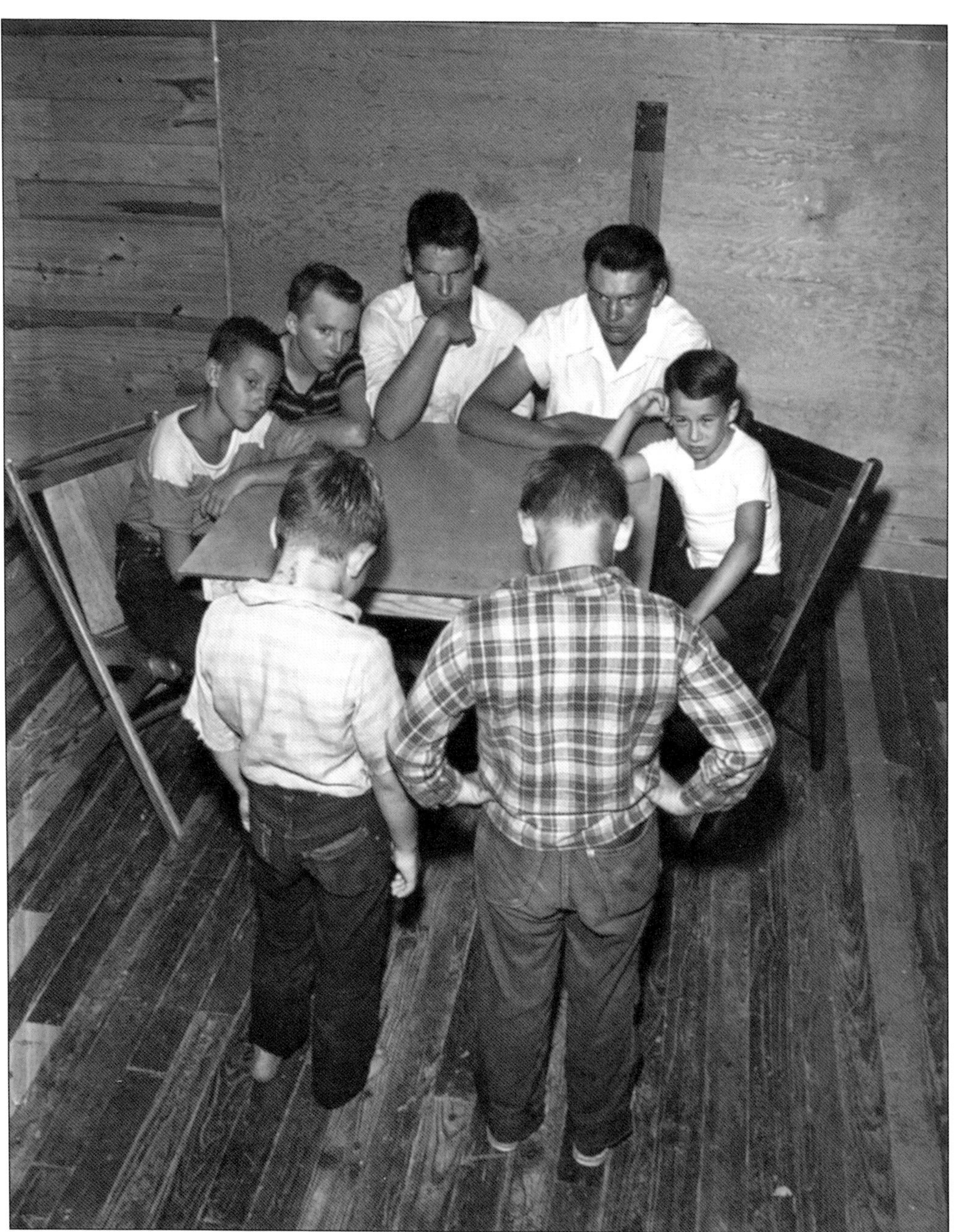

This image shows council members of the River Oaks Boys Club sitting around a table, deciding the fate of two young members. The caption in the *Fort Worth Star-Telegram* evening edition on July 29, 1950, reads, "A youngster is not likely to repeat an offense once he has had to face the hard but fair members of the River Oaks Boys Club disciplinary council." Sitting at the table are Bobby Loyd, Paul Adams, Jimmy Nettles (president), and Kiah O'Brien. It was likely a minor offense. The boys look pretty scared straight. (Courtesy of the *Fort Worth Star-Telegram* Collection, University of Texas at Arlington Libraries.)

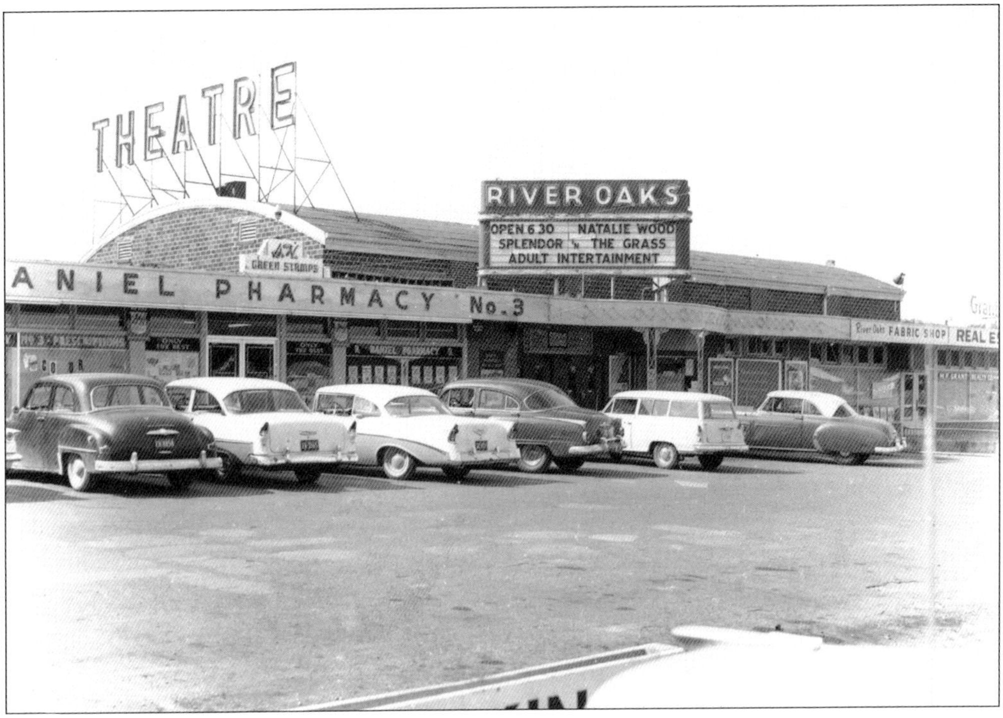

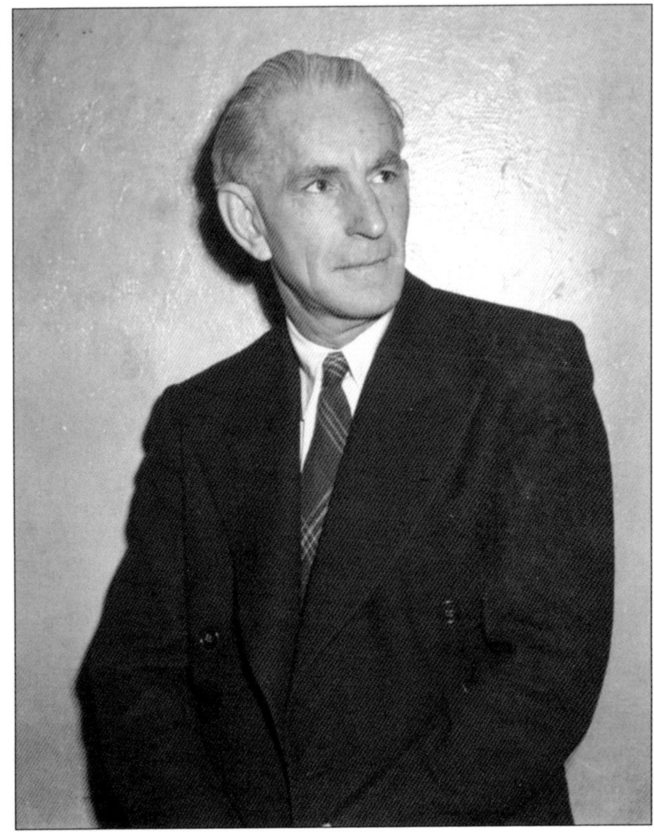

The River Oaks Theater is seen here in 1961. The theater was located behind the strip center on River Oaks Boulevard. The entrance was in front of the shopping center. Patrons would pass through a hallway to see the films. The building behind the shopping center is no longer standing. The theater was operated by the regional chain Interstate Theater Circuit, which operated over 150 theaters in Texas and the Southwest. Limie Stillwell was the manager of the River Oaks Theater and is seen here in a photograph dated April 23, 1945. In the 1940s, movie patronage was at its peak. Stillwell brought many great films to the patrons of the River Oaks Theater. (Above, courtesy of David Bloomfield; right, courtesy of *Fort Worth Star-Telegram* Collection, University of Texas at Arlington Libraries.)

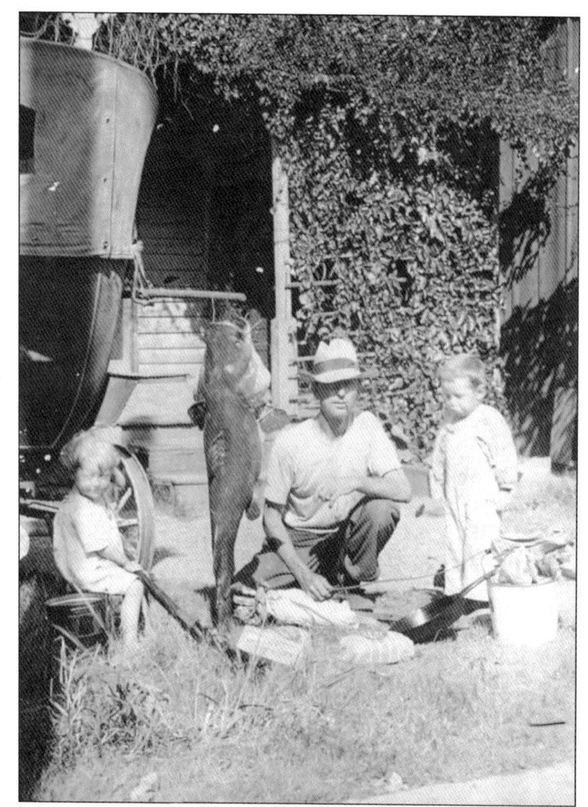

Besides football and maybe deer hunting, fishing is about every Texan's favorite sport. River Oaks is located near the Trinity River, and Lake Worth is a stone's throw away, so many residents enjoyed the sport. As a consequence of fishing's popularity, fried catfish is a favorite food for many Texans, along with barbeque and chicken fried steak. (Both, courtesy of the River Oaks Historical Society.)

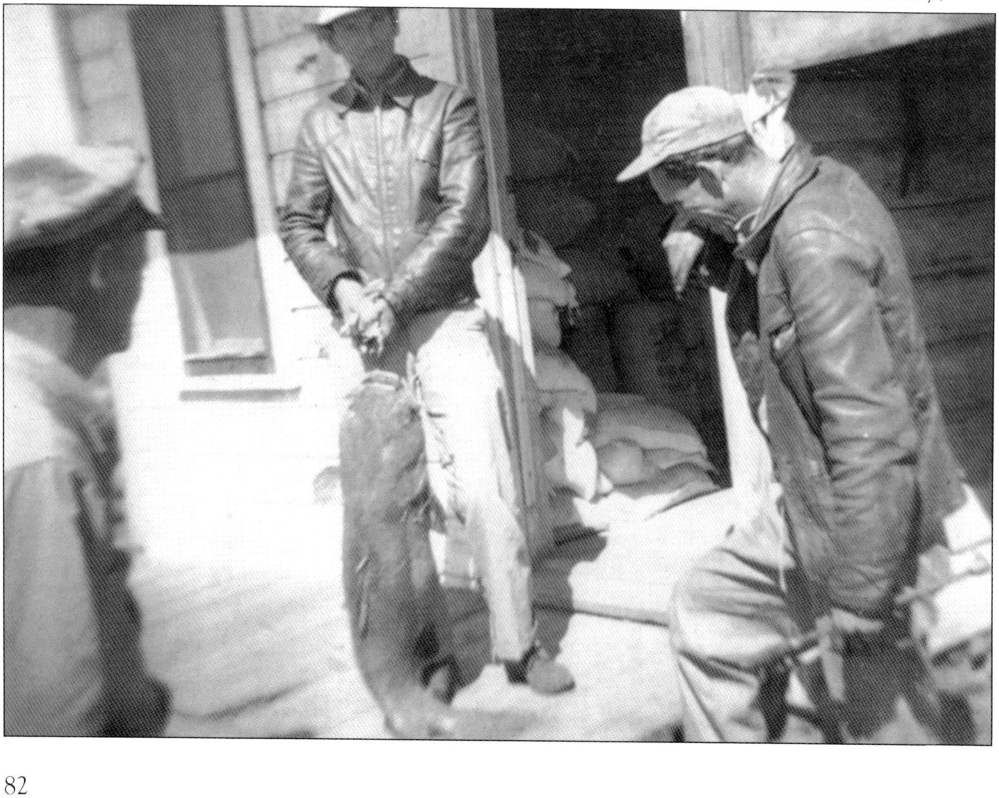

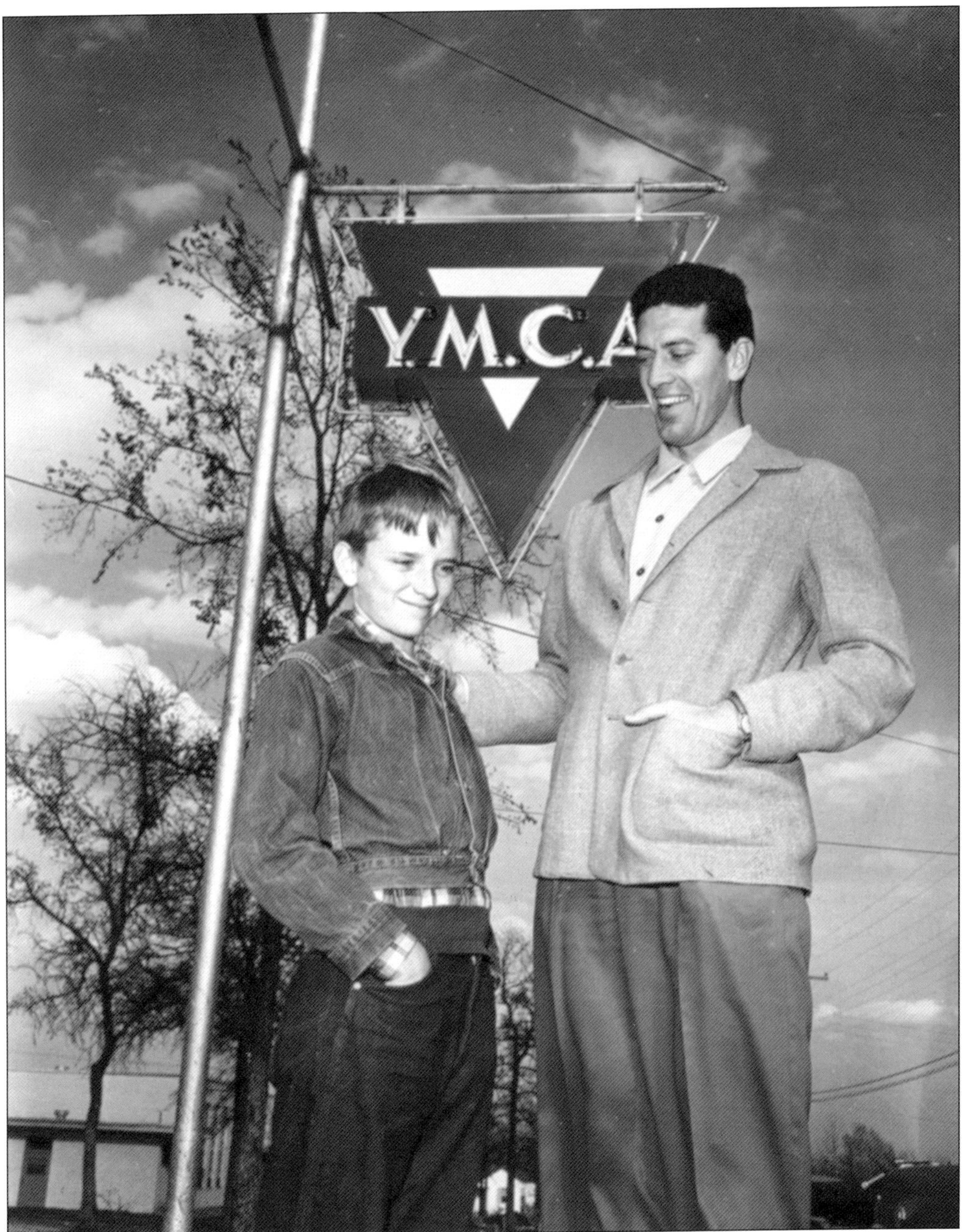

Bob Bond, director of the River Oaks Youth Men's Christian Association Branch, poses with Gerald Graham of 1211 Harvard Street, a young club member, standing in front of the new neon sign that hangs in front of the River Oaks YMCA building on the Castleberry School grounds. This picture appeared in the *Fort Worth Star-Telegram* on March 5, 1951. (Courtesy of the *Fort Worth Star-Telegram* Collection, University of Texas at Arlington Libraries.)

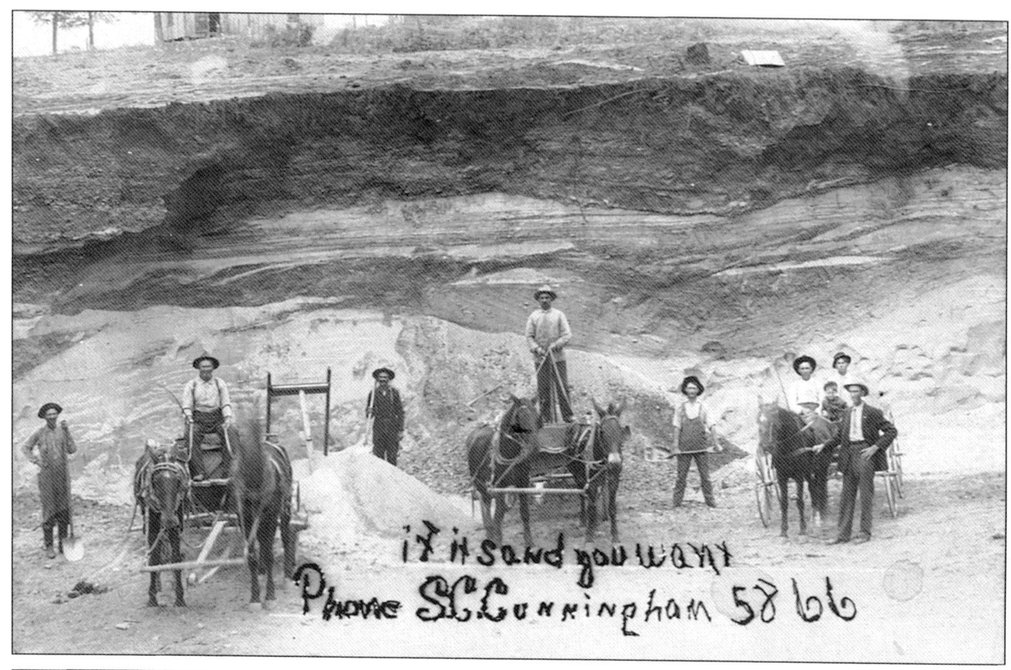

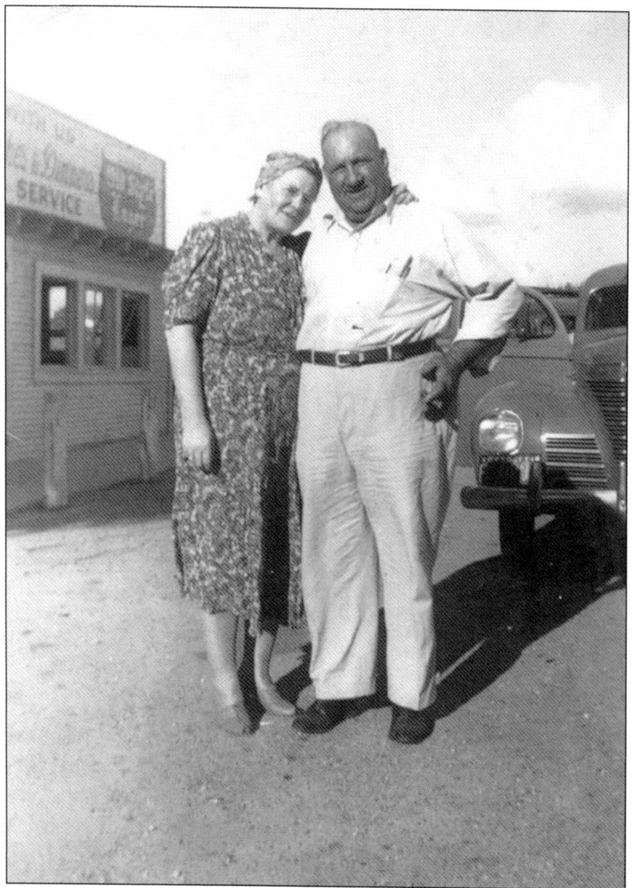

The Crystal Springs Dance Pavilion, located at 5653 White Settlement Road on the southeastern edge of River Oaks, is generally credited as the birthplace of Western swing. Crystal Springs was an open-air ventilated dancehall where people from surrounding towns as far as 90 miles away would dance through the cool breeze wafting off the river on hot Texas summer nights. "Papa Sam" Cunningham owned the land and operated a sand and gravel pit on the very property that would eventually become a celebrated dancehall. In 1918, Papa Sam was excavating sand and gravel for the US Army's nearby Camp Bowie when he discovered a natural spring filling the hole with water as fast as he dug it. His wife remarked, "Look, Sam, that water is clear as crystal," and thus his property was called "Crystal Springs." (Both, courtesy of *The Birth and History of Western Swing* and Cary Ginell.)

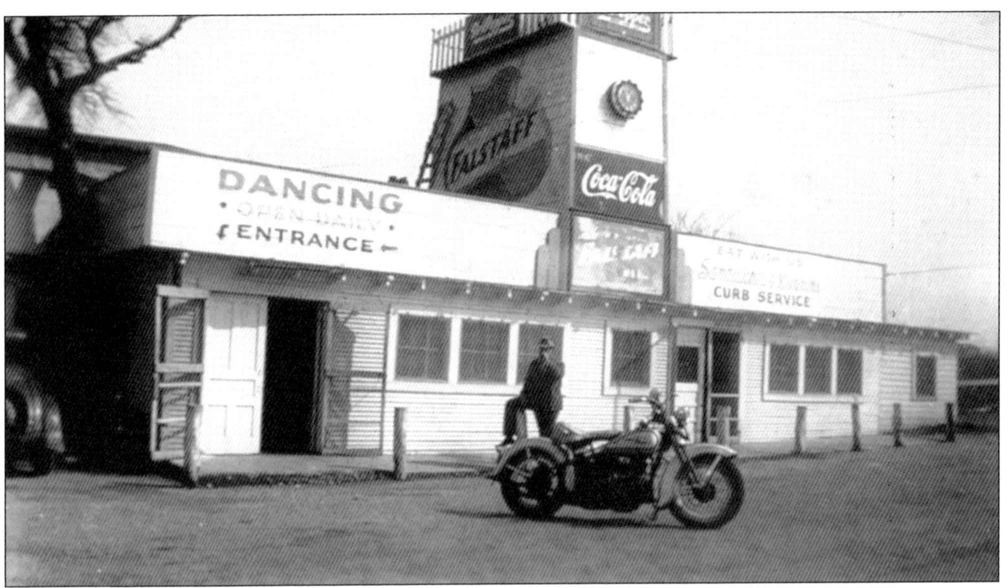

A crystal-clear spring filling the sand and gravel pit is not very good for a sand business. Papa Sam Cunningham fought a losing battle against Crystal Springs until 1925, when he decided to embrace the water. He dug a hole in the ground, and it quickly filled with water and became a small lake for swimming. Near the lake, he built a concrete swimming pool, also filled with spring water. He added some picnic tables and moved a large open-air wooden barracks building from Camp Bowie and turned it into a dance pavilion. The place was far from fancy, but the pavilion had ceiling fans for summer and a coal-burning stove for winter. Eventually, Papa Sam added a huge wooden dance floor. With the help of such performers as Bob Wills and Milton Brown, the dance hall became one of the most popular night spots in the area for dancing, drinking, and most importantly, listening to a new music genre. (Both, courtesy of *The Birth and History of Western Swing* and Cary Ginell.)

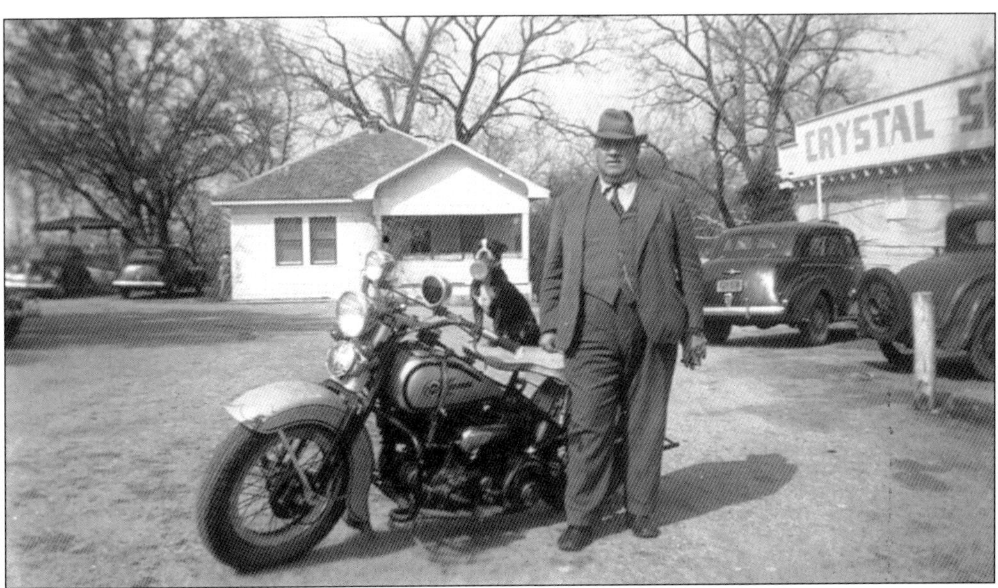

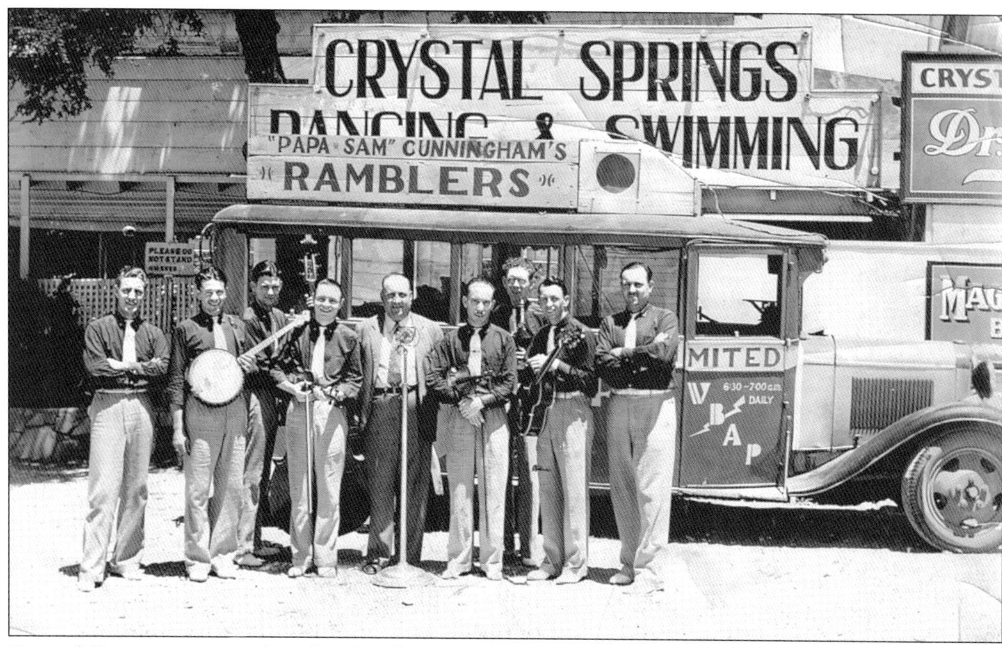

Crystal Springs remained under family control until the end. After World War I, the returning doughboys and their ladies came to swim in the springs and hear music. The music venue grew and in 1925 moved into a new building constructed on the premises. This structure had a capacity of about 1,000 people and could accommodate approximately 800 people on its dance floor. People walked, drove, and even took the Crystal Springs shuttle bus from downtown Fort Worth to hear Milton Brown and His Musical Brownies play. Crystal Springs continued to prosper as a country music venue until the 1960s. In December 1966, a fire completely destroyed the structure, and it never reopened. (Both, courtesy of *The Birth and History of Western Swing* and Cary Ginell.)

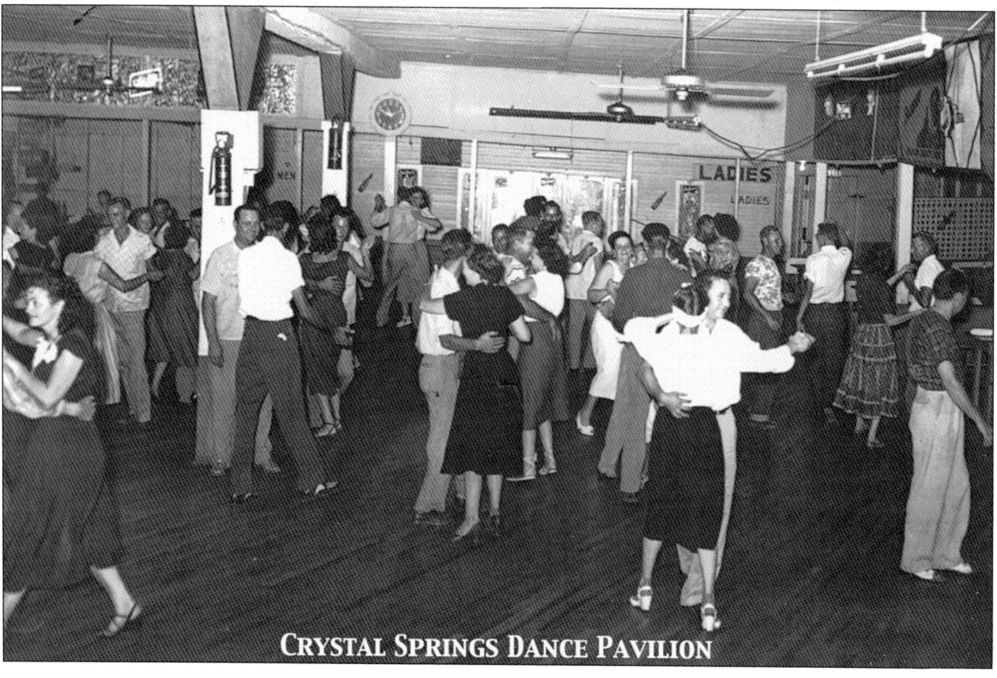

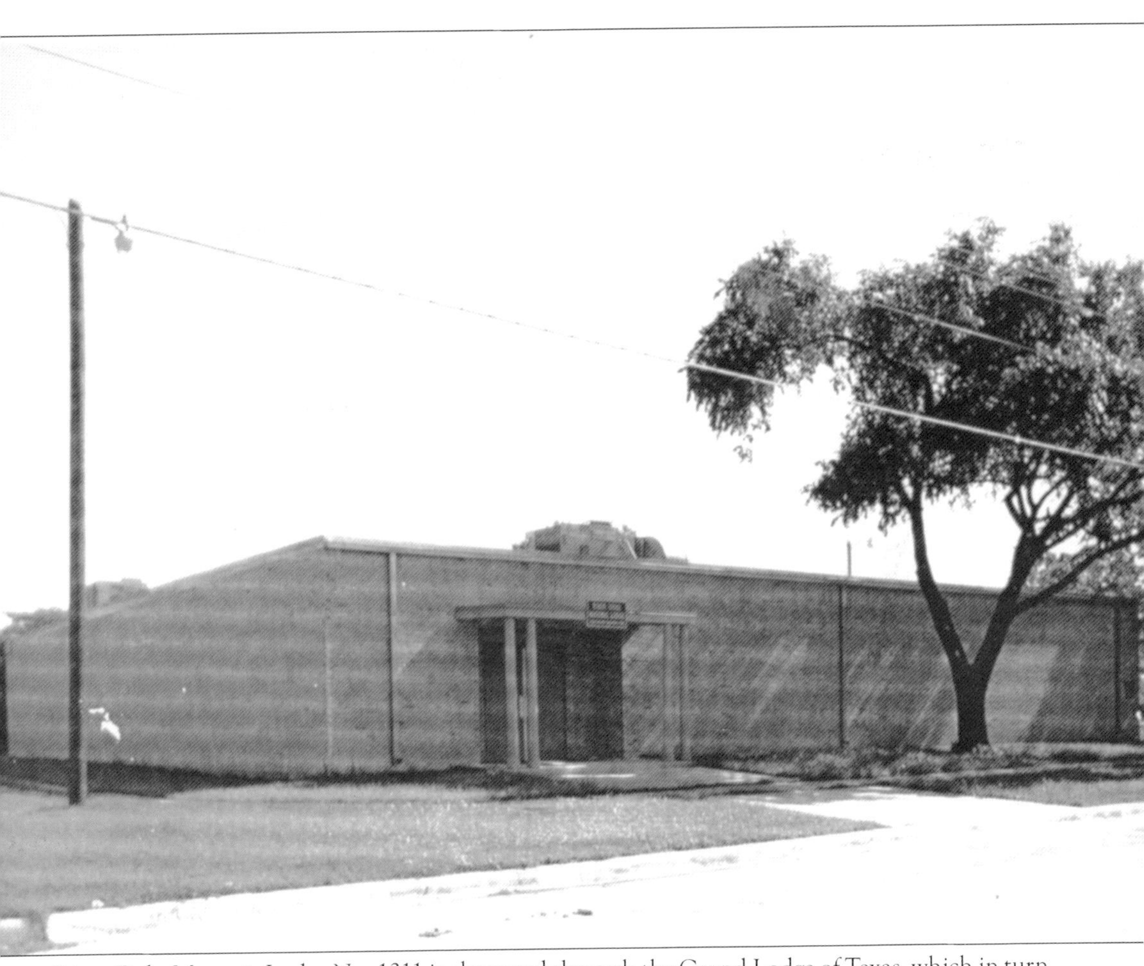

River Oaks Masonic Lodge No. 1311 is chartered through the Grand Lodge of Texas, which in turn is recognized by the United Grand Lodge of England. The lodge was chartered on December 20, 1948. The lodge has since sold the building to the City of River Oaks and meets at the Masonic temple in downtown Fort Worth. (Courtesy of the River Oaks Historical Society.)

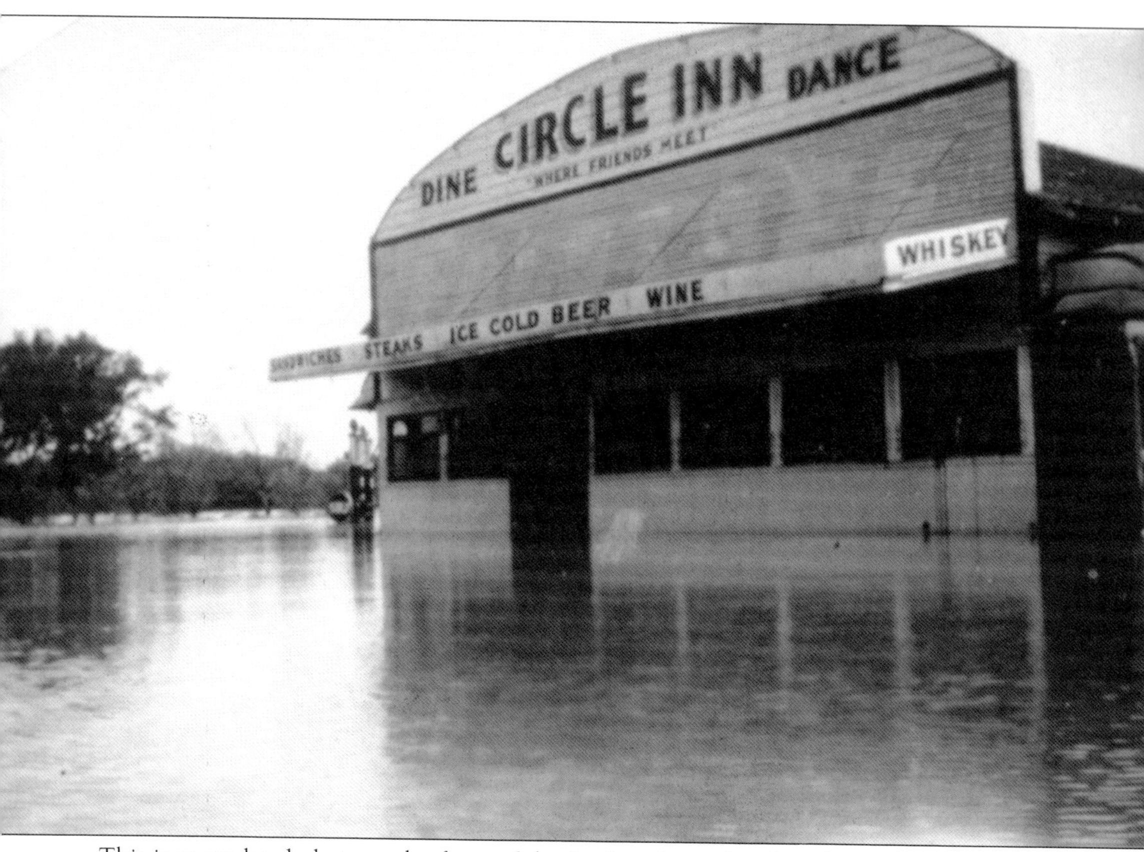

This is an undated photograph of one of the few bars located within the city of River Oaks. On the back of the photograph, someone wrote, "Circle Inn Beer Joint, 'Circle in and stagger out.' " The Circle Inn was located on the corner of Ohio Garden and Isbell Roads. (Courtesy of the River Oaks Historical Society.)

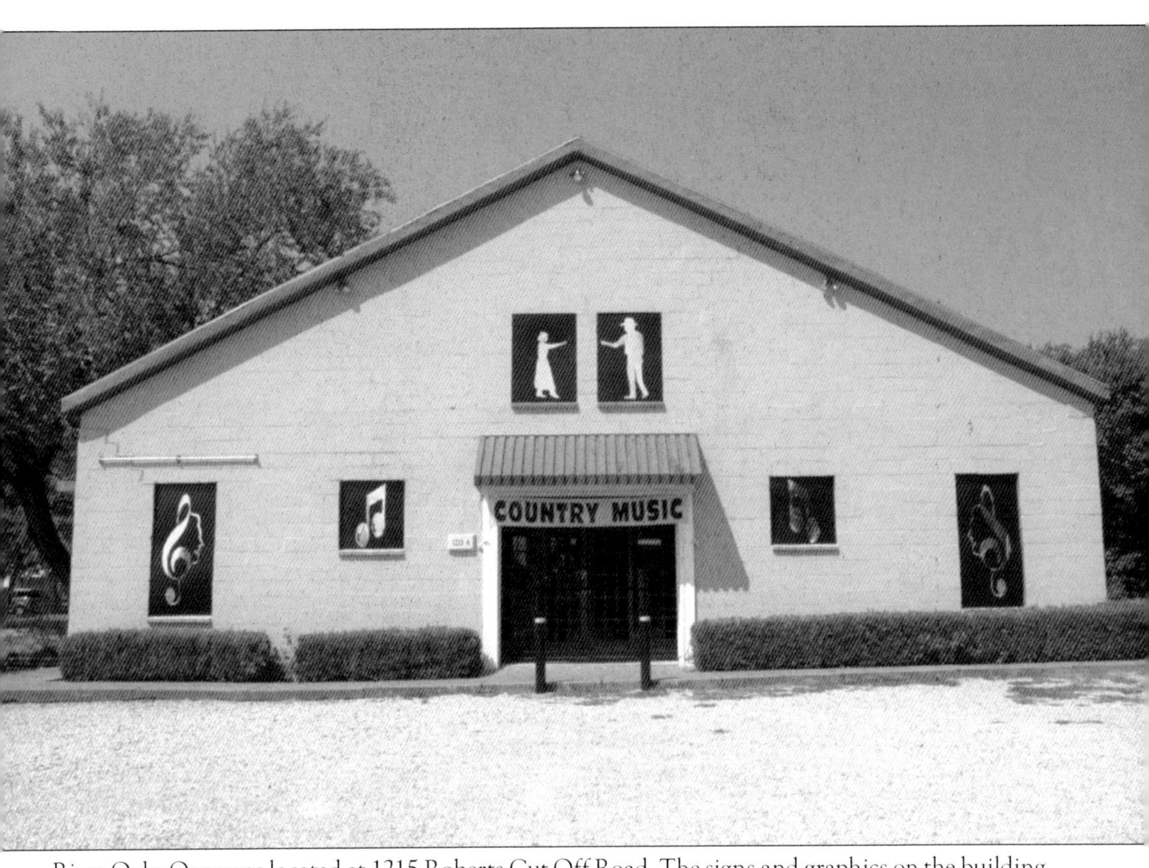

River Oaks Opry was located at 1215 Roberts Cut Off Road. The signs and graphics on the building were created by Shirley Bloomfield and Shirley Wheat. The River Oaks Opry provided wholesome entertainment for the citizens of River Oaks. (Courtesy of the River Oaks Historical Society.)

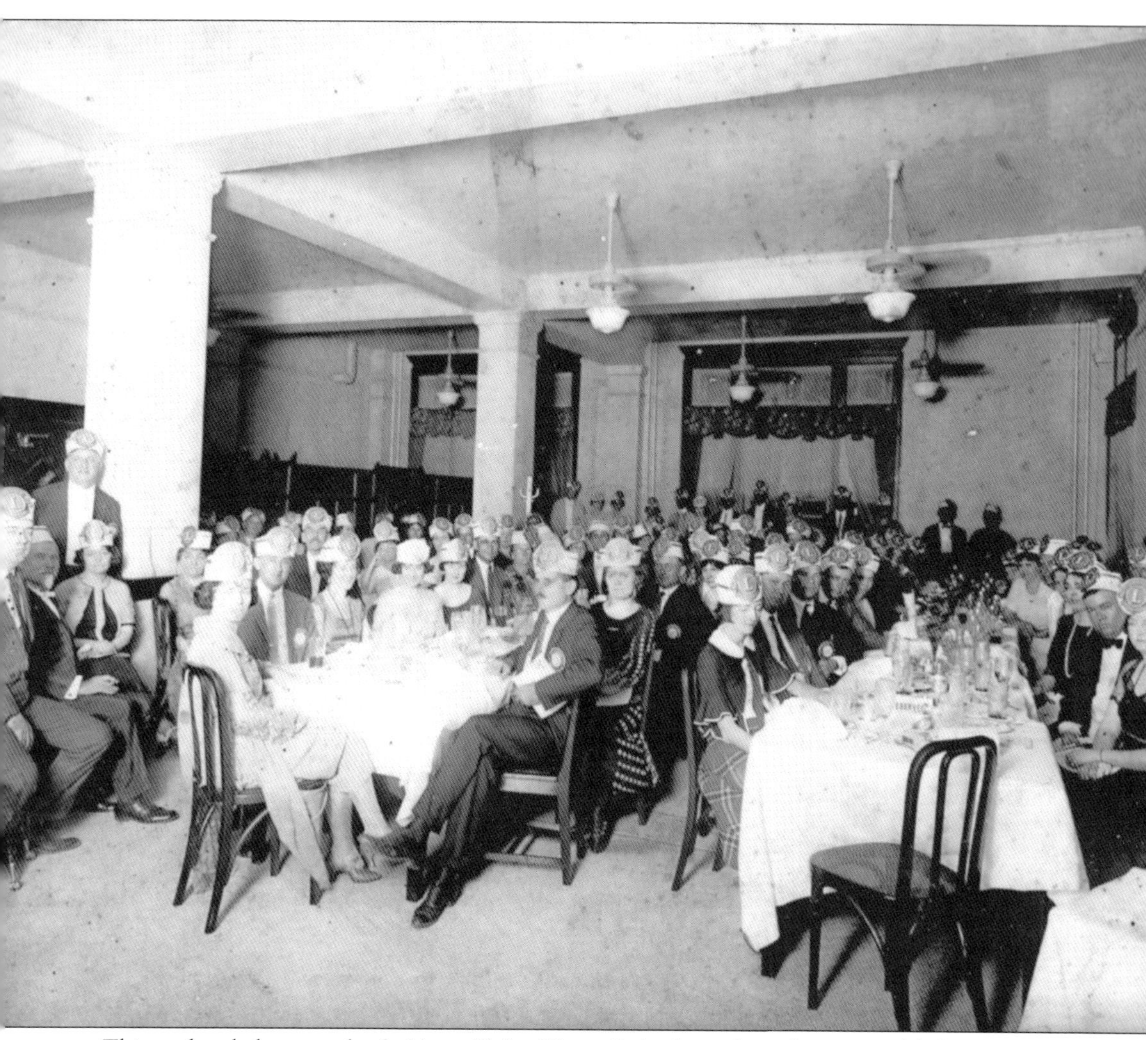

This undated photograph of a Lions Club of River Oaks fancy dress dinner was likely taken at John Knox Presbyterian Church. The Lions met at John Knox before securing their permanent building. The Lions Club's mission is to serve their communities, meet humanitarian needs, encourage peace, and promote international understanding. (Courtesy of the River Oaks Historical Society.)

Six

Business and Military Connections

The businesses located at Willett's Corner were the first to serve local residents in what was largely a rural area in 1938. With the opening of Consolidated Aircraft Corporation and Carswell Air Force Base, now NAS JRB Fort Worth, other businesses opened in the area to serve the burgeoning bedroom community. Most commercial businesses in River Oaks are located up and down River Oaks Boulevard. Due to land limitations of only 1.9 square miles, the city's commercial corridor is relatively small. Still, the city boasts an eclectic group of restaurants, including Italian, Mediterranean, Mexican, Chinese, down-home cooking, and several fast-food chains. The closing of the lone grocery store in River Oaks has concerned citizens, but there are several options for major grocery stores just outside the city limits on either end of River Oaks Boulevard. The major loss to the city is in lost tax revenue, not as an inconvenience to citizens.

The main driver of economics in the city of River Oaks has always been its proximity to the bomber plant and Carswell Air Force Base. The city has always benefited from employees and military personnel finding it convenient to live in River Oaks. With cuts in military budgets in the 1990s, the city's population slowed. Current mayor Darren Houk noted, "It kind of became a sleepy little town as everything grew away from the metroplex. Now, people are realizing how great it is to actually be close to Fort Worth. We're getting some of the people that moved away who are now seeking out neighborhoods like River Oaks. Close enough to the action but still have that small-town feel. As River Oaks grows, it is committed to maintaining the small-town charm of the community while bringing it back to its full potential." The City of River Oaks is committed to improving the quality of life for its citizens by attracting new businesses and strategically investing in projects supporting business development. The city, along with county and state entities, is developing a master plan to redo River Oaks Boulevard, incorporating modern urban designs that will improve access and safety and enhance economic development along the boulevard. The plan includes wider sidewalks, bike trails, benches, and beautification efforts.

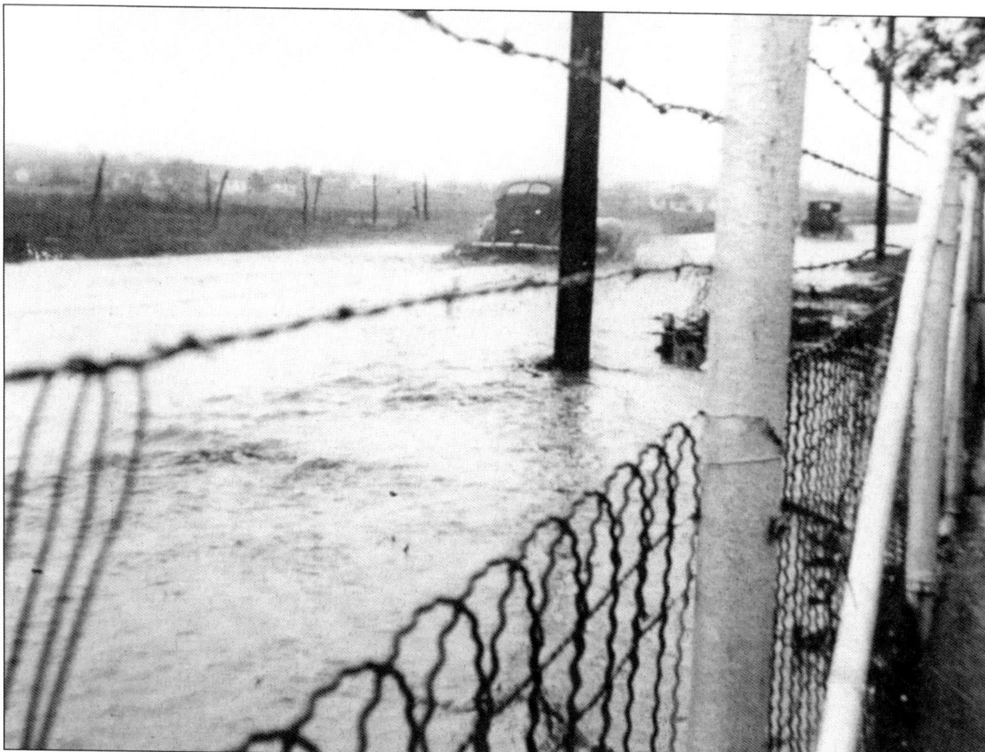

Before the construction of the modern-day levees around the Trinity River, much of River Oaks was susceptible to flooding. The flood of May 17, 1949, was among the worst in the city's history. The above photograph was taken from the Estes and Sons business on the corner of Yale Street and River Oaks Boulevard, then known as Highway 183. Yale Street still suffers from flooding and was nicknamed "Yale Canal." Flooding was so severe that Carswell sent over 100 military police into River Oaks and Fort Worth to aid citizens and prevent looting. The flood of 1949 led to extensive flood control measures. Levee improvements were made, and Marine Creek Lake and Cement Creek Lake were created. Both are tributaries of the Trinity River. Further improvements were started in the 1950s and 1960s. Lake Benbrook was created, the levees were bolstered, and the river channel was straightened and widened. (Both, courtesy of the River Oaks Historical Society.)

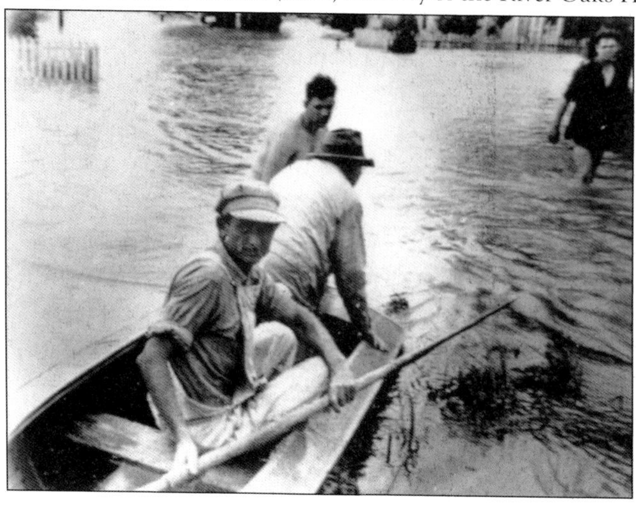

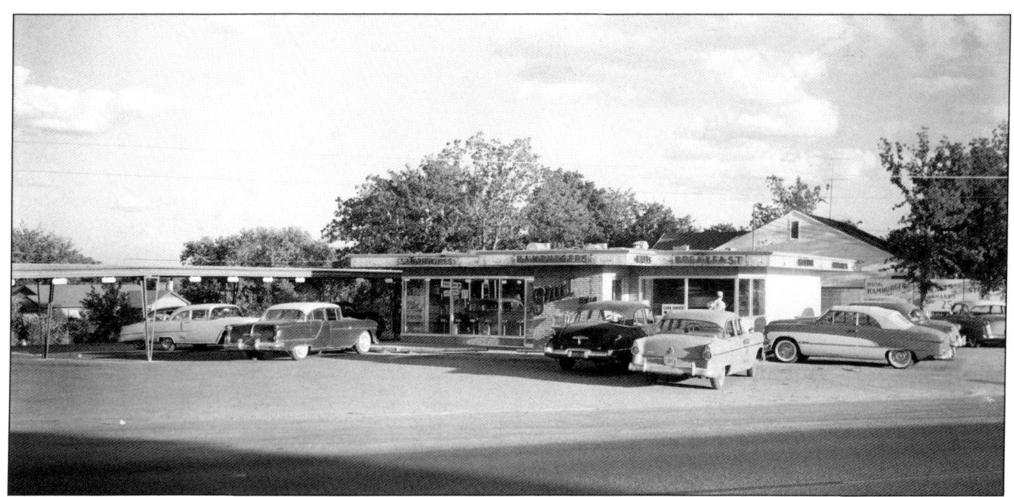

The Griddle System was a small fast-food hamburger chain in North Texas that started in the late 1950s. Most were closed by the mid-1960s, including this one on River Oaks Boulevard. A former employee remembers getting paid $1.00 an hour and working shifts that lasted from 11:00 a.m. until 2:00 a.m. It was their first and last job in the food industry. (Courtesy of the River Oaks Historical Society.)

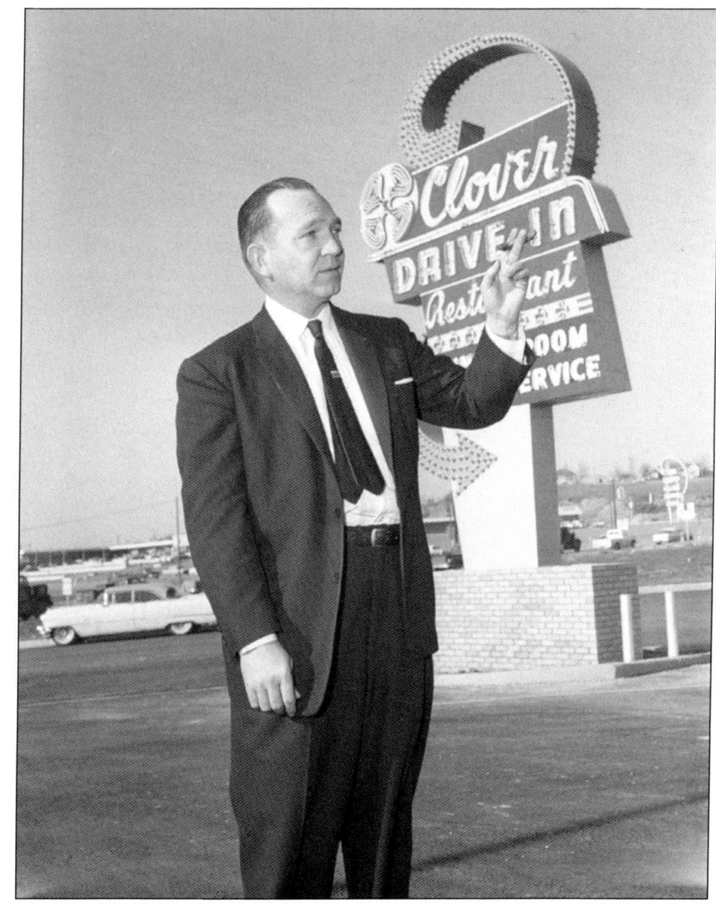

In this February 20, 1959, image, operator Herman Allen is at the opening of his new restaurant, Clover Drive-In, at 2028 Jacksboro Highway on the edge of River Oaks. The restaurant seated 140 people inside and had plenty of room for parked cars served by car hops. The drive-in remained open 24 hours, seven days a week. The Clover Drive-In was the second location of the burgeoning chain. Author Mark A. Nobles remembers tasting his first cherry Dr. Pepper at this location. It changed his young life. (Courtesy of the *Fort Worth Star-Telegram* Collection, University of Texas at Arlington Libraries.)

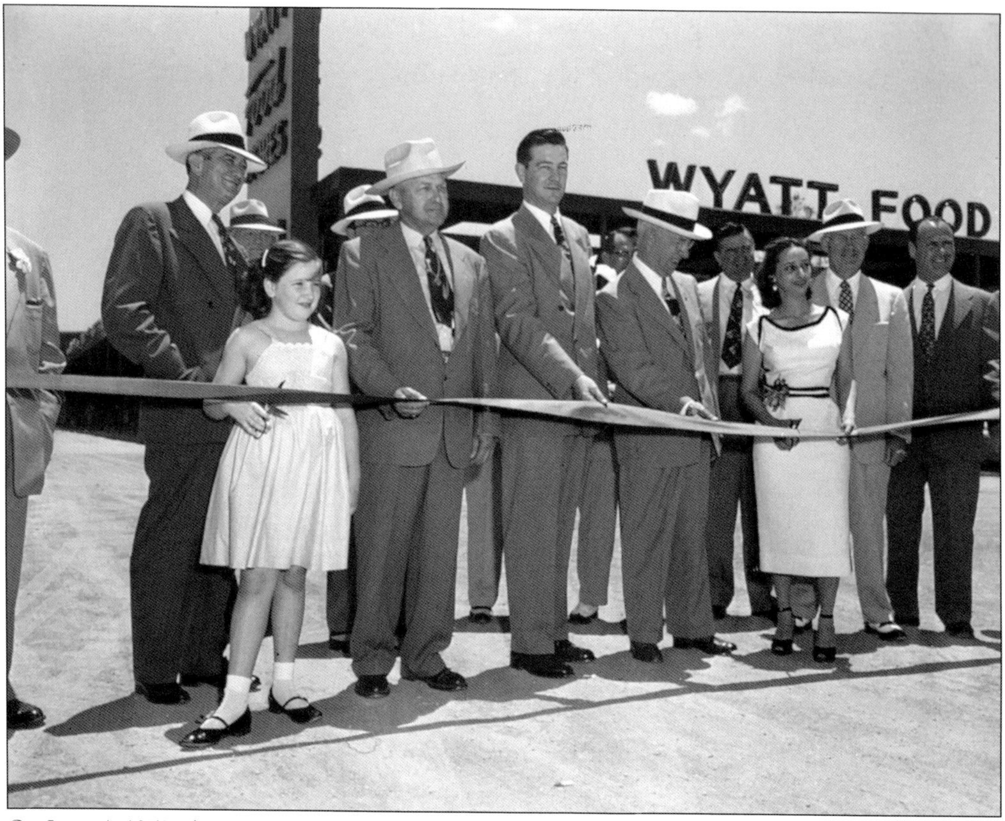

On June 4, 1952, the Fair Oaks Shopping Center opened on River Oaks Boulevard. In attendance were Jo Marie Lilly (left) and Jo Ann Sarazan (right) shown cutting the ribbon, formally opening the Fair Oaks Shopping Center. Others in the photograph are, from left to right, Lionel W. Bevan Sr., president of the Fair Oaks Building Corporation; Mayor J.R. Edwards; Artice Lilly, secretary of the corporation, and Erle White, president of White Auto Stores. (Courtesy of the *Fort Worth Star-Telegram* Collection, University of Texas at Arlington Libraries.)

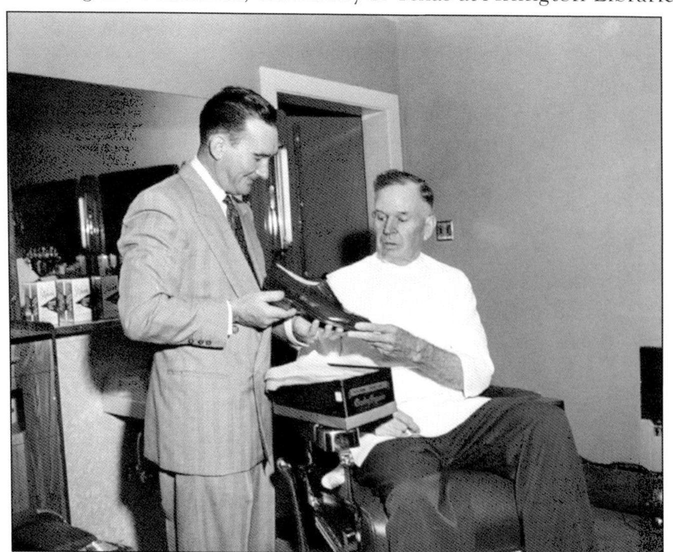

The shopping center featured the Fair Oaks Men's Shop, a barbershop and men's apparel combination business that was the first of its kind in Fort Worth. (Courtesy of the *Fort Worth Star-Telegram* Collection, University of Texas at Arlington Libraries.)

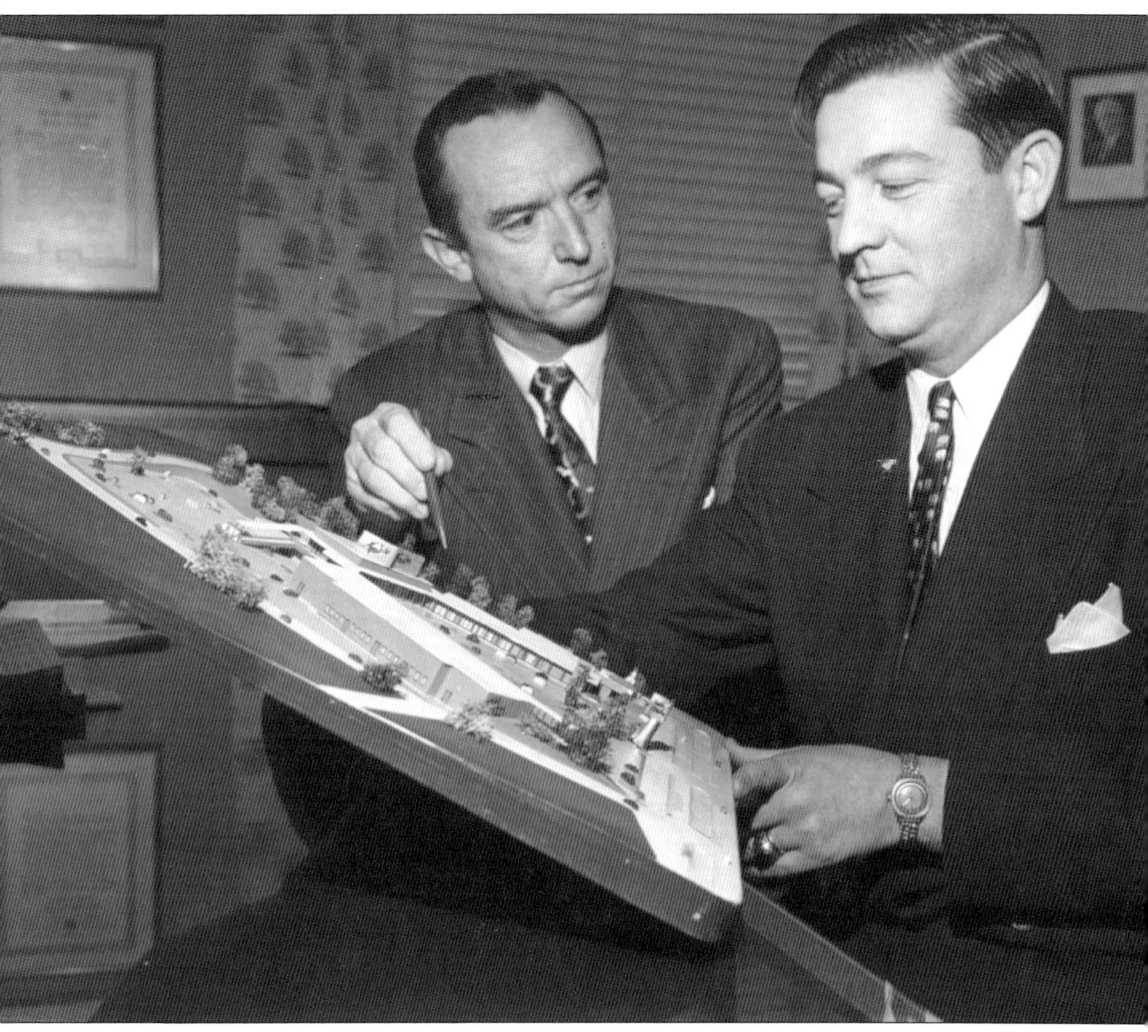

A.G. King (left) and Lionel Bevan Jr. are pictured examining a scale model of the Fair Oaks Shopping Center. King was with W.G. Clarkson & Company, architects, and Bevan was president of Fair Oaks Building Corporation. The photograph is dated January 17, 1951. (Courtesy of the *Fort Worth Star-Telegram* Collection, University of Texas at Arlington Libraries.)

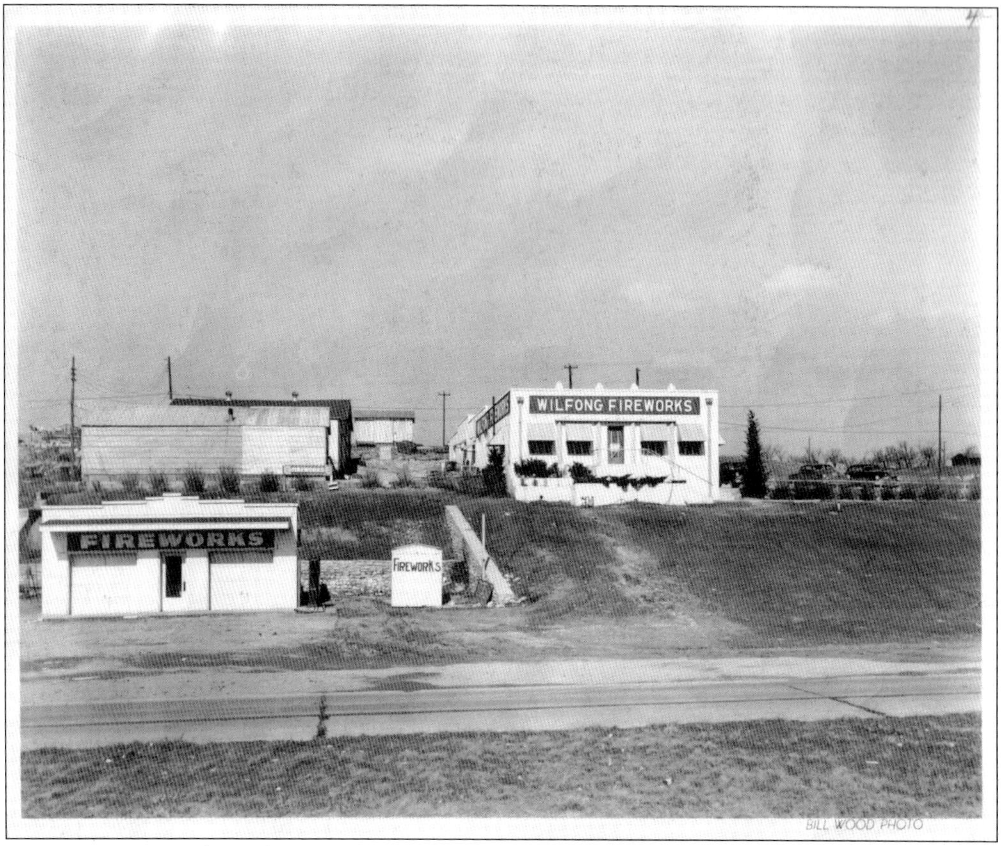

On June 19, 1953, the Wilfong Fireworks Company on Jacksboro Highway, on the eastern border of River Oaks, exploded, creating a mushroom cloud that could be seen for miles. It was the height of the Cold War, and since the factory was located close to Carswell Air Force Base, local residents thought a nuclear bomb had exploded over the area. Several people were injured, and nearby homes and apartments were destroyed or damaged, but no one was killed. Employees of Wilfong credited this to strict safety measures employed by the company. (Courtesy of the River Oaks Historical Society.)

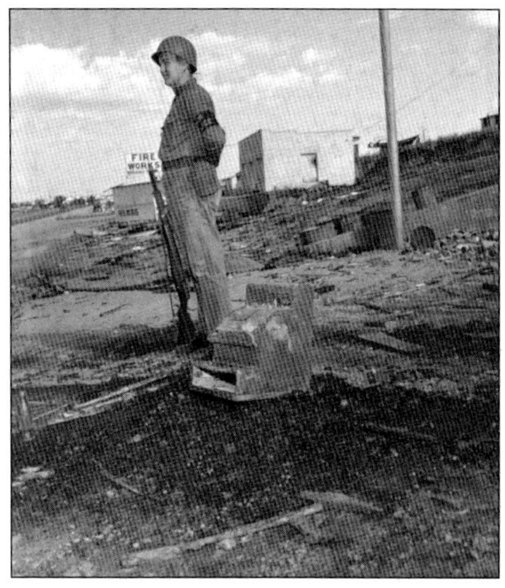

A1c. Walter Crone of the Carswell Air Police is shown over the blast area of the Wilfong Fireworks Company. A charred cash register lies forgotten along Jacksboro Highway. Not only has Carswell been an economic driver for the city of River Oaks, the base has never hesitated to send funds and/or manpower to aid the city in times of need and disaster. (Courtesy of the *Fort Worth Star-Telegram* Collection, University of Texas at Arlington Libraries.)

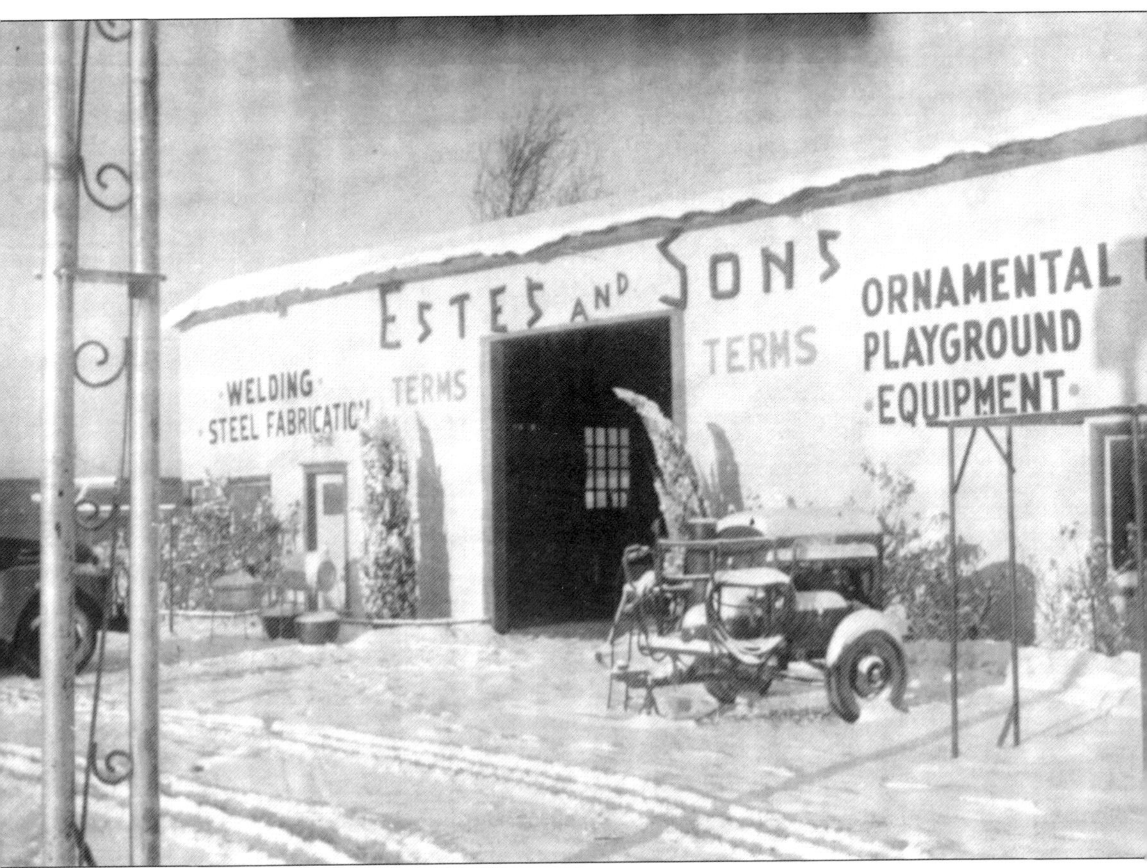

Located at Yale Street and River Oaks Boulevard, Estes and Sons Welding and Steel Fabricating is a great example of the blue-collar businesses that have always called River Oaks home. It is pictured here in an undated, snow-covered winter photograph. Mr. Estes and his sons fabricated ornamental iron or swing sets for River Oaks residents and even offered credit at reasonable terms. (Courtesy of the River Oaks Historical Society.)

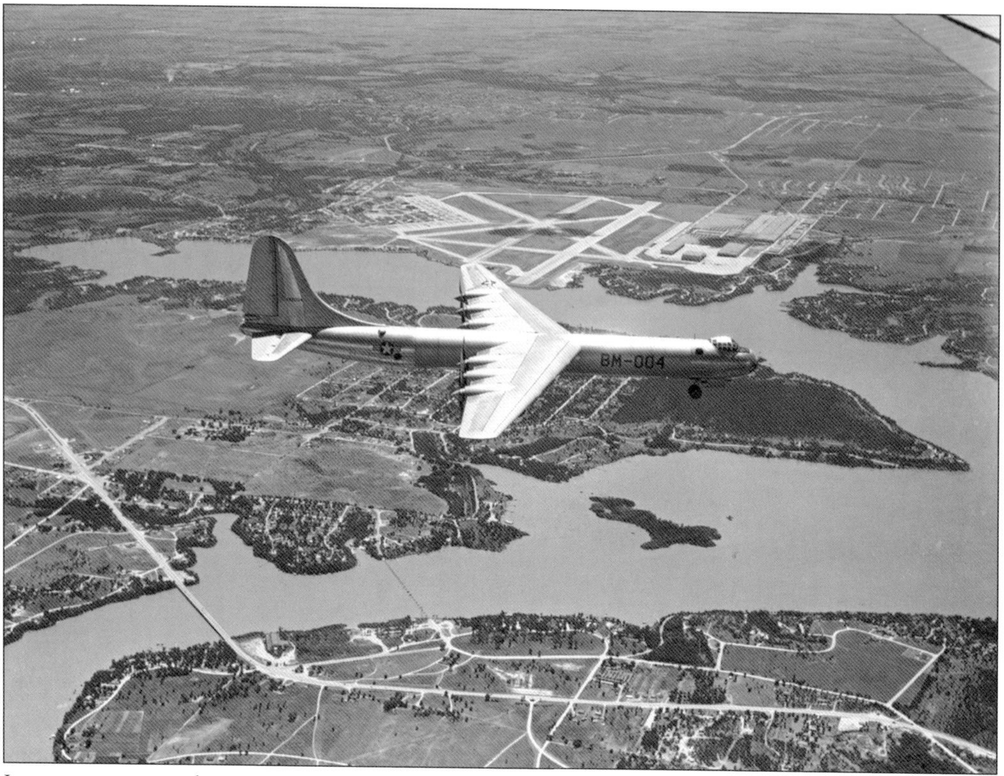

Living next to a military installation has many benefits but also comes with hazards. The B-36 was one of the largest bombers ever built and often rattled and broke windows in River Oaks. There is always the possibility of a mishap with planes landing and taking off. Fortunately, no major damage to the city has been recorded. (Both, courtesy of the *Fort Worth Star-Telegram* Collection, University of Texas at Arlington Libraries.)

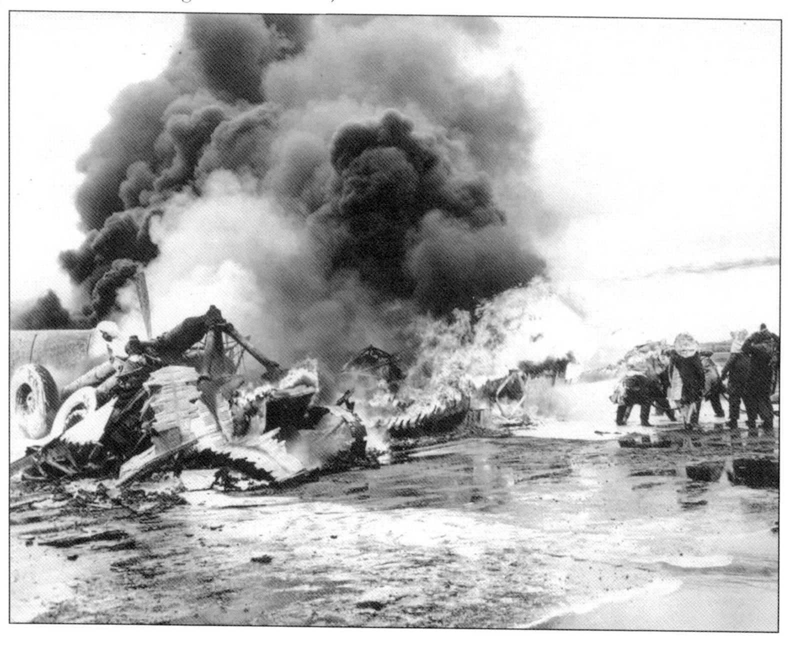

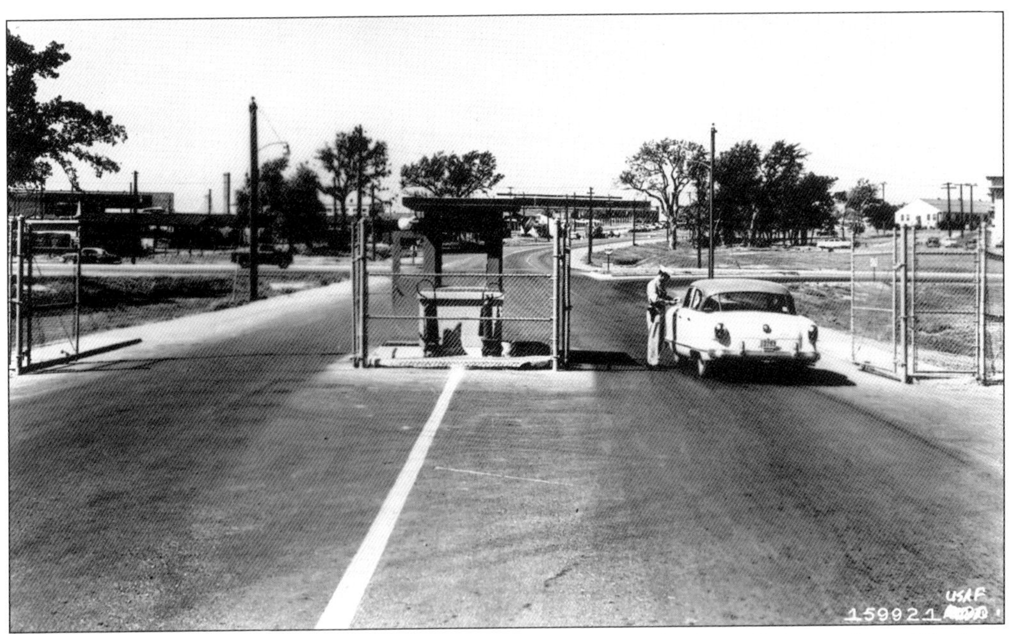

The East Gate is the main entrance to Carswell Air Force Base for River Oaks residents. The base was named after Medal of Honor recipient Maj. Horace S. Carswell Jr. (1916–1944). In 1940, the City of Fort Worth filed an application with the Civil Aeronautics Administration asking for a primary pilot training airfield for the Army Air Corps. In May, Gen. Jacob E. Fickel visited Fort Worth on an inspection visit. At the same time, the Fort Worth Chamber of Commerce was trying to convince aircraft manufacturers to build an aircraft assembly plant in the area. Consolidated Aircraft, wanting to build in the area, suggested to the Air Corps that they jointly build an airfield adjacent to the heavy bomber plant they wanted to build in Fort Worth. On June 16, 1941, Pres. Franklin D. Roosevelt approved $1.75 million to construct an airfield next to the Consolidated manufacturing plant. The Army wanted to have the airfield ready quickly before the plant was put into production, and construction of the "Lake Worth Bomber Plant Airport" began almost immediately. (Both, courtesy of the *Fort Worth Star-Telegram* Collection, University of Texas at Arlington Libraries.)

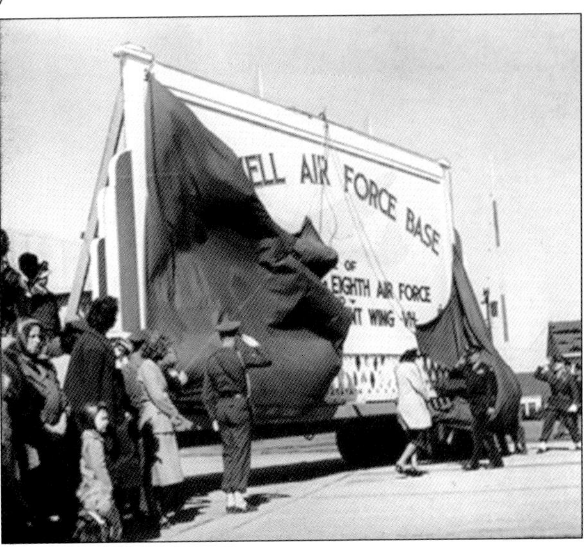

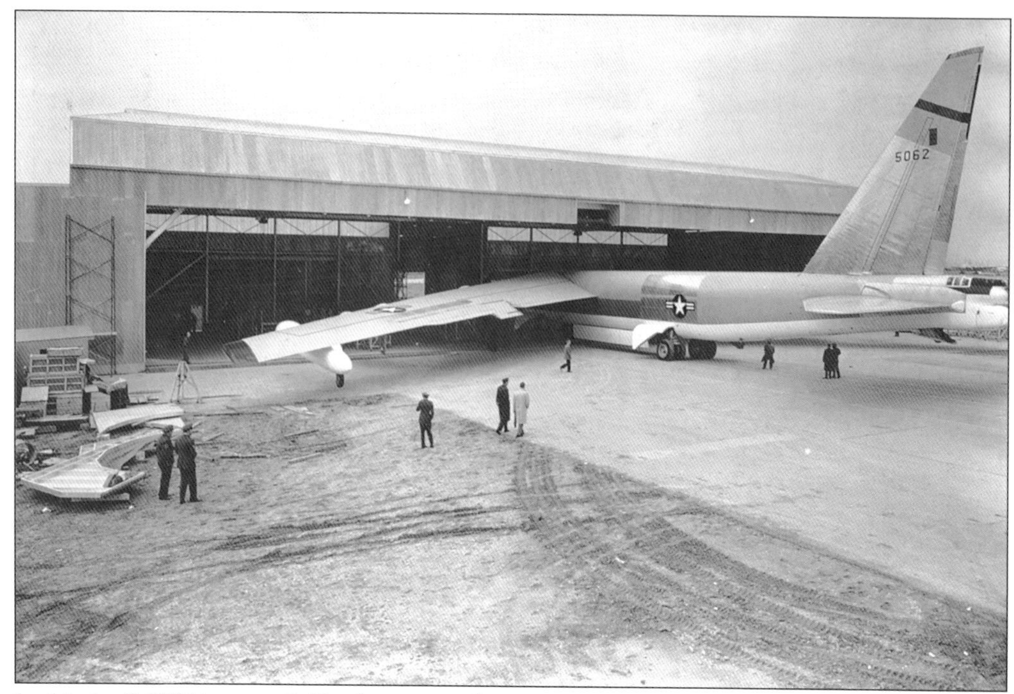

In this April 1957 image, a B-52 is being towed into a maintenance dock structure built specifically to fit the full wingspan of the bomber. During the 1992 Air Force reorganization, the Strategic Air Command was disestablished. Carswell's 7th Bomb Wing and its B-52Hs were assigned to the newly created Air Combat Command. Carswell Air Force Base was selected for closure under the Defense Base Closure and Realignment Act of 1990. As part of the closure, the 7th Bomb Wing from Carswell was relocated to Dyess Air Force Base. (Courtesy of the *Fort Worth Star-Telegram* Collection, University of Texas at Arlington Libraries.)

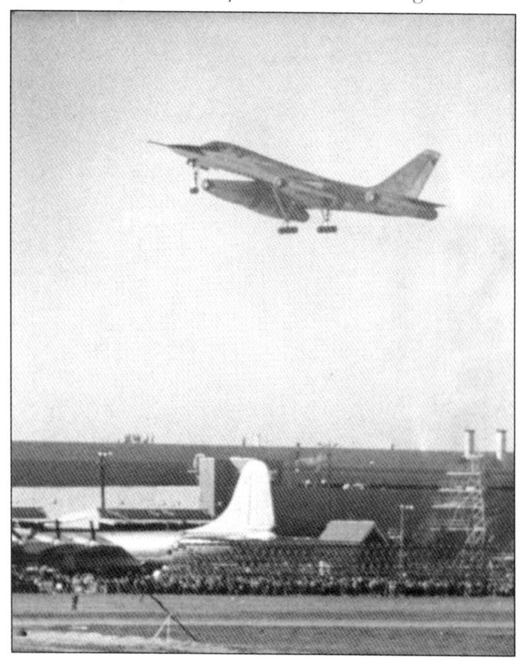

During a test flight in November 1956, a Convair B-58 Hustler with landing gear deployed flies over the Convair factory with a parked B-36 bomber as a crowd of spectators looks on. In 1993, Congress directed the establishment of the nation's first joint reserve base under the Base Realignment and Closure authority. Carswell ceased US Air Force (USAF) active duty operations on September 30, 1993. On October 1, 1993, the Air Force Reserve's 301st Fighter Wing assumed base responsibilities, establishing Carswell as Carswell Air Reserve Station. The USAF ended operational control of Carswell on September 30, 1994, with the transfer of the property to the US Navy. (Courtesy of the *Fort Worth Star-Telegram* Collection, University of Texas at Arlington Libraries.)

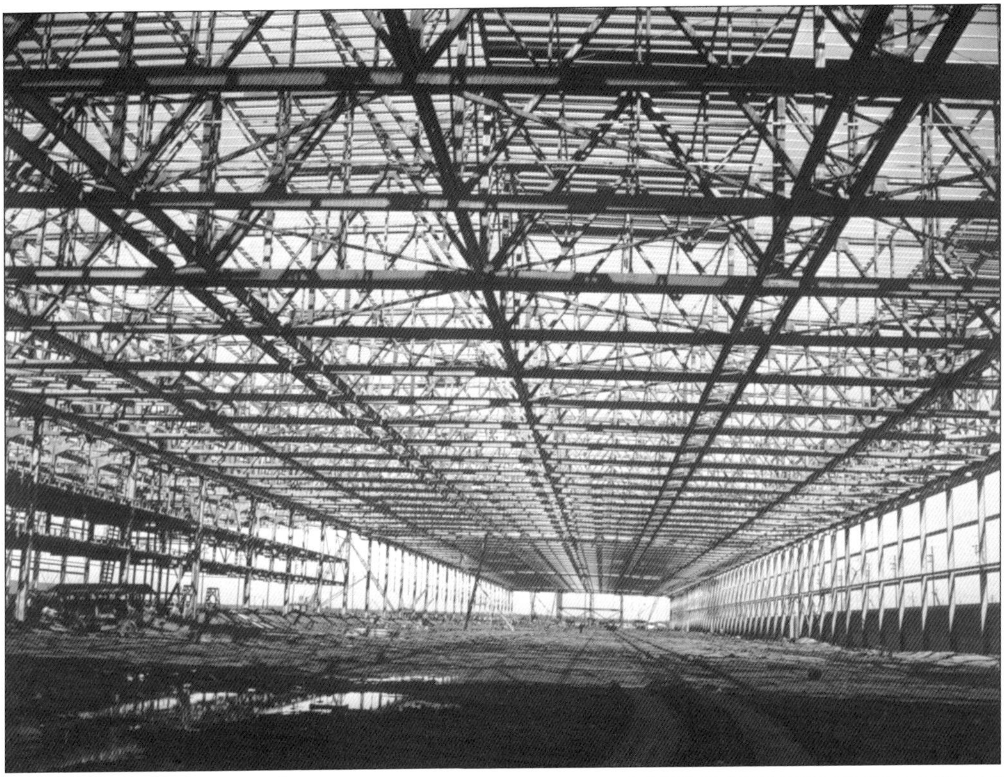

In June 1941, construction began on Government Aircraft Plant 4 in Fort Worth. In December of that same year, the Japanese bombed Pearl Harbor, starting the largest arms buildup in history. Construction of Government Aircraft Plant 4 took less than nine months. When Consolidated took over the plant on January 1, 1942, it hired a workforce of 25,000 people, mostly local farmers with limited mechanical skills. The first B-24 was built and delivered less than one year after the April 1941 ground-breaking ceremony. The last Fort Worth B-24 rolled through the doors of the assembly building on December 26, 1944. A few months, earlier the War Department had announced that Government Aircraft Plant 4 would switch production to the new B-32 Dominator. After a short ceremony commemorating the last of the 2,743 B-24s and 291 C-87s built at the plant, employees resumed work on the new B-32s already filling the production line. (Both, courtesy of the *Fort Worth Star-Telegram* Collection, University of Texas at Arlington Libraries.)

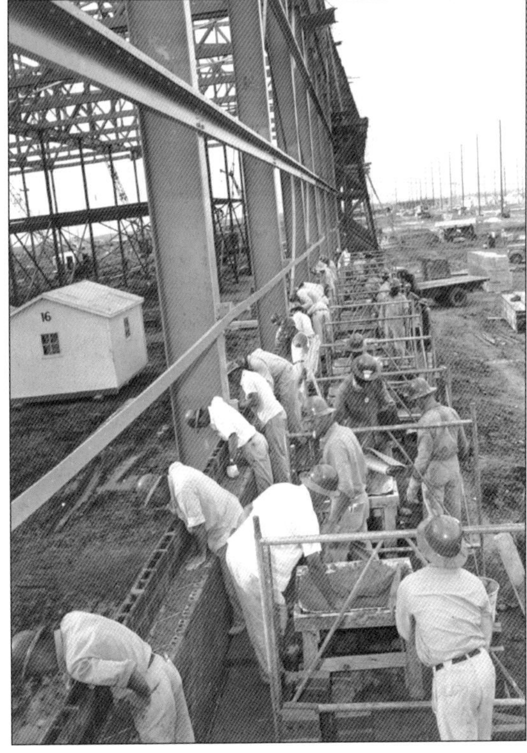

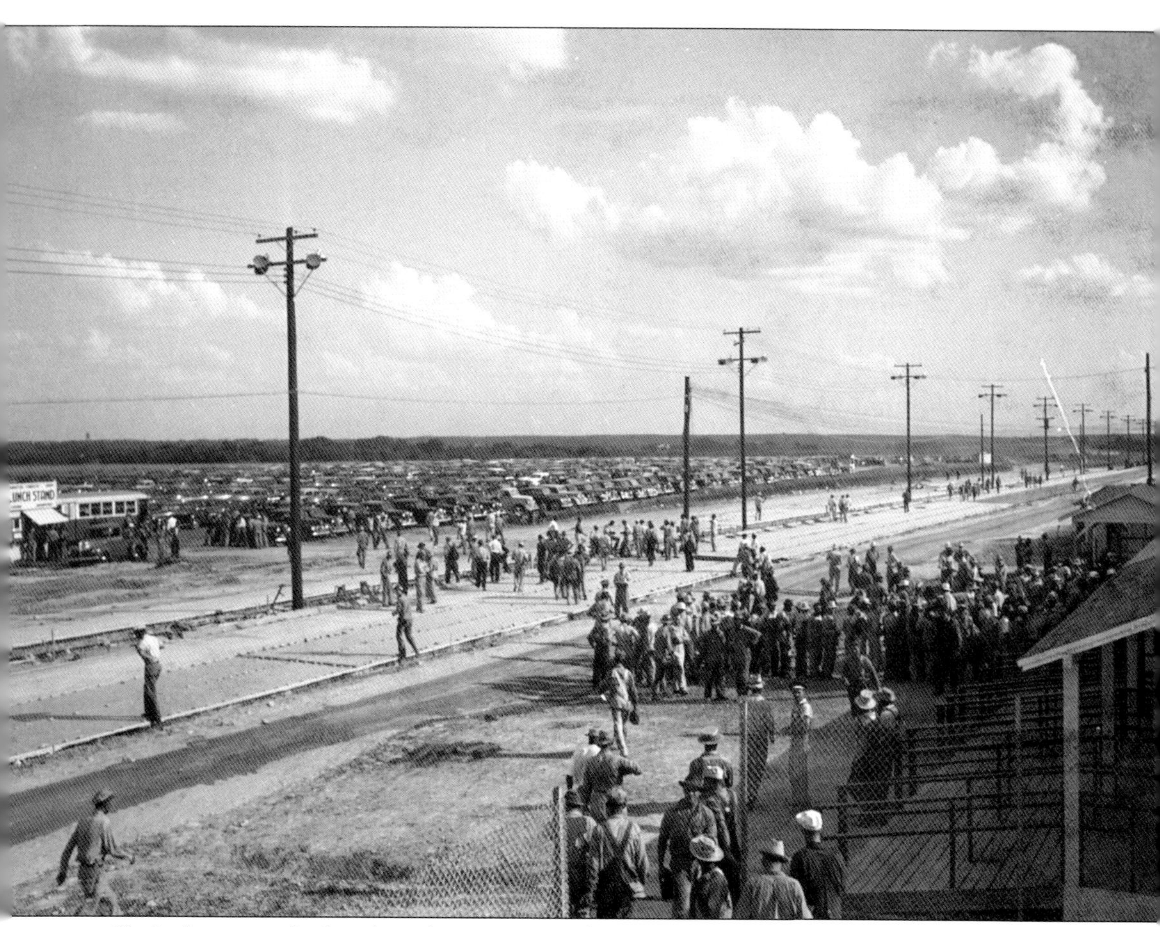

Shift change at the bomber plant is pictured on September 19, 1941. To satisfy the blackout conditions necessary during the war, the plant had no windows. This meant the plant needed a lot of lights and air-conditioning to combat the hot Texas summers. The electric bills at the time were equivalent to $282,000 per month in today's dollars. More than 30,000 people worked at Air Force Plant 4 during World War II. (Courtesy of the *Fort Worth Star-Telegram* Collection, University of Texas at Arlington Libraries.)

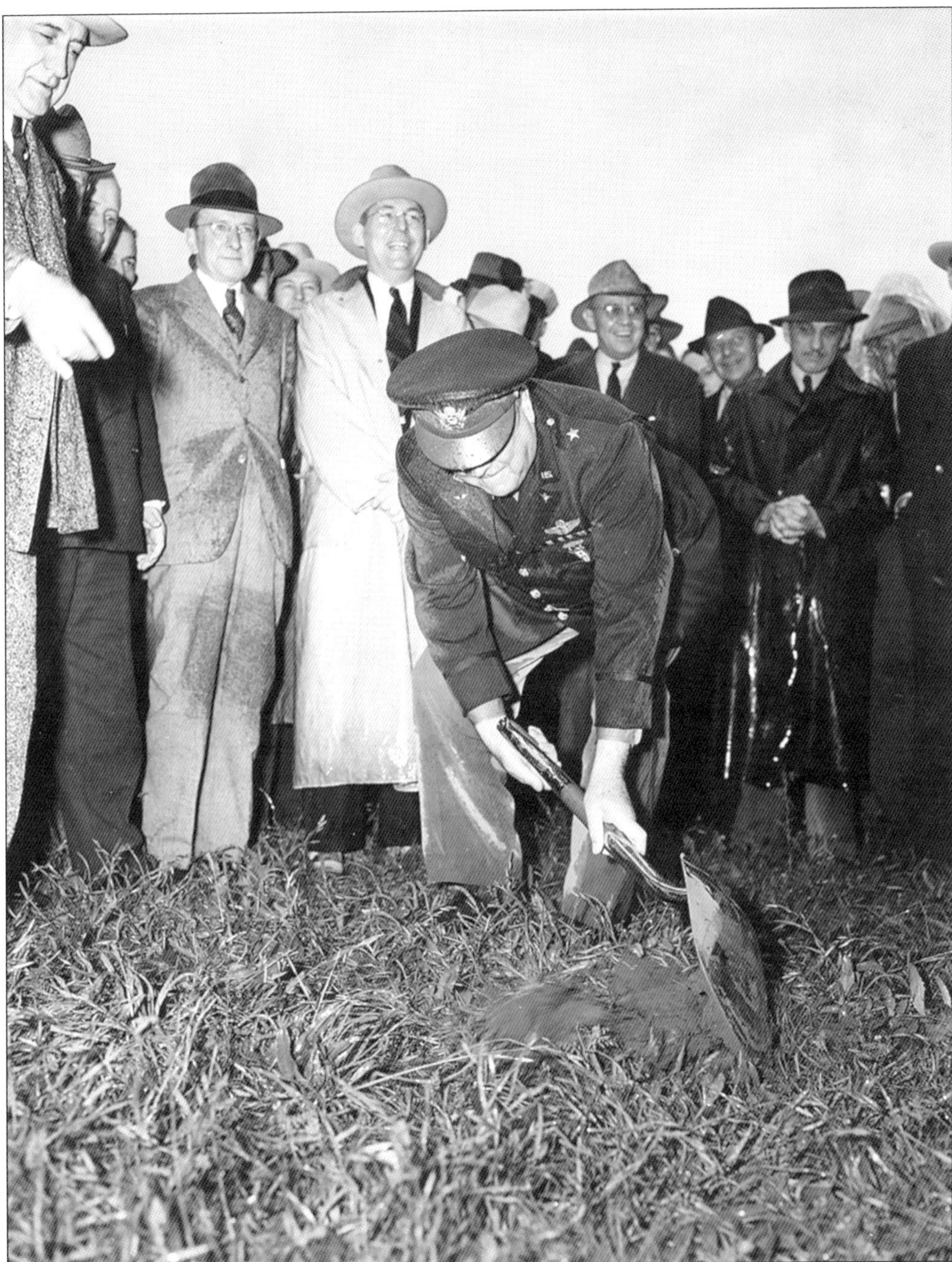

At ground-breaking ceremonies for the Lake Worth bomber plant on April 18, 1941, in Fort Worth, Brig. Gen. G.C. Brant turns the first spade. He is watched by, from left to right, Amon Carter, Sam Bothwell, Albert S. Low, Col. Lawrence Westbrook, and Col. S.L. Scott. Consolidated sold to General Dynamics and General Dynamics sold its aircraft manufacturing interests to Lockheed Martin. Plant 4 is now Lockheed Martin Aeronautics' divisional headquarters. Today, the F-35 Lightning II Joint Strike Fighter is being produced on the assembly line at the plant. (Courtesy of the *Fort Worth Star-Telegram* Collection, University of Texas at Arlington Libraries.)

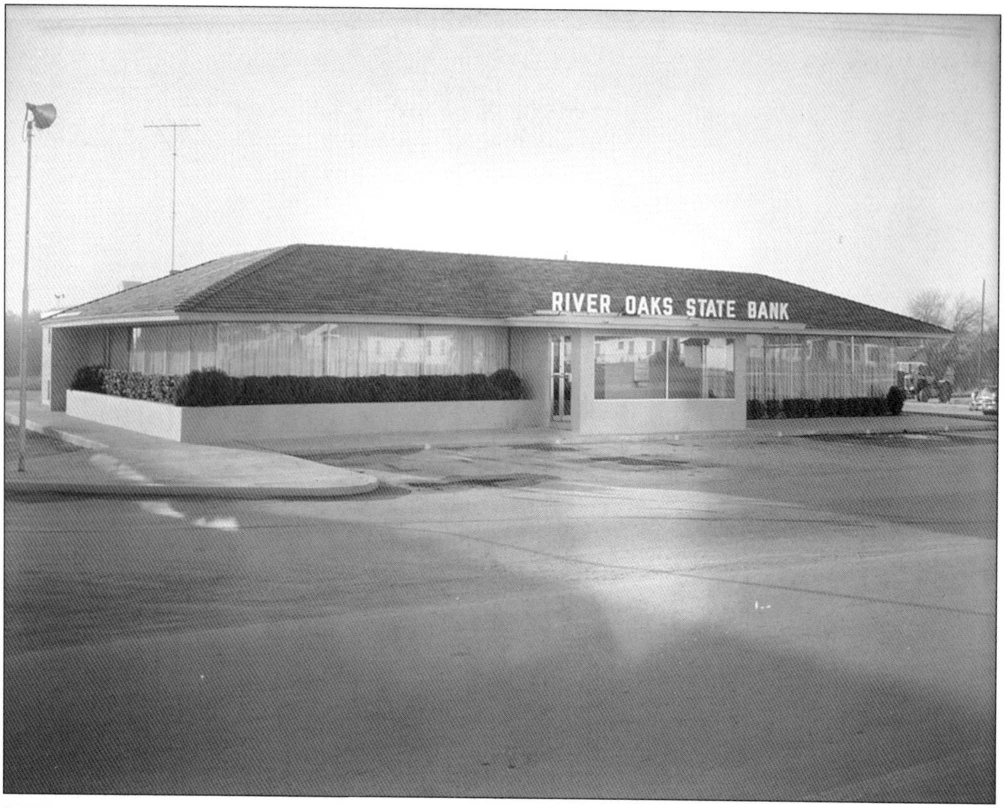

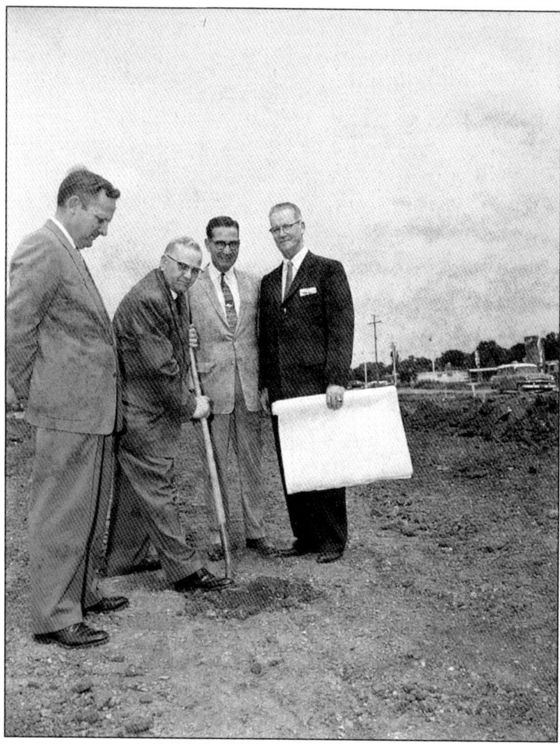

River Oaks has always been business-friendly and welcoming to entrepreneurs. In the days before banking conglomerates, River Oaks attracted independent banks to help finance new businesses and serve the citizens of the city. River Oaks State Bank and Securities Bank were both located in River Oaks. (Both, courtesy of the *Fort Worth Star-Telegram* Collection, University of Texas at Arlington Libraries.)

Seven

Auto-Racing Culture

With a high number of River Oaks residents being associated with the military or aircraft manufacturing, it is of little surprise that these people would have a need for speed and a bit of a reckless nature. The city of River Oaks has a long history of car and motorcycle racing clubs and has produced more than its fair share of prominent drivers, both male and female. Tarrant County and North Texas in general have a storied motorsports history, and there was no shortage of racetracks in the area for these young men and women to test their meddle. Drag racing saw a huge boom in popularity in the late 1940s, when an influx of mechanically minded men returned from World War II. They soon turned their interests to modifying older cars to see how fast they could make them go. As the drag racing culture spread, cities and towns not only here but across the country felt the negative effects of street racing, which pushed folks to find a safer place to race. During the 1950s, the proliferation of car clubs inspired the construction of drag strips. The first purpose-built drag strip, known as the Santa Anna Drags, appeared in Southern California. Soon enough, drag strips began popping up across the country, including several in Tarrant County. One could bet the boys from River Oaks were regular contestants and brought home trophies to prove it. At one point, there were three different car clubs in River Oaks, and out of these groups sprang an International Motor Sports Hall of Fame member and an International Hot Rod Association Hall of Fame member—not bad for a tiny city that has never had a population much greater than 8,000. Drivers from River Oaks took their skills from backroads around Carswell Air Force Base to drag strips, NASCAR ovals, and even the "Brickyard" of the Indianapolis Motor Speedway. There are likely more car haulers and overstuffed trophy cases in River Oaks than in any other city of comparable size.

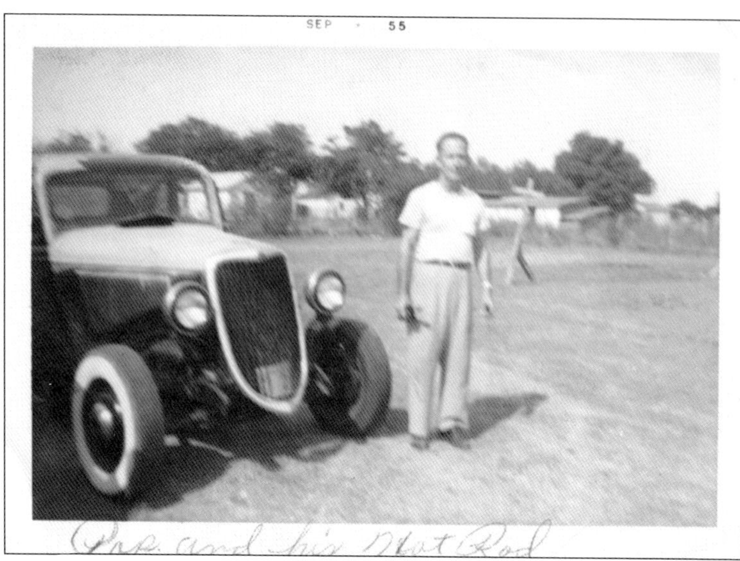

Hugh Willett, owner of Willett's Corner, River Oaks' first commercial area, proudly stands next to his hot rod in an undated photograph on his property. While some car enthusiasts drove their way to fame, others, like Willett, simply derived pleasure from the sport as a pleasant diversion. (Courtesy of Shirley Bunker.)

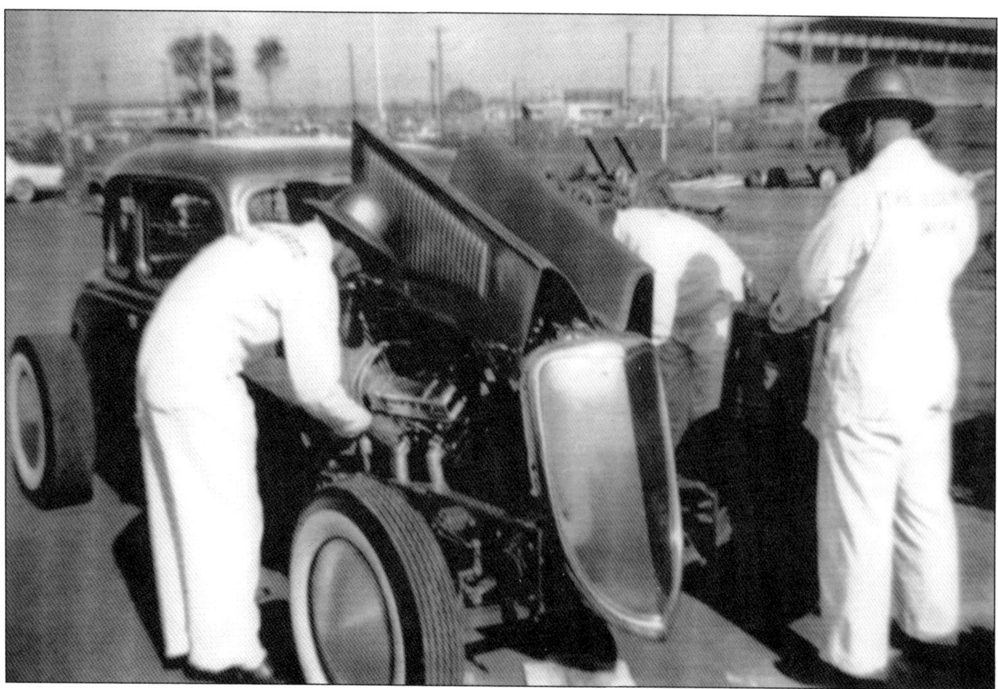

Two men from a car club called the Golden Rods are working on their car before a race. The Idlers had a lot of competition, but the rivalries only made everyone work harder. (Courtesy of Linda Claridge.)

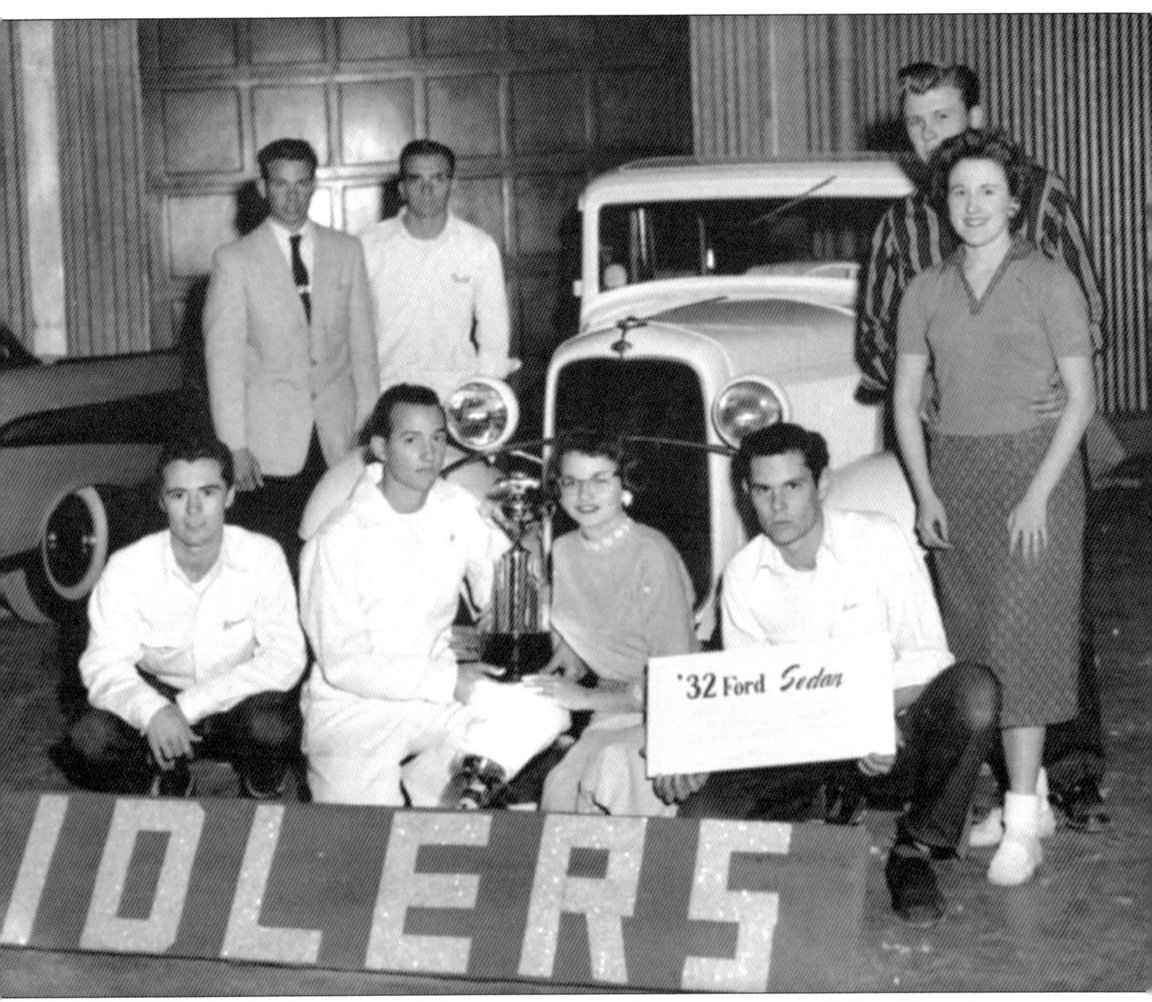

The Idlers were one of three car clubs in River Oaks beginning in the 1950s. The clubs were groups that met to help each other build and work on their individual cars, share tools and expertise, and have a common work area. As the racing culture galvanized and came together, the racers left the danger of street racing to formal racing on tracks. (Courtesy of Jack Atkinson.)

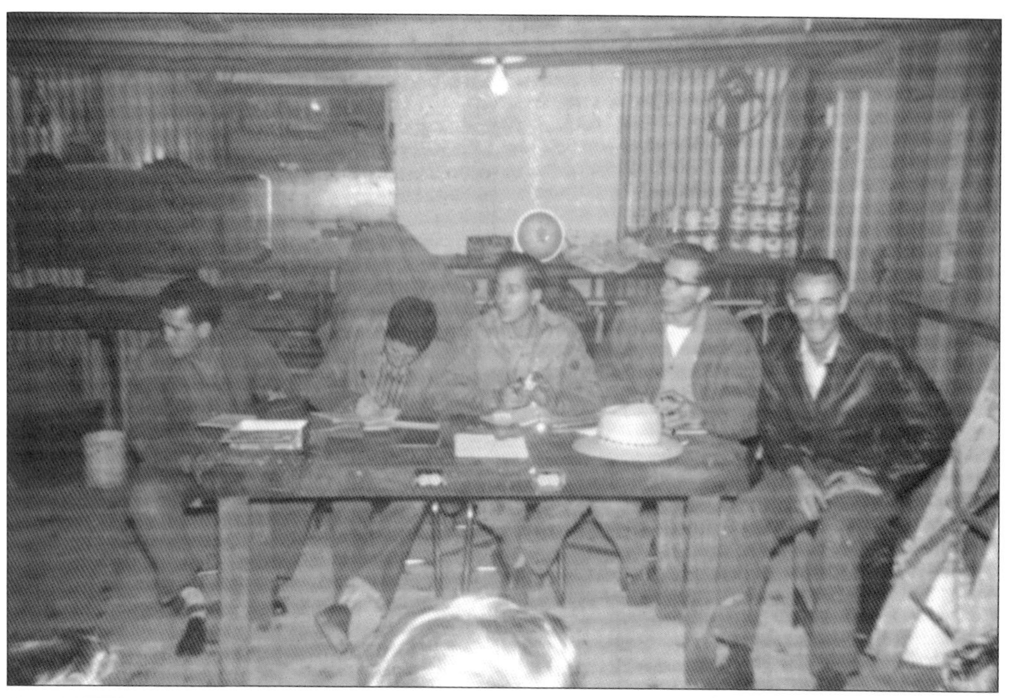

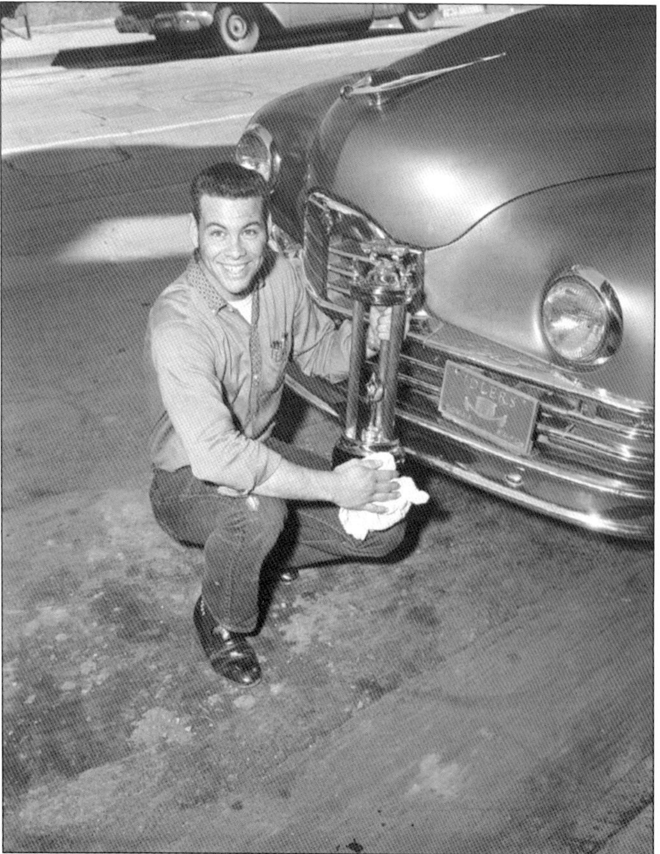

The Idlers hold a meeting in their garage. Seated from left to right are Hank Dixon, Ed Ousley, Bobby Loyd, Gerald Graham, and Jack Parnell. Car clubs were not groups of people wrenching on jalopies and drinking lemonade—officers were elected, dues were paid, and rules were made to be followed. (Courtesy of Linda Claridge)

Jack Atkinson is shown holding a trophy in front of his 1950 Packard. While still a student at Castleberry High School, Atkinson entered the car in his first race in 1955. He won first place at the Tarrant County Modified Auto Association open drags. Atkinson had a long career in drag racing and was mayor of River Oaks as well as serving on the city council. (Courtesy of the *Fort Worth Star-Telegram* Collection, University of Texas at Arlington Libraries.)

J.W. Claridge began his love for racing in 1955 at the Eagle Mountain Lake National Guard Base drag racetrack. He won the Ninth Annual World Drag Racing Championship in his class in 1963 at Green Valley Raceway. In 1983, *Car Craft* magazine nominated his team for its All-Star Drag Racing Team of the Year, and he was inducted into the National Hot Rod Association (NHRA) Division 4 Drag Racing Hall of Fame in 1987, the same year that the Texas Senate presented a resolution to the Claridge Racing Team for its contribution to the sport of drag racing. His wife, Linda Claridge, won over 40 awards before it was popular for women to drag race. When their son Johnny turned 17, he started drag racing, and he continued to race for 33 years. When Johnny started racing, J.W. became his tutor and mechanic. They began crisscrossing six states chasing NHRA division points. In 1982, Johnny placed fourth in the world, and he went on to win back-to-back Super Gas titles among his numerous awards. (Both, courtesy of Linda Claridge.)

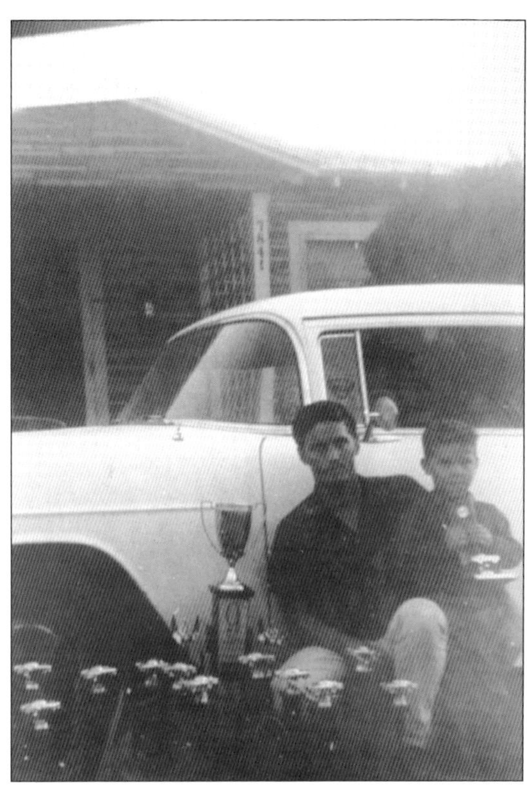

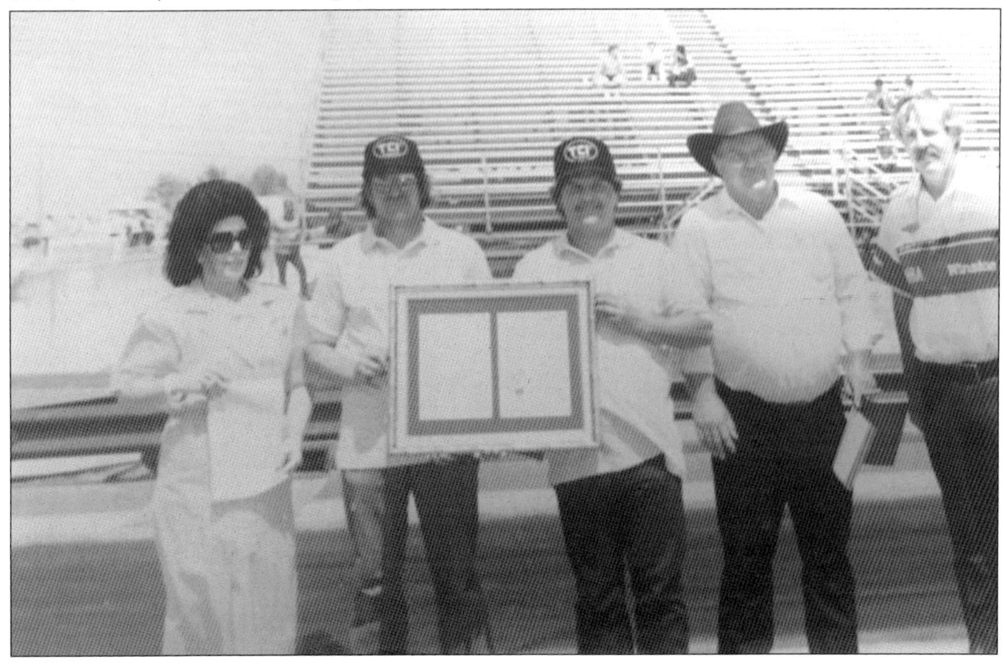

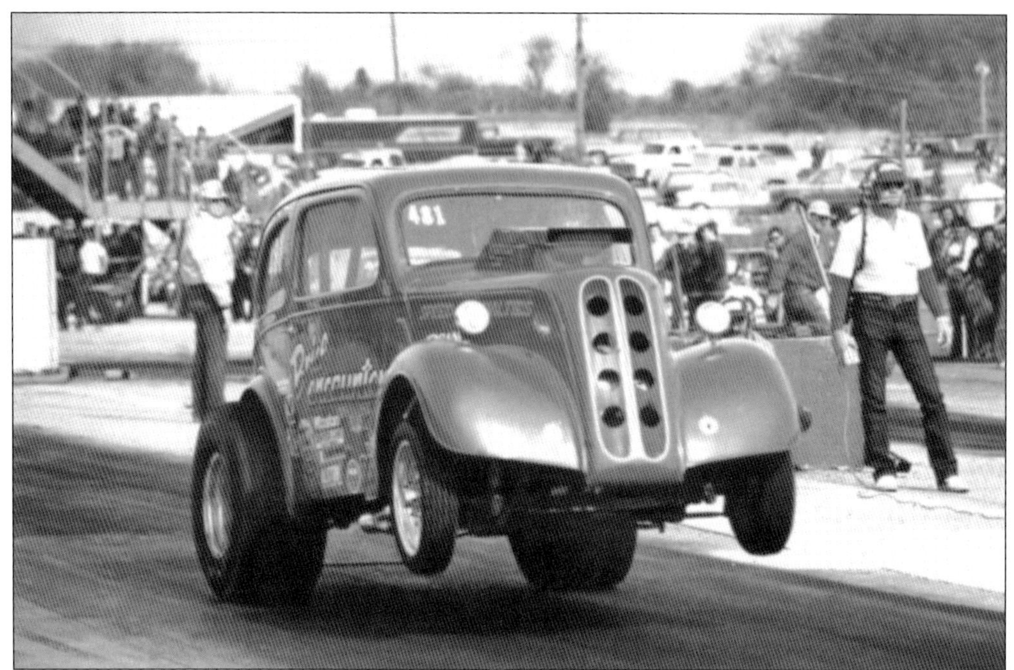

J.W. Claridge is widely known in the racing field for his ability to answer questions regarding American-made cars with high-performance engines. This outstanding man has unique mechanical talents that have been an invaluable aid not only to the Claridge Racing Team but also to many other racing participants. J.W. passed this talent on to Johnny, who is currently a supervisor for Reher-Morrison Racing Engines. In over 50 years of drag racing, the Claridge family has campaigned a 1950 Mercury, 1955 Chevrolet, 1948 Anglia, 1927 Roadster, Dragster, Chevy II, and 1969 Camaro. Throughout the years, drag racing has given the Claridge Racing Team an opportunity to develop its competitive and winning skills while spending time together. During the 2009 season, race fans looked for the team's 1967 Camaro with its new paint job and orange racing stripes. (Both, courtesy of Linda Claridge.)

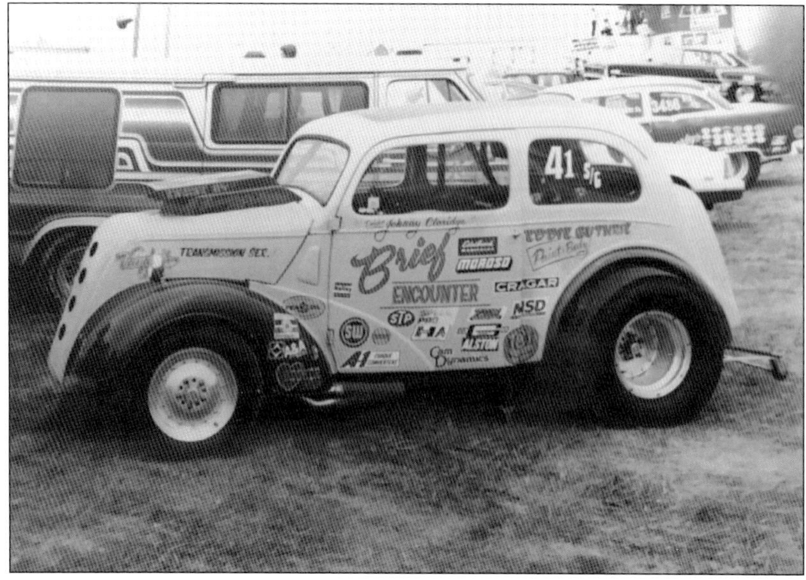

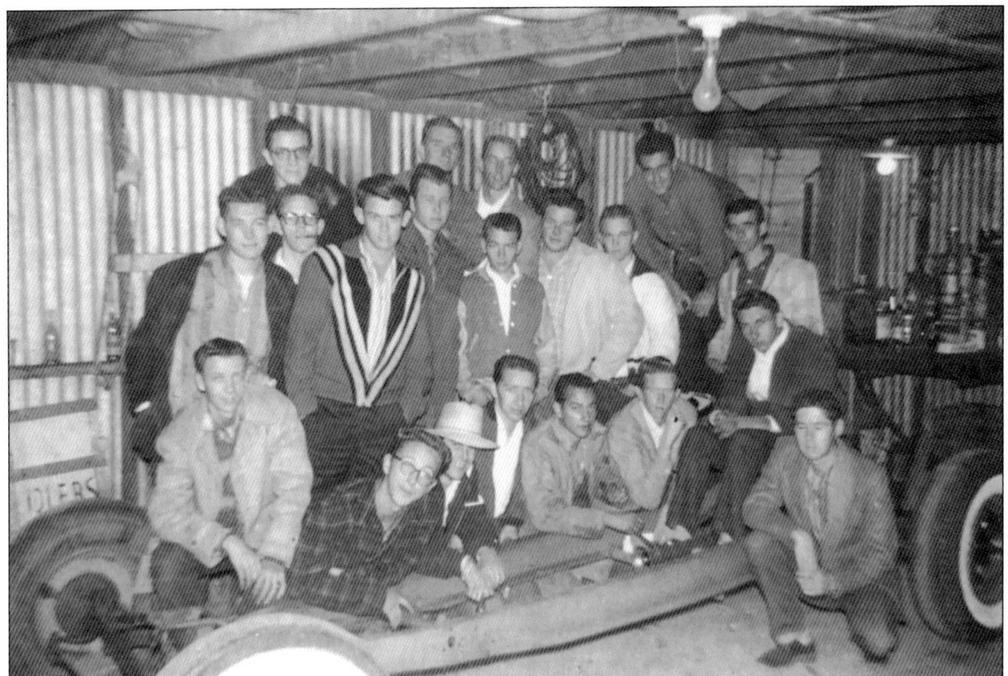

Pictured in November 1957, the Idlers are in their workshop on Ohio Gardens Road. Johnny Rutherford, top row, third from left wearing a white shirt, and the car club are reportedly shown with the chassis of Rutherford's first-ever race car, a 1932 Chevy Coupe. Rutherford's interest in racing started at an early age in River Oaks. His father, like many in River Oaks, was employed in aviation but was also interested in race cars. Young Rutherford grew up around airplanes, boats, and anything else that moved fast. One fateful Saturday night when he was nine years old, Rutherford's father took him to a midget race, and something clicked. He knew he wanted to be a race car driver. After that, everything was racing related. (Courtesy of Linda Claridge.)

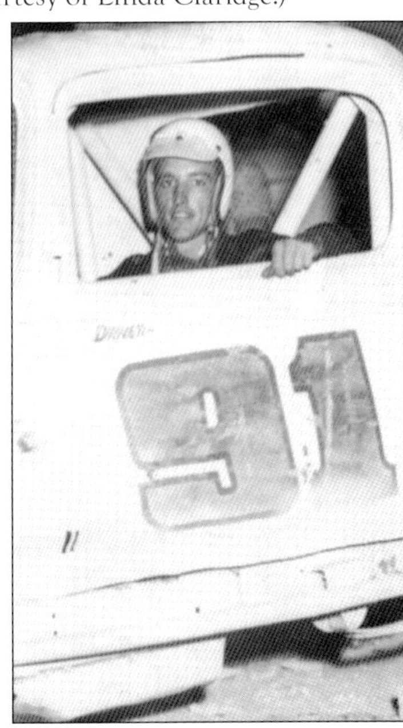

Johnny Rutherford is pictured at the Devil's Speed Bowl in Dallas in the late 1950s. Rutherford credits the Idlers with helping him build his first race car and taking him to the Devil's Bowl Speedway for his first races. Rutherford only raced in the North Texas area for a year and a half before moving to the Midwest to race in the International Motor Contest Association sprint car division. By 1963, he was making his first start at the Indianapolis 500. Rutherford won his first Indy 500 in 1974 and is one of only ten drivers to win the race more than three times. Rutherford won in 1974, 1976, and for the last time in 1980. (Courtesy of American Heritage Auctions.)

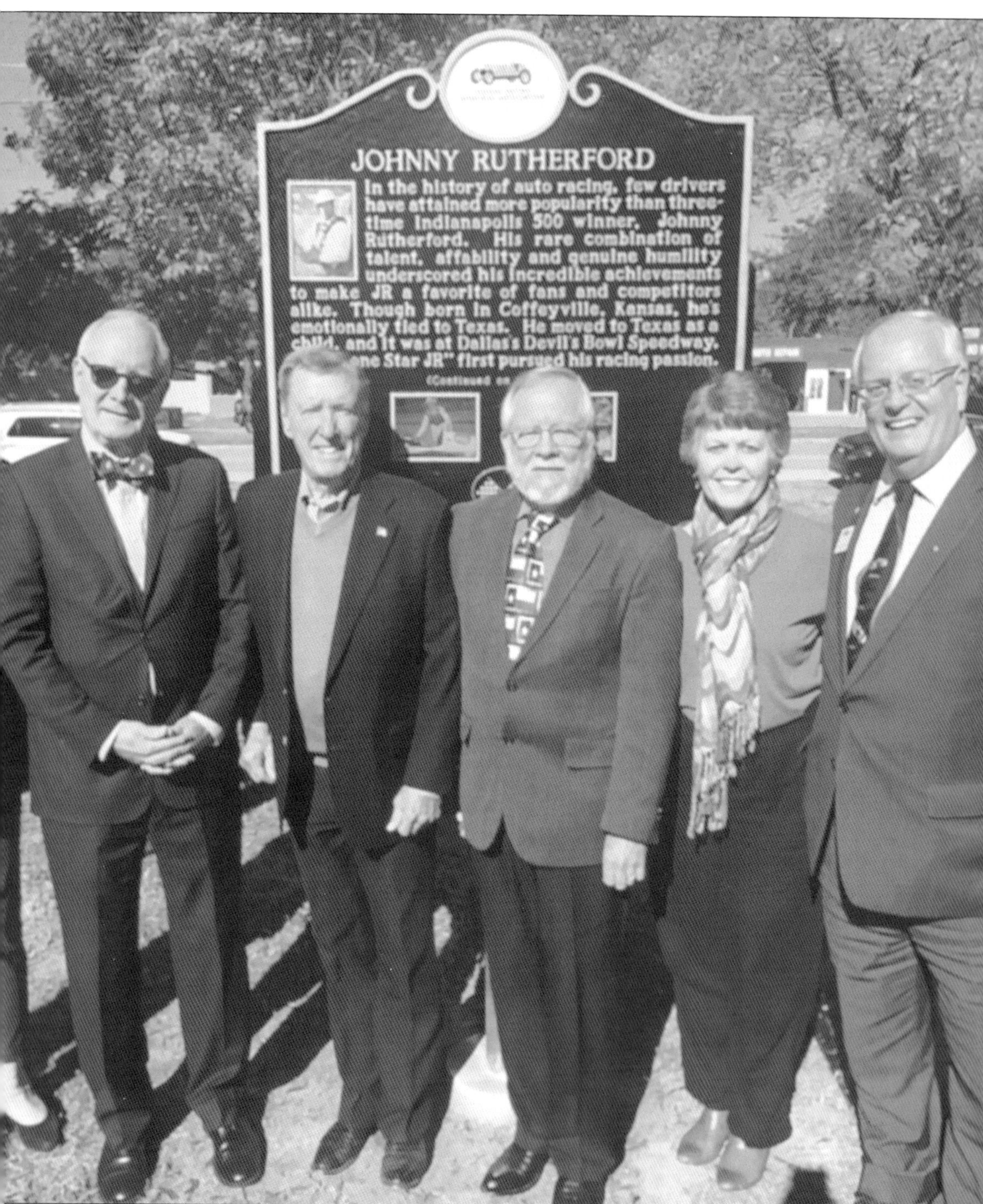

The City of River Oaks honored Johnny Rutherford by renaming Coates Park Lone Star JR Park. "Lone Star JR" is Rutherford's nickname. The American Racing Memorial Association (ARMA) sponsored the historic marker. In attendance were, from left to right, the marker's sponsor Bill Blaylock, Johnny Rutherford, River Oaks mayor Herman Earwood, ARMA member Therese Eutsler, and ARMA cofounder Mark Eutsler. (Courtesy of the Crawford, Indiana, *Journal Review*.)

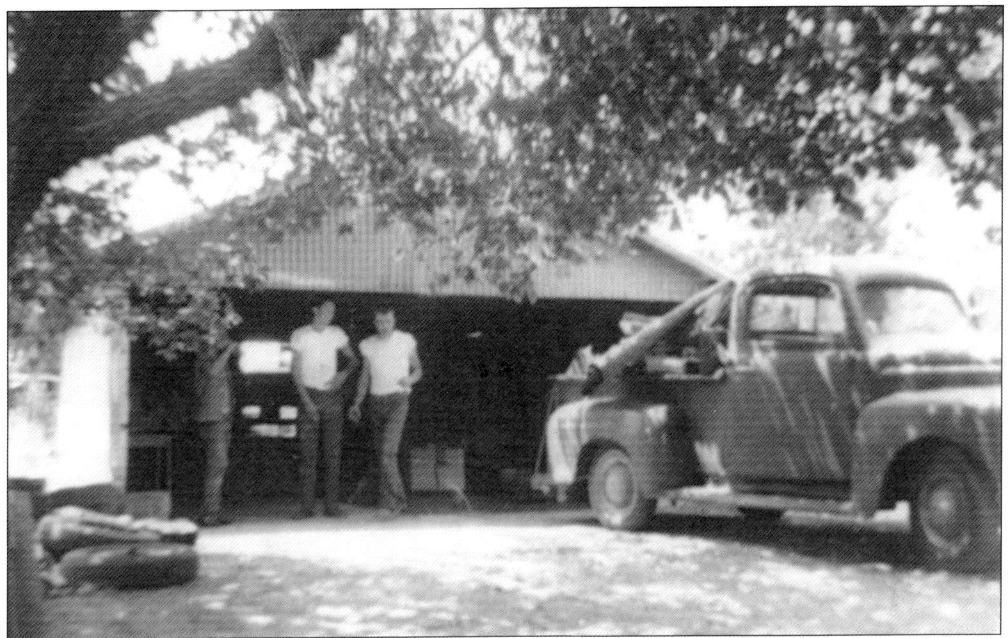

Idlers Wilber Kenzee (left) and Gene Brozen take a break at the Idlers' garage. It does not get any more 1950s car culture than two young men having a smoke break during a wrenching session wearing jeans and white T-shirts. The only thing better would be if they each had a pack of smokes rolled up in their left sleeve. (Courtesy of Linda Claridge.)

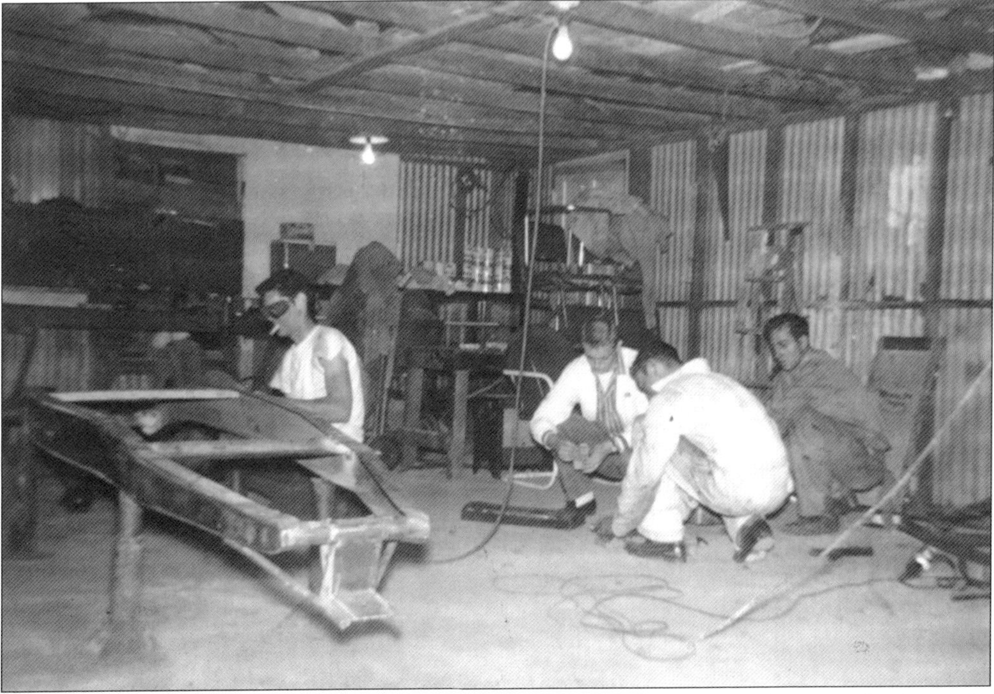

Before cars were mostly computers, all one needed was a space under a shade tree and a few tools. Luckily, these Idlers had a tin garage and extension cords for electricity to build their dreams of speed. (Courtesy of Linda Claridge.)

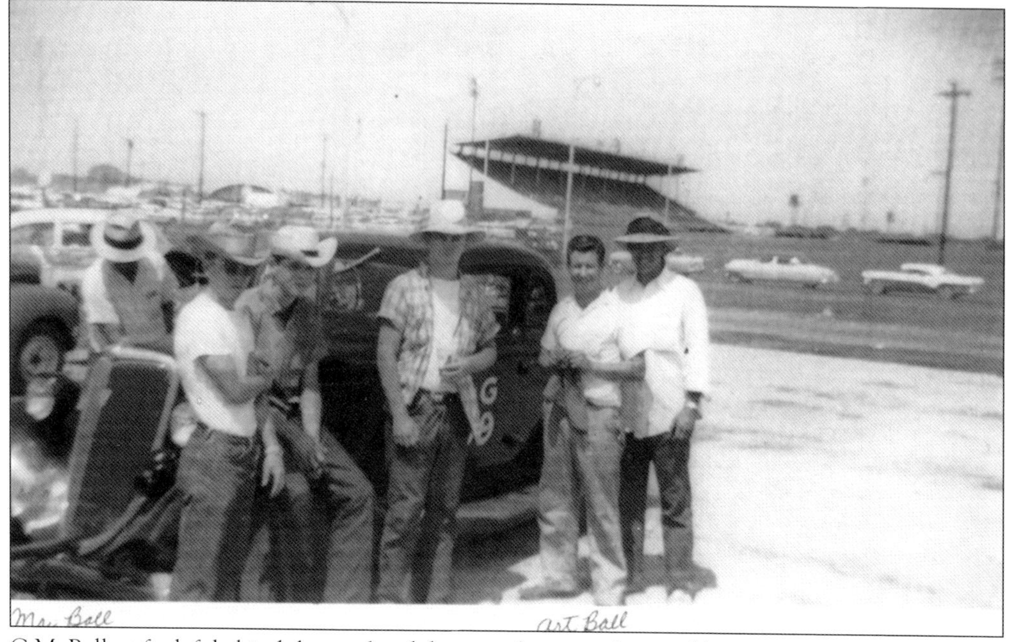

C.M. Ball, at far left behind the car, head down and wearing hat, and his son, Art Ball, second from right, stand with friends at the Southwest Regional Championships, held at the Eagle Mountain Lake National Guard Base track in 1960. The pair were ready to drag for the pride of River Oaks. (Courtesy of Linda Claridge.)

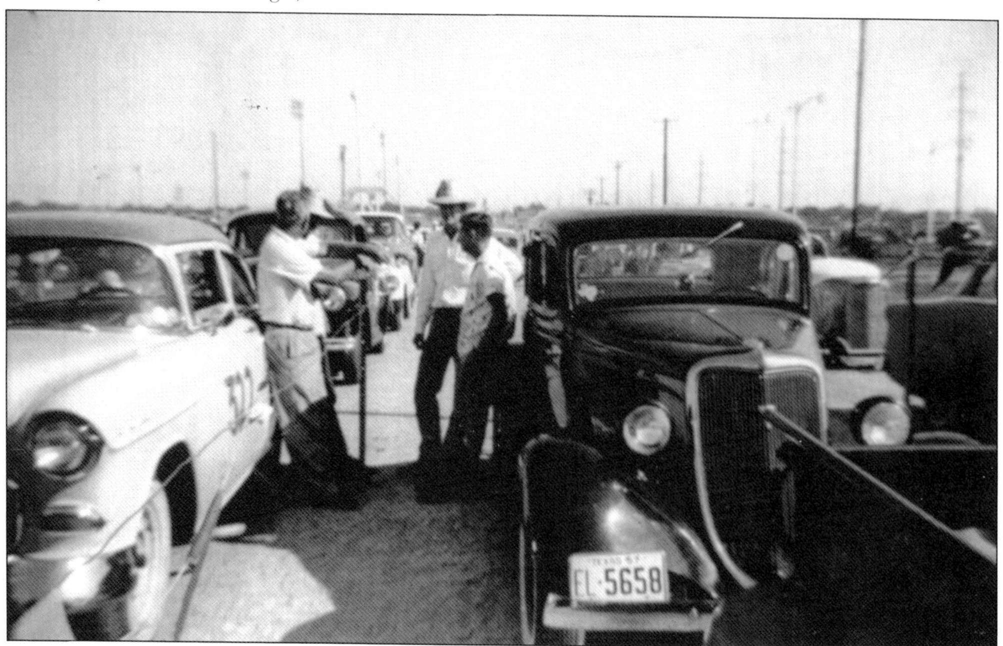

Rutherford and Claridge were not the only members of the Idlers to attain substantial success and notoriety. On August 31, 1957, Johnny Loveless, seen here wearing the hat, qualified for the National Hot Rod Association Drag Racing National Finals in Oklahoma City. Loveless, like most people, did not earn his living from racing. It was a passion. Loveless owned a neighborhood grocery store in River Oaks. (Courtesy of Linda Claridge.)

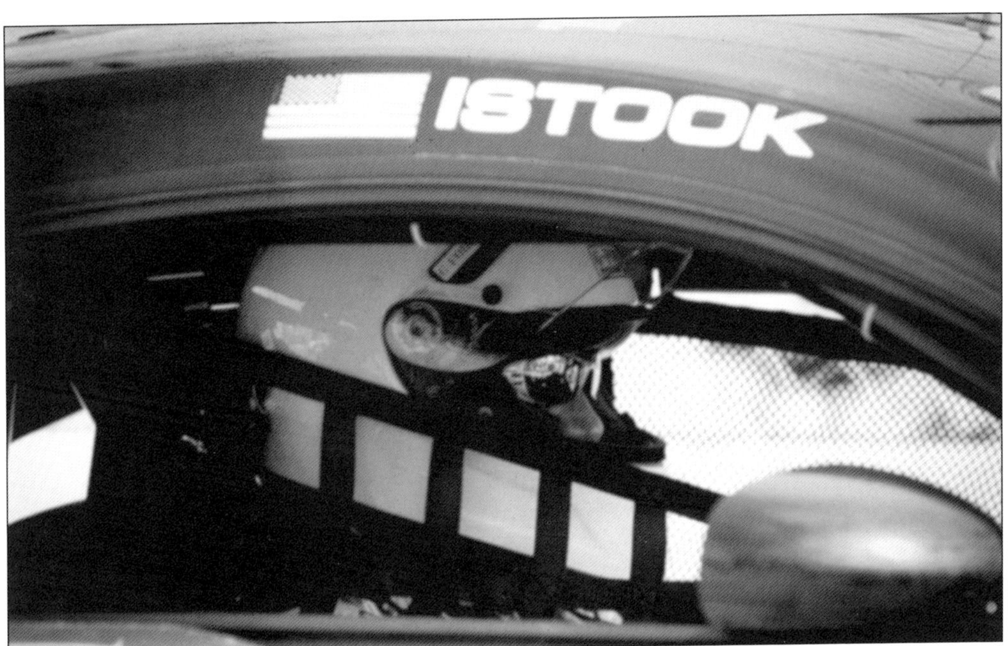

Longtime River Oaks resident Don Istook is a legend for Audi enthusiasts in America. He has built and raced special Audi race cars for decades. Some of Istook's most memorable cars include the Audi S4 racers that battled it out in the Grand Am Cup series in the early 2000s. He has also raced various Audi TT race cars. Currently, Istook races an Audi TT RS in the Sports Car Club of America Pirelli World Challenge. (Courtesy of Don Istook.)

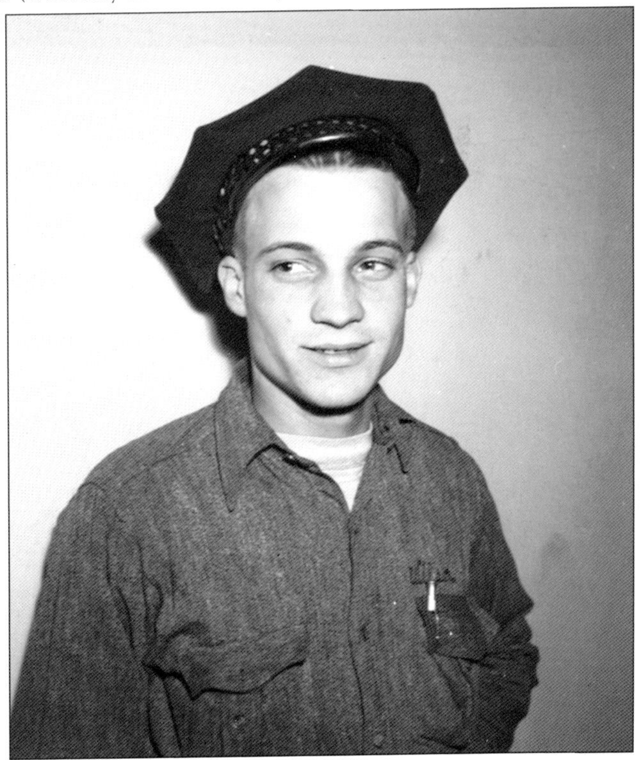
In December 1940, M.A. Wilson became the Texas Motor Transportation Association (TMTA) straight truck-driving champion of Texas. The contest was held in Dallas, and Wilson was only 22 years old at the time. The TMTA began in 1936, and the championships started in 1937. The contest allowed drivers to demonstrate their driving and inspection skills, knowledge, and professionalism. The drivers underwent a written examination, a pre-trip inspection test, and a driving skills test. (Courtesy of the *Fort Worth Star-Telegram* Collection, University of Texas at Arlington Libraries.)

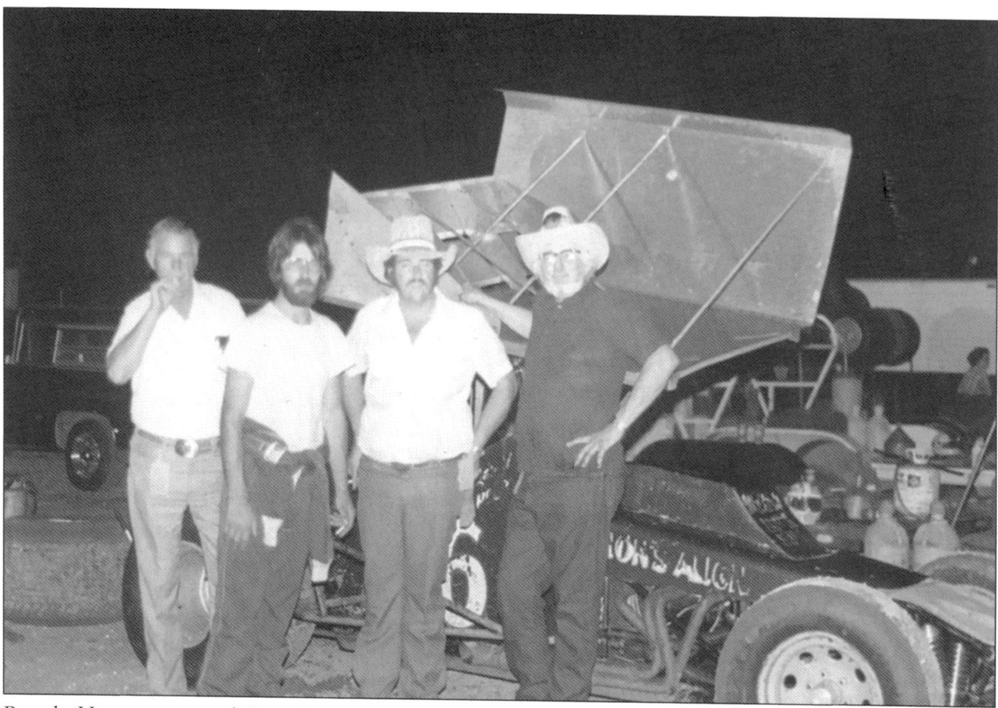

Randy Hooper, second from left, and Vernon Hooper, fourth from left, stand by their modified race car getting ready for a race in this undated picture. The younger Hooper began racing quarter midget cars at the age of nine. He won his class in his first year of driving. (Both, courtesy of Randy Hooper.)

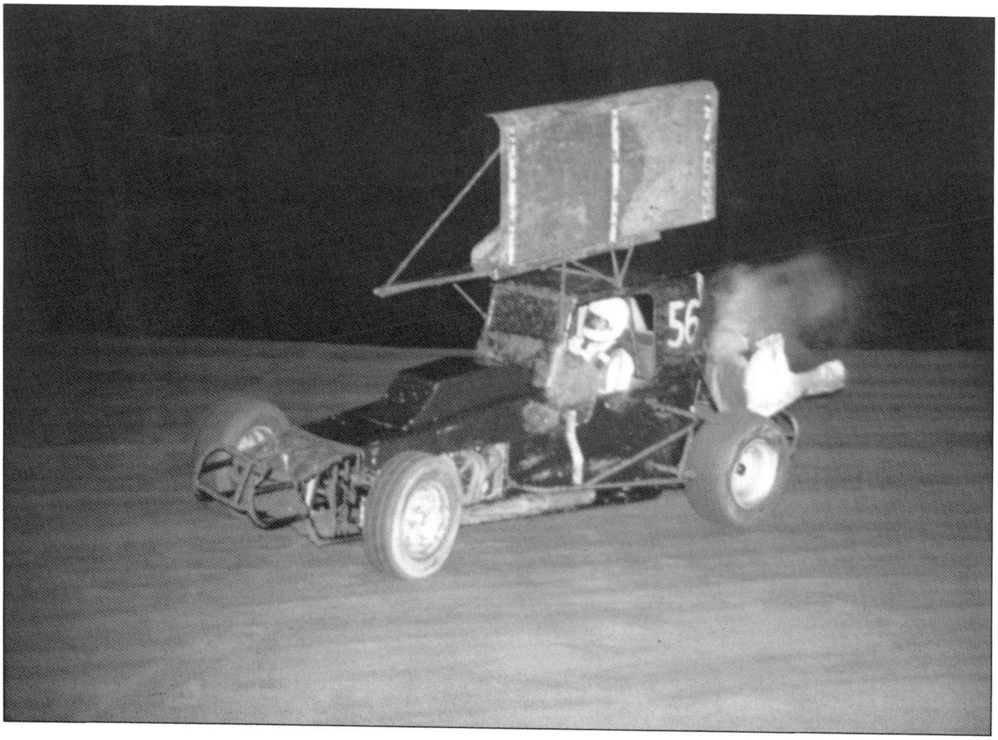

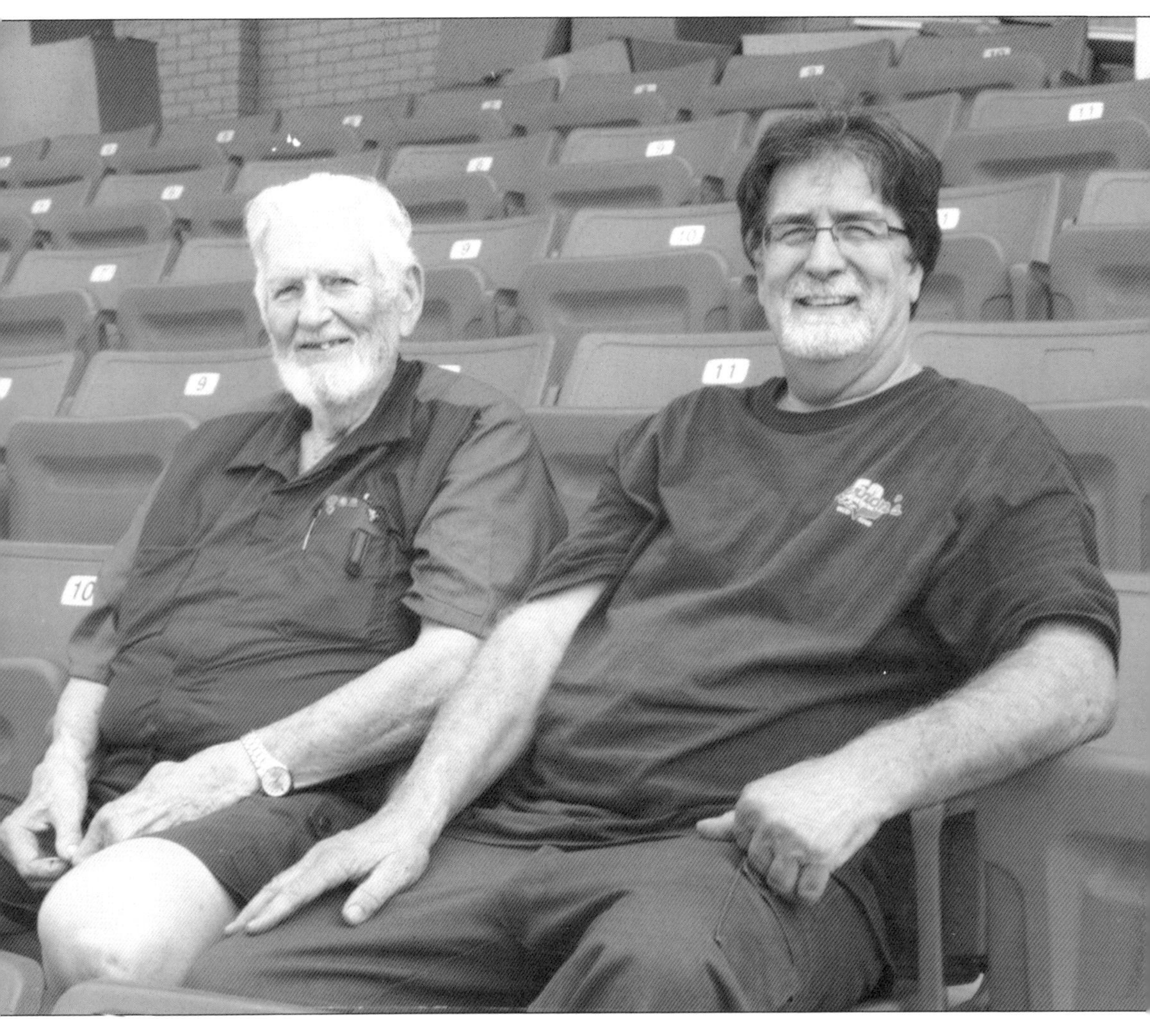

The father-and-son team of Vernon and Randy Hooper has been racing at tracks across Texas ever since, collecting trophies. The Hoopers have been fixtures in the River Oaks car culture for generations. Their annual fish fries at Vernon's Automotive became legendary and became a magnet for area racing participants and enthusiasts. (Courtesy of Randy Hooper.)

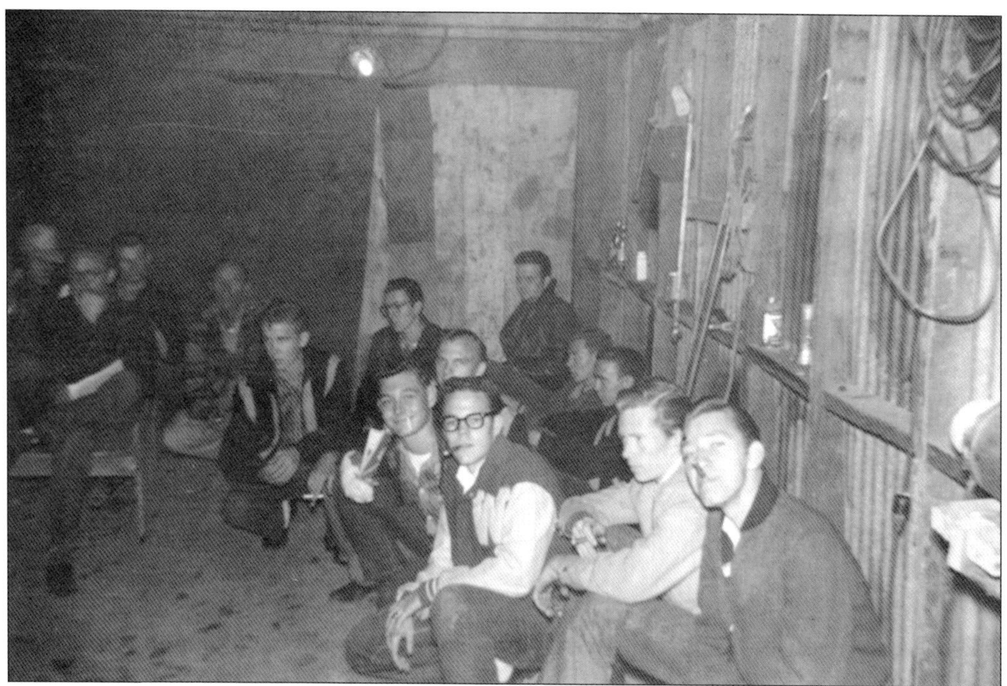

Sporting two future racing hall-of-famers and a slew of winning drivers across a wide range of racing classifications, the young men (and at least one woman) who plied their need for speed on dirt tracks of Tarrant County and beyond have given great pride to the city of River Oaks. Perhaps the city should consider a checkered flag for the new city logo. (Both, courtesy of Linda Claridge.)

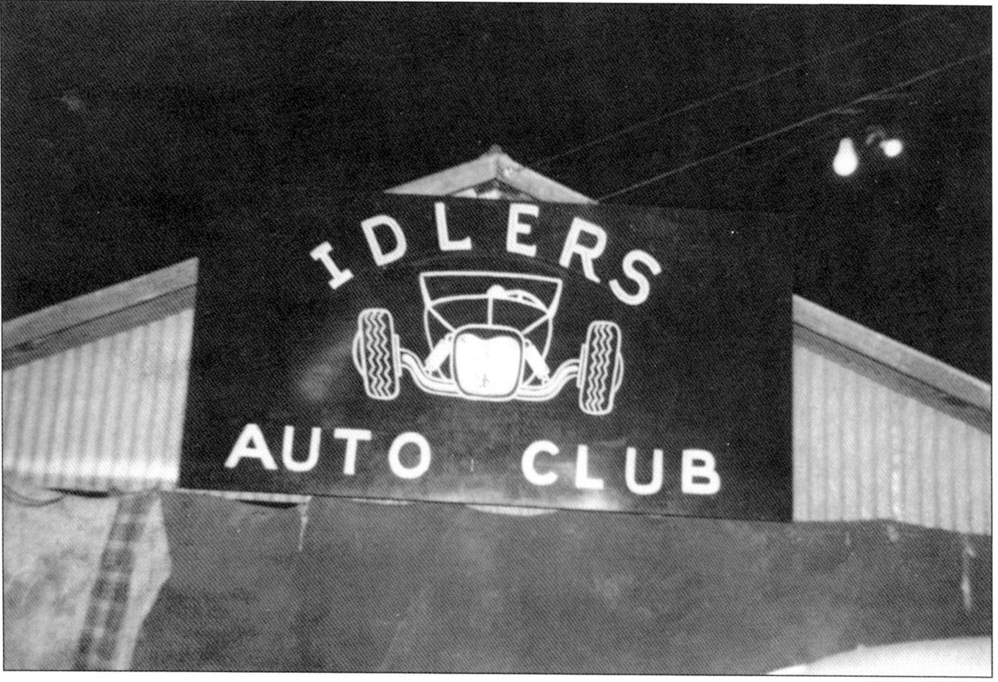

Eight

MODERN DAY

The city of River Oaks has never been flashy or the next big thing. It has never wanted to be flashy or the next big thing. River Oaks has always been comfortable being River Oaks—proud of its history and populated with good, hardworking people who look after and support each other. While other cities look to growth and industry, due to being landlocked on all sides, the City of River Oaks has been forced to look inward and take care of its citizens. The city has replaced 65 percent of the existing water lines and has relined over 10,000 feet of old existing sewer mains. In 2013, the City of River Oaks participated in a sub-regional planning study referred to as Planning for Livable Military Communities. Through that effort, River Oaks Boulevard (State Highway 183) was identified as an important transportation facility. This corridor master plan addresses the feasibility of strategies to support modern urban design, improve access and safety, and enhance economic development potential along the boulevard. The Texas Department of Transportation, the City of Fort Worth, and the City of River Oaks are proposing to improve Meandering Road from State Highway 183 to Anahuac Avenue and LTjg Barnett Road from Meandering Road to the east side of the West Fork of the Trinity River in Tarrant County. These infrastructure improvements will greatly impact the city's livability and attractiveness to new residents and businesses.

No one can say what the next 75 years will hold for the city of River Oaks, but one thing that will continue to hold true is that the citizens of the city hold the key to its future. The City of River Oaks will continue to build its infrastructure, parks, and services in an effort to enhance residents' quality of life. Creative entrepreneurs will continue to be attracted to the city and provide good food and great services to clientele inside and outside the city limits. As the city slogan clearly states, the city of River Oaks will always cherish its past and embrace its future.

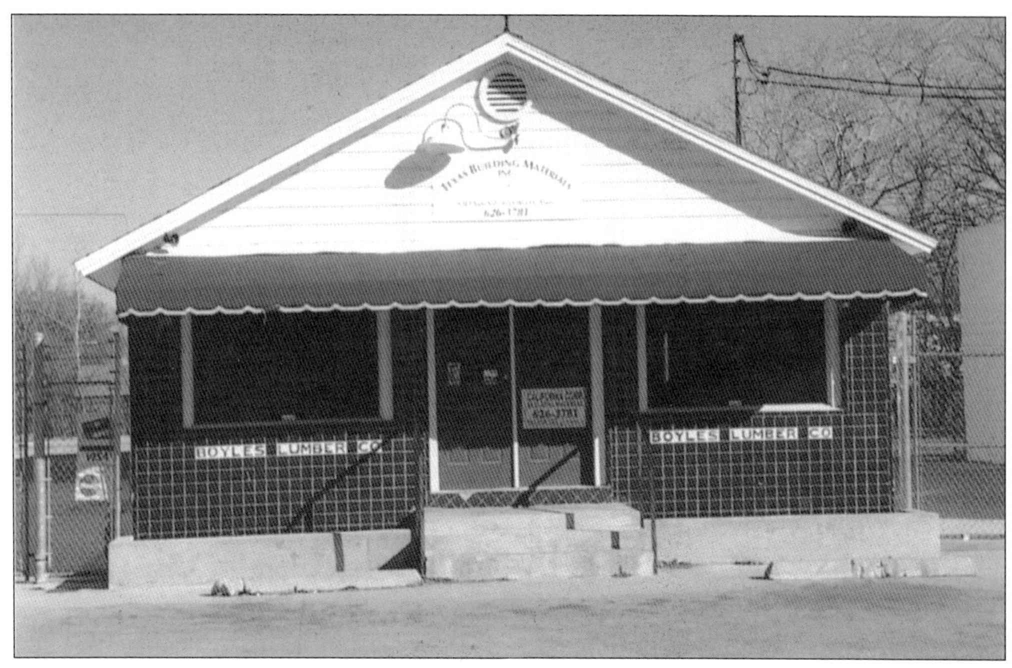

The original River Oaks Community Center was purchased in 1999. The property had to be de-annexed from Fort Worth before opening. The building was located on Churchill Street. In 2005, a new, larger, more versatile property was purchased at 5300 Blackstone Drive, right on the corner of Roberts Cut Off Road. The new facility opened in 2006 after some remodeling to convert the church into a multipurpose community center. (Both, courtesy of the River Oaks Event Center.)

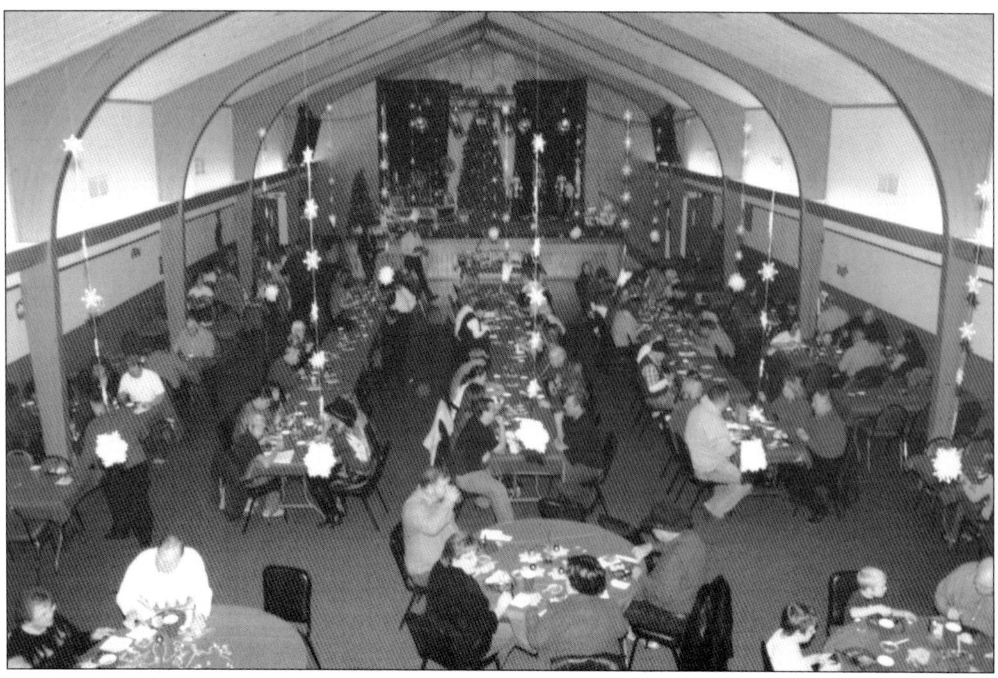

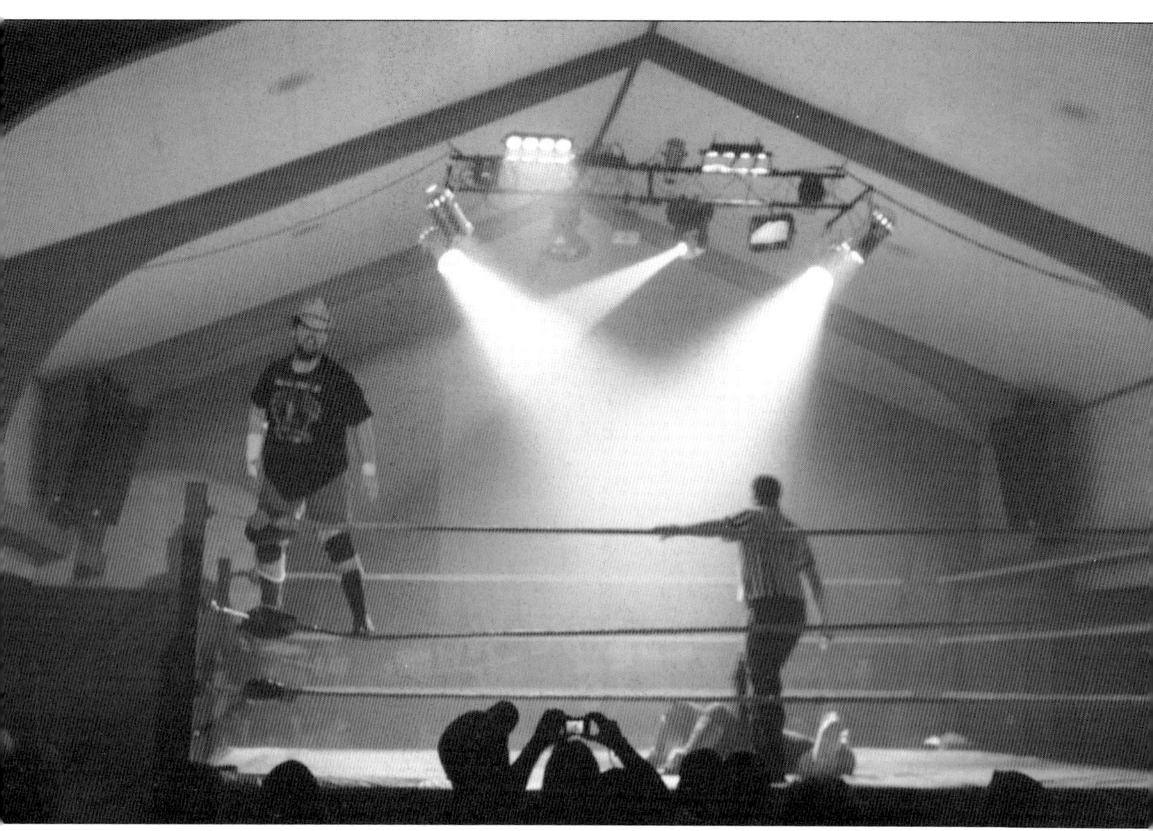

The River Oaks Community Center has hosted almost every event imaginable—even wrestling. In 2023, River Oaks decided to change the name to the River Oaks Event Center to better reflect the diverse nature of acts and shows being brought to the center. The new event center still hosts community-minded events like a food bank, karaoke, and exercise and sewing classes that serve the community. (Courtesy of the River Oaks Event Center.)

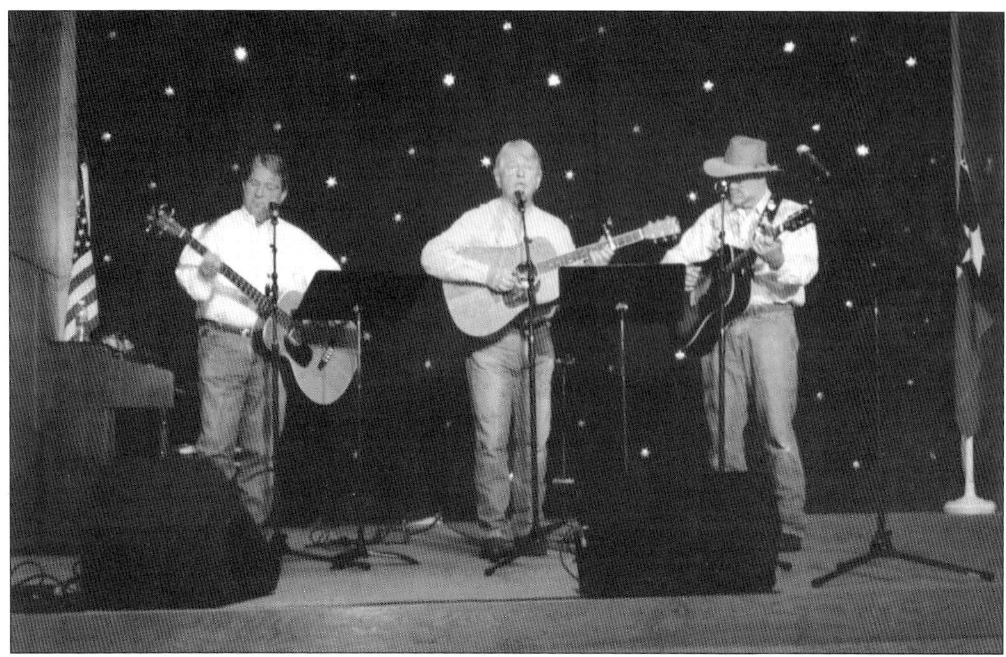

The River Oaks Event Center now seeks out live bands, both local and touring, playing everything from blues to country and western. It also books Vegas-style celebrity impersonators, and the facility is available to rent for private events and shows. The newly positioned event center is meant to bring a broader range of entertainment to the citizens of River Oaks and to entice people outside the city limits to come and experience all the city has to offer. River Oaks Event Center directors Shirley Wheat (left) and Shirley Bloomfield (right) are pictured at an undated event. (Both, courtesy of the River Oaks Event Center.)

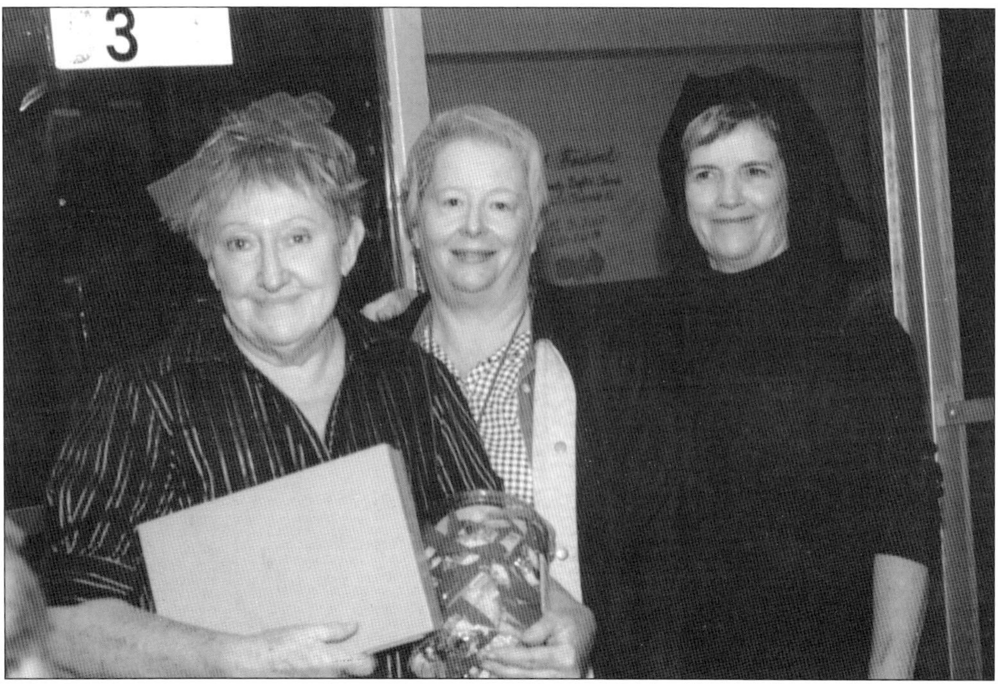

Castleberry High School graduates Paulina Espinosa and Raul Sanchez opened Blurrberry Barbershop on October 3, 2022. Espinosa graduated with a cosmetology degree and Sanchez has a barber's license. Having both a cosmetology license and barber's license enabled the couple to offer a full line of services for the entire family. Espinosa and Sanchez flank customer Darren Houk during Blutrrberry's ribbon cutting ceremony in 2022. (Courtesy of Blurrberry Barbershop.)

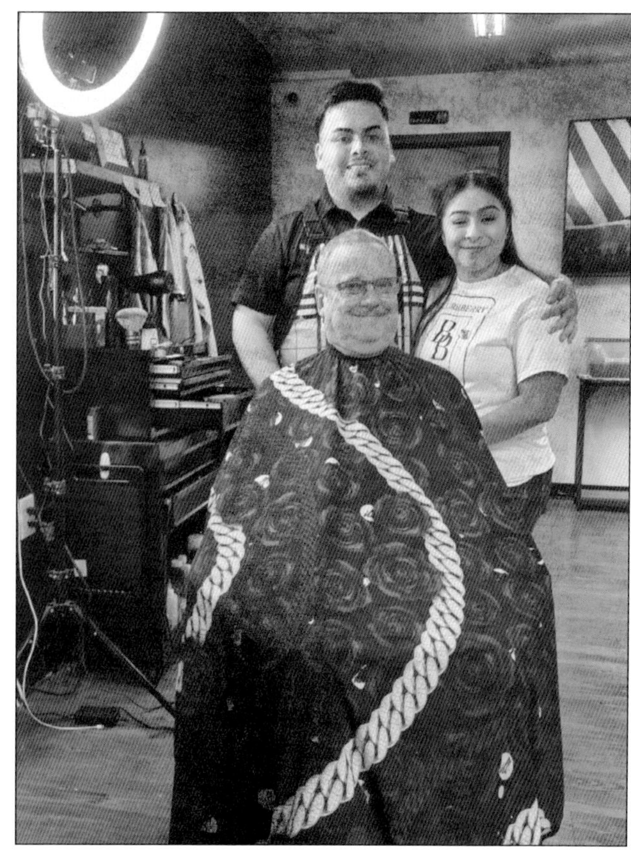

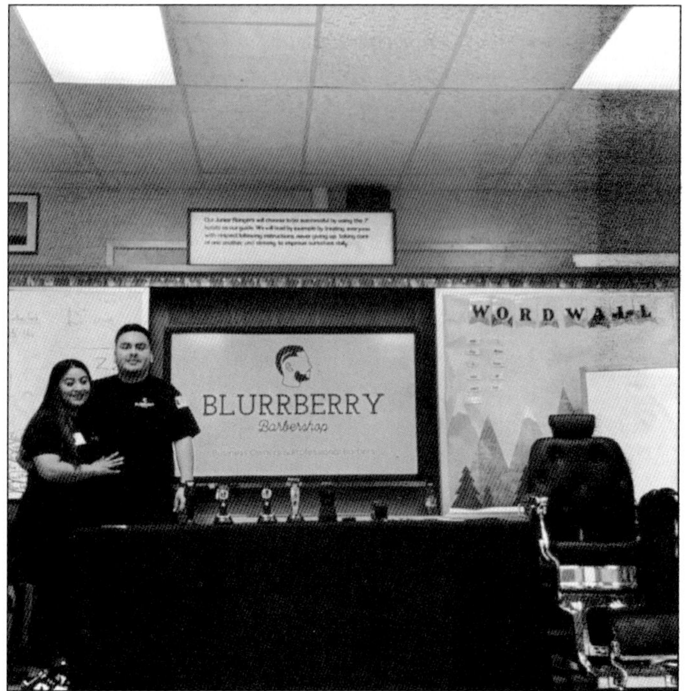

Paulina Espinosa and Raul Sanchez talk to students about a career in barbering during Career Day at CISD. After working for other salons for several years, they found that for the fees they paid to other barbershops and salons, they could open their own business. Both attended CISD schools and had many friends and family living in the area, so opening Blurrberry in River Oaks was an obvious choice. (Courtesy of Blurrberry Barbershop.)

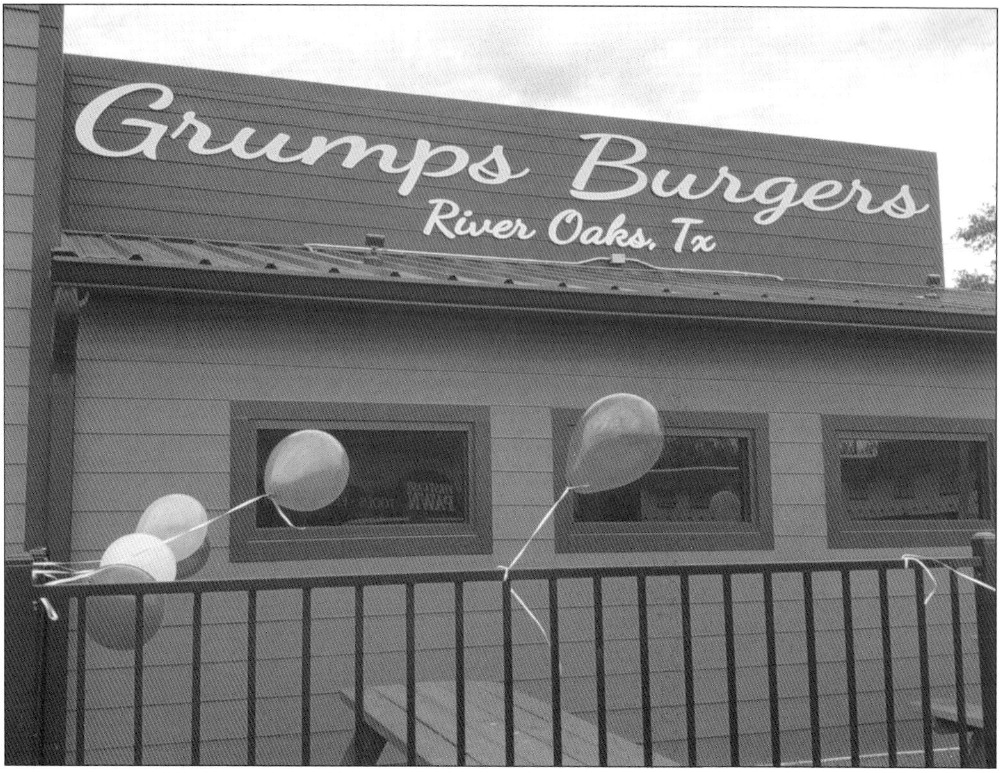

Collier Albright, owner of Grumps Burgers and holding ceremonial scissors below, founded the company in 2001 with the goal of opening a burger chain that was fun, clean, had a casual atmosphere, and was service-oriented and priced reasonably. They would be places where friends and family could gather and enjoy themselves without feeling rushed. Grumps in River Oaks was the sixth location. Since its ribbon-cutting ceremony in December 2022, the city of River Oaks has opened its arms to Grumps, and the company has been a huge supporter of the community. Grumps has supported local schools and charitable events and hosted community events. (Both, courtesy of Grumps Burgers.)

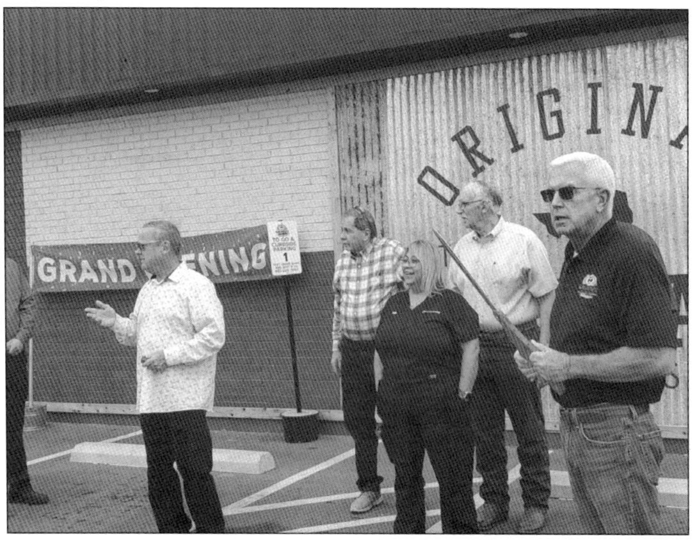

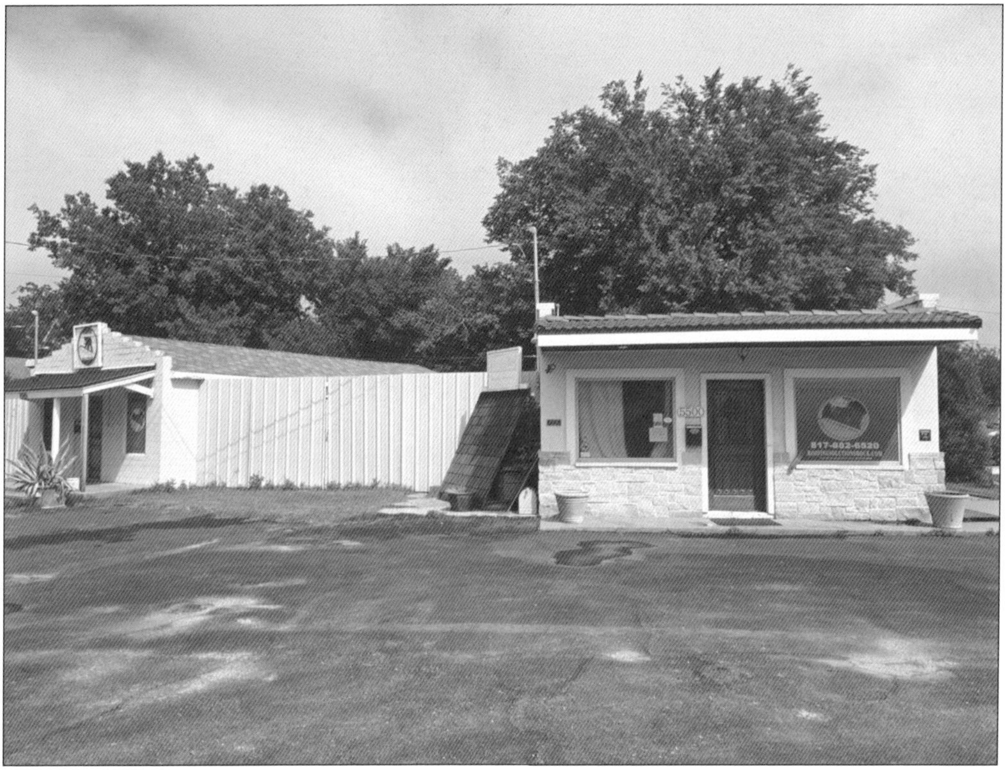

In 2010, Roofing Solutions by Darren Houk bought several properties that were once Willett's Corner. Both buildings on the property went through extensive remodeling. The last business to occupy 5500 Meandering Road was a defunct snow cone stand. Roofing Solutions now has its showroom and offices in the old snow cone stand. The building on the left is used as a warehouse for roofing materials. Roofing Solutions is a residential and commercial roofing company serving River Oaks and all of Tarrant County. Both properties are eligible for historic designation, but there are no current plans to apply for such. (Both, courtesy of Darren Houk.)

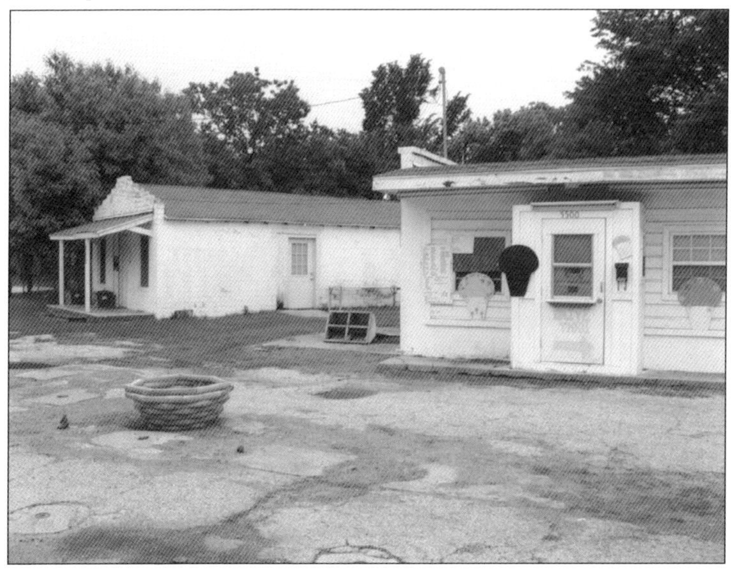

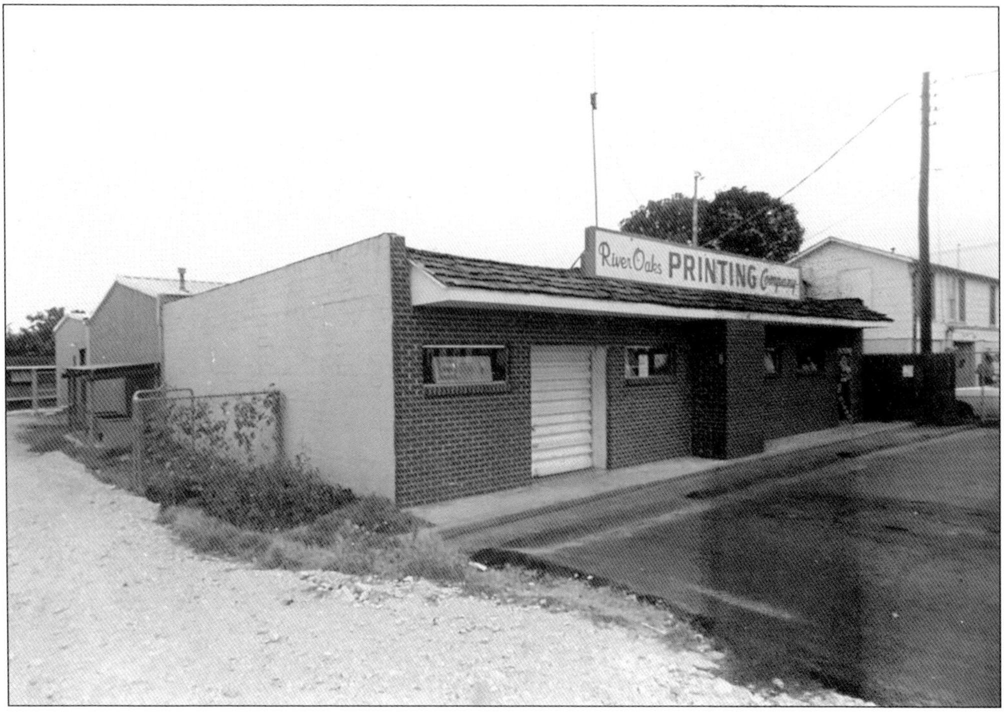

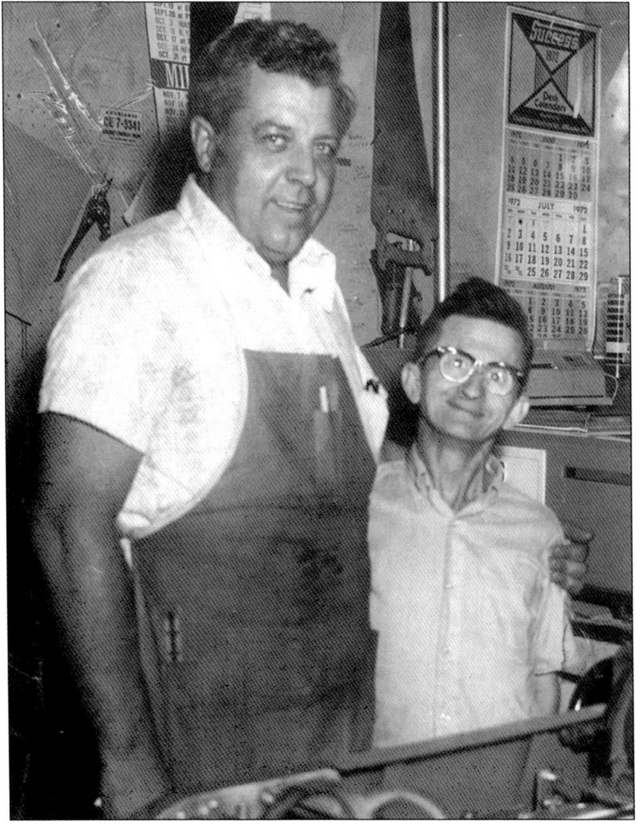

Robert. J. "Bob" Machos founded River Oaks Printing in 1951. Machos started working at the young age of six by growing and selling his own produce. He also had five paper routes as a young man. He was a master craftsman and spent his life making River Oaks Printing Co. Inc. a successful, thriving printing operation. Machos passed away in 2001, but his dream and his business continue to thrive. His sons and grandchildren oversee the day-to-day operations of this third-generation family business. River Oaks Printing celebrated its 70th year in business in 2021 and is considered to be one of if not the oldest continually operating businesses in River Oaks. (Both, courtesy of the Machos family.)

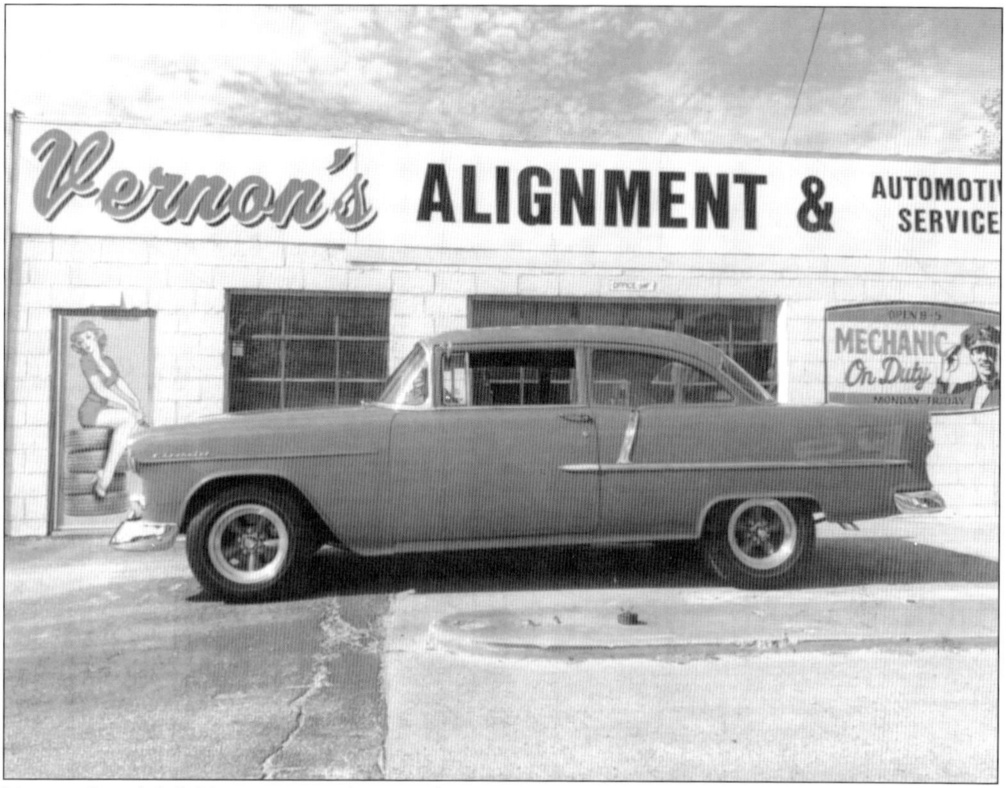

Vernon Randolph Hooper started Vernon's Automotive in 1960 on the edge of River Oaks. Hooper was a lifelong resident and booster of the city. Vernon's Automotive and Alignment is a full-service auto repair shop that also performs alignments and other front-end work. Hooper owned and operated Vernon's Alignment for 61 years before his death in 2021 at the age of 91. He was a longtime member of the River Oaks Lions Club. After his "semi-retirement," he loved to travel across the country in one of his many motor homes to Lions Club functions and auto races. Vernon and his son Randy Hooper held season tickets for and attended almost every home game of the Castleberry Lions football team. Randy Hooper continues the legacy and operates the shop to this day. (Both, courtesy of Randy Hooper.)

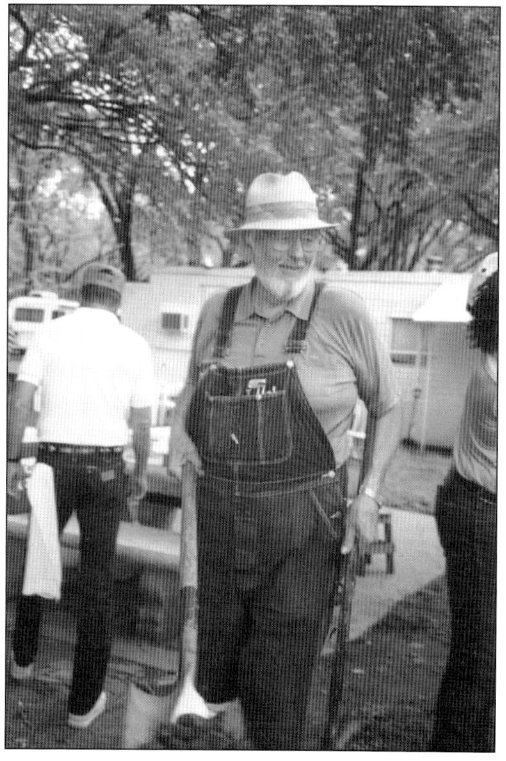

Discover Thousands of Local History Books Featuring Millions of Vintage Images

Arcadia Publishing, the leading local history publisher in the United States, is committed to making history accessible and meaningful through publishing books that celebrate and preserve the heritage of America's people and places.

Find more books like this at
www.arcadiapublishing.com

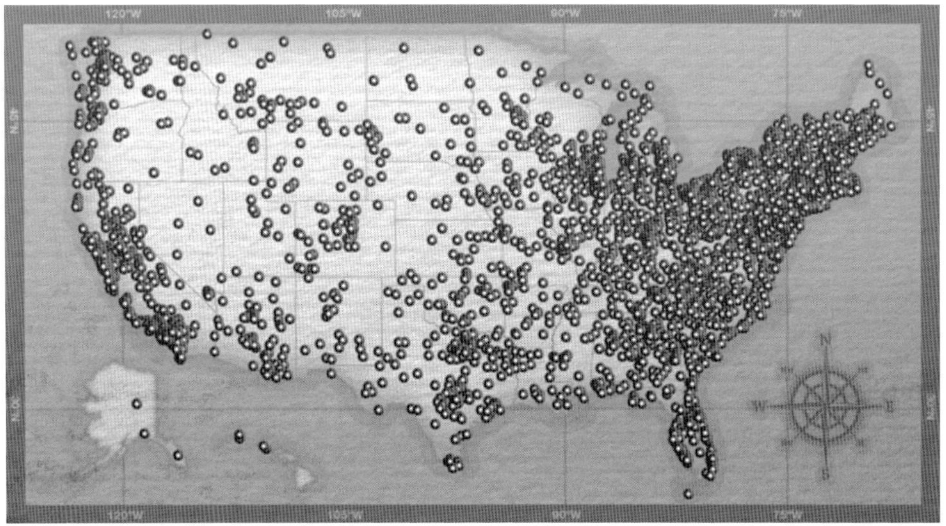

Search for your hometown history, your old stomping grounds, and even your favorite sports team.

Consistent with our mission to preserve history on a local level, this book was printed in South Carolina on American-made paper and manufactured entirely in the United States. Products carrying the accredited Forest Stewardship Council (FSC) label are printed on 100 percent FSC-certified paper.

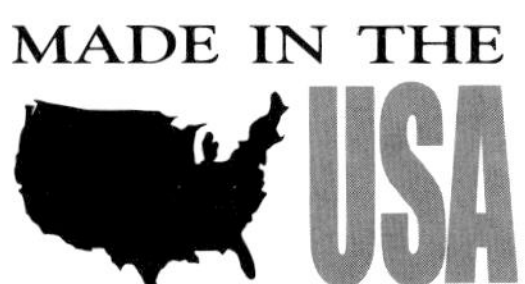